Locomotives of the
Great Central Railway

The period from the turn of the Century to the First World War is thought of generally as being the golden age of the British railway system. As the epitome of that era there could be no better example, surely, than a Robinson Atlantic. Christened *Jersey Lilies*, these were engines with grace, beauty and flowing lines - the creation of an artist and much more than a mere piece of functional machinery.

Elegance and confidence combined seem to ooze from No.258 as she stands outside Gorton Works, newly built in December 1905. One of four compound Atlantics classified 8D and 8E by the G.C.. 258 has been finished in the photographic or 'shop' grey applied to give a clear rendering on the orthochromatic plate emulsions of the day. In an age when mass-production and economics seem to rule everything, one can only marvel at the beautifully - executed lining and panelling - all carried out for what was, essentially, a moment's work.

Collection of G.H.Platt

Locomotives of the

Great Central Railway

Volume One :- 1897 - 1914

by
E.M.Johnson

IRWELL
PRESS ▬▬▬▬

Maximum Efficiency

Equip your Engines with the "Robinson" Locomotive Superheater and ensure maximum efficiency.

THE

"ROBINSON"

LOCOMOTIVE

SUPERHEATER

is used by over 60 Railway Companies in different parts of the world with the most satisfactory results.

The Superheater Corporation, Ltd.,

14, NEW BURLINGTON STREET, LONDON, W.

Published by
IRWELL PRESS
3, Durley Avenue, Pinner, Middlesex, HA5 1JQ
Printed & Bound by Netherwood Dalton & Co. Ltd, Huddersfield

Contents

Foreword

It was decided to split this Great Central locomotive history into two main sections. That from the formation of the company in August 1897 until the start of the first World War and then onwards from there until the end of 1922. This is in contrast to other histories which have attempted to cover the entire company history in one volume and others that have broken the locomotives down into types or classes.

I felt that neither of these approaches suited what I wanted to say about Great Central engines. The 'type approach' would have meant huge sections of the 4-4-0, 4-6-0 and 2-8-0 classes. The latter would have bordered on the impossible as the 8K 2-8-0 spills over into two sub-sections: the ROD variants and the Gresley/Thompson rebuilds which are almost subjects for a book in their own right!

Even so, there are still problems. It was felt that to begin with the

Pollitt 11A 4-4-0s would have cut off the development of the MS&L/GC 4-4-0 in mid stream; so reference is made to the preceding Class 2/2A and Class 11 engines, leaving some scope for their fuller description in a later work. A similar problem arises with the 0-6-0 Goods engines and these have been similarly dealt with.

1914 onwards will include the 2-6-4 or 'Heavy Tanks' built from the end of that year and classes constructed thereafter. Coverage will be extended also to the first of the celebrated 'Directors' - the Class 11E of 1913 which have had to be omitted from this volume owing to pressure on space. This subsequent volume will also include the steam railmotors and absorbed engines from the Lancashire, Derbyshire & East Coast and Wrexham, Mold & Connah's Quay railways, excluded from this volume owing to lack of space.

We journey to Penistone to look at the final development of Robinson's first express locomotive, the 11B 4-4-0. Reference to the relevant chapter shows the original 1901 design as being refined gradually to incorporate innovations in boiler and firebox design allied to cylinder layout and including such improvements as superheating. Confronted by 11D (the final version of the class) no.1027 we should take note of the longer smokebox required to house the superheater headers. Above the boiler handrail is carried the pipe for the brake ejector, this required the lower cab spectacle to be reduced from the original oblong shape to a square pattern (compare this picture with no.1042 at Mexborough.) The nicely rounded original dome cover has been replaced by the flatter-topped pattern worn by no.1026 at Guide Bridge and 4-column safety valves are carried indicating a Sharp, Stewart engine. 1027 was superheated in 1920-confirmed by a plate in the main frames-which puts the picture in the late G.C.era.

Railway Revivals collection

Locomotives of the Great Central Railway

It would be difficult to determine precisely the appeal of the pre-1923 railway companies. Their stubborn independence with regional and often local identities were obvious hallmarks. Observers would note definite traffic patterns and peculiarities; even the less enthusiastic would take in such things as the beautiful and colourful locomotive and coaching stock liveries. Station buildings along with such subtleties as the design of signals and signalboxes all helped to form what would nowadays be termed a 'Corporate Identity.'

Of all the companies that disappeared into the melting pot at the end of 1922, the Great Central Railway certainly had all these qualities and posessed as well one other unique feature: the company had, to its ultimate detriment, been the last one to arrive in the capital. This late 19th century thrust, the last great entreprenurial exercise of the Victorian railway era, fired by the legendary Watkin, produced a superb piece of railway.

It was on August 1st.1897 that the Manchester Sheffield & Lincolnshire Railway changed its name to that of 'Great Central.'Thus was formed the last of the 'Great' British railway companies taking a provincial and esssentially cross-country line to the same status as the other luminaries that shared the hallowed prefix to their names.

Engrossed with a hugely ambitious and expensive piece of railway - the line from Annesley, south of Sheffield to Marylebone cost over £3 million - it is interesting and appropriate to look back at the condition of the locomotive stock and its associated engineering environment at that time. Railways have the awkward habit of being prodigious soakers-up of money; aside from the construction of the London Extension Line itself, money had to be raised for the building of the necessary locomotives and rolling stock. This was achieved by the setting up of an independent company known as the Railway Rolling Stock Trust Ltd. This company purchased the necessary equipment and retained ownership until the Great Central had paid for it. A very necessary piece of high finance, best described as a sort of grandiose hire-purchase agreement! Construction began southwards in the autumn of 1894. Harry Pollitt-appointed Locomotive Engineer in 1893-had inherited a mixed bag of locomotives from his predecessor, ThomasParker. Many of these had double frames, a continuation of practice from the Sacre era which had begun as far back as 1859. So, in the February of 1898, the first full year of the Great Central's existence, we find Pollitt addressing the Locomotive, Carriage and Wagon Committee of the newly-formed company. His statement was

Great Central grace and power at Guide Bridge. Atlantic no.267 on a Down express nears the end of its journey.

Collection of G.H.Platt

unequivocal: although the company's locomotive stock had been augmented rapidly during the last few years - (Pollitt had built some fine 4-4-0s, the latter had included period refinements such as piston valves)-there had been no proportionate increase in appliances or machinery to cope with repairs.

Increases in workshop space had been provided at the company's Gorton Works in Manchester but nothing appeared to have been done about equipping them with any machinery that could have been described as modern.

Pollitt complained strongly of excess handwork being undertaken in the shops and put forward a submission to the committee for the extensive installation of modern powered machinery-much of it pneumatic and hydraulic-in the Boiler Shop, Erecting Shop, Turning Shop, Smithy and Iron Foundry. His estimate-over £40,000. a colossal sum of money in those days-was deferred, understandably, until the Committee could meet at Gorton and assess the situation for themselves on the spot. Although the rendezvous did take place, a decision was postponed until the next meeting. They did approve, however, repairs to the Brass Foundry roof at a cost of £95.00! An inspection was also made of the Gorton coaling stage; the minutes record the 'inadequate and antiquated appliances for coaling engines.'

Subsequent to producing his report, Pollitt and the Locomotive Committee visited the works at both Crewe and Derby. Whilst the reports do not exactly eulogise over what was observed, Crewe's highly organised, efficient and well laid-out workshops lit by the LNW's own electricity, made an obvious impression. Likewise, the spacious facilities seen at Derby with such, then, innovations as laboratory testing of materials and the extensive use of pneumatic and hydraulic tools were noted.

Services proper on the London Extension began on March 15th 1899. Doubtless because of pre-occupation with this - Pollitt did not get sanction for his new machinery until the May of that year when authorisation of £61,660 was approved by the GC Board. This included £8,799 for the construction of the new Gorton coaling stage.

Express motive power for the 'New Line' was provided by Pollitt's 11A 4-4-0s and although competent enough machines for the lightweight trains concerned, the actual number of engines available for traffic was reaching crisis proportions. In the spring of 1899 arrangements were made to borrow a number of locomotives from sympathetic companies. The Great Eastern loaned 5 engines, 3 or 4 were requested from the G.N. and the North Eastern pledged a further 3. Gorton works were fully occcupied at that time, British locomotive builders had full order books and neighbouring Beyer,Peacock & Co. were suffering the effects of a lengthy strike. Thus, recourse had to be made to overseas builders for the badly needed engines. An order for 20 2-6-0 tender engines was placed with Messrs.Burnham Williams at their Baldwin works in Philadelphia. Incidentally, the same company supplied the Midland Railway with

similar locomotives at about the same time. Still the G.C.'s engine problems were not over. Construction in Philadelphia did not proceed as quickly as the company anticipated, even though the 2-6-0's were to be dispatched to England more or less as 'kits' for assembly at Gorton. Pollitt himself went to the U.S.A.to assess the situation at first hand and cabled a report home from the Waldorf Astoria Hotel in New York. However, the 'Yankees' as the engines became known, did materialize and though all were reported to be at work by May 1900, events were to prove them to be a poor investment.

Pollitt gave the following report on the G.C. motive power stock to the Locomotive, Carriage and Wagon Committee on September 5th.1899:

CONDITION OF LOCOMOTIVES as at 31st August 1899

In good condition on G.C.line	*384*
Requiring repairs	*124*
In good condition on C.L.C.line	*146*
Requiring repairs	*31*
In good condition on M.S.J & A	*5*
Requiring repairs	*3*
Working on N.W & L.Railway	*7*
Total number of engines working	*700*
Under repair at Gorton	*86*
Under repair at running sheds	*54*
Under repair at Yorkshire Engine Co	*13*
Total number under repair	*153*
Waiting at Gorton to go into shops	*5*
Waiting at running sheds to go into shops	*5*
Standing at Gorton - worn out	*39*
TOTAL ENGINE STOCK	*902*

Following production of his report Pollitt recommended to Edward Chapman (the Deputy Chairman) that, with the development of the London Line, further batches of locomotives would have to be built. He also suggested that the G.C.adopted the practice of neighbouring companies and carried out light repairs at the various depots, concentrating heavy repairs at Gorton.

Subsequent to this report, William Pollitt (the General Manager) reported to the Board that the Great Eastern Railway had arranged to lend four additional engines, making the total loaned by them seventeen and that the G.C. would then have forty-six engines on loan.

With the dawn of the new century, its London Extension firmly established, Great Central locomotive matters were about to take aa momentous step forward. In June of that year the Chairman, Sir Alexander Henderson, announced that he had had very strong recommendations from the Chairman of the Waterford & Limerick Railway in Ireland in favour of one Mr.John.G.Robinson as a suitable candidate for the

POLLITT'S STATEMENT SHOWING DETAILS OF ENGINES TO BE CONSTRUCTED
(5th September 1899)

NUMBER	TYPE	DATE OF ORDER	WORKS	COST
25	Side tank Goods	1/4/98		£2,200 each. 8 are already at work, 8 more by 31/12/99. The order should be complete by June 1900.
6	Single driving wheel Passenger	31/1/99	Gorton	£2,900 each. one engine by Christmas next, 2 per month until March 1900.
16	Side tank Goods	5/5/99	Beyer Peacock	£2,995 each. 2 by February 1900. 3/4 per month after February. Finish June 1900.
20	Goods tender*	5/5/99	Burnham Williams, Philadelphia U.S.A.	£2,600 each. Order should be complete in 6 months.
6	Side tank Goods	26/7/99	Gorton	£2,700 each. Delivery to commence in July 1900. 2 per month.

* The so-called 'Moguls' were ordered as a substitute for 20 class 9H 0-6-0 Goods tender engines, on order but with no hope of delivery in the immediate future.

Class 2 4-4-0 no.566, with round-topped boiler, longer smokebox and Robinson chimney, stands in front of the turntable and water tower at Manchester Central. The date of the picture is unknown, but 566, built in 1890, is known to have received her new smokebox in 1901 and was reboilered with the standard no.1 Belpaire in February 1916. In typical Robinson fashion, extended cabs, as sported by this locomotive, were applied to the class as a whole from 1912. Thus, we are left with a photograph taken inside an approximate 4-year span. 566 was withdrawn in August 1931.

Collection of G.H.Platt

post of Locomotive Superintendent. Henderson and Pollitt (Sir William the General Manager) met S. W. Johnson of the Midland Railway who also gave Robinson a very strong recommendation. Robinson was invited to attend a Locomotive, Carriage and Wagon sub-committee and give particulars of his experience. His appointment was duly ratified by the G.C.Board in June 1900 at a salary of £1200 p.a.in the first year, £1350 the second and finally to £1500 in the third year. An interesting comparison of salaries paid to 'Executives' in those days is made by recounting that H.A.Ivatt had asked for, and got, a salary of £2500 from the G.N.R. in 1895. Robinson took office as Locomotive Engineer on Monday, July 2nd.1900. He wasted no time in assessing the company's locomotive stock for, on 31st.July he was able to report to the L.C.& W. Committee that he had been able to inspect engines that had been standing at Gorton for several *years*. About 40 of these were stated to be worn out, obsolete and beyond repair. Pollitt's assessment of the situation the previous year had echoed much the same thing. A horrendous catalogue of worn cylinders and wheel tyres, flawed crank axles, cracked or broken frames, and dilapidated boilers and fireboxes had added up to a thoroughly woeful situation. A suggestion was put that 40 locomotives be built and charged to the Revenue Account. Permisssion was also sought to break up 20 of the redundant engines immediately. Precisely what type of locomotive was in Robinson's mind is not recorded. We do know that he reduced the order for Pollitt's Singles from 10 to 6 engines; just 4 of the Class 13 4-2-2s were built during the first 4 months of his regime albeit with some design alterations (Q.V.) By the Autumn of 1900 however, Robinson was finding his feet. On October 4th he submitted a long address to the Locomotive, Carriage & Wagon Committee. His initial point concerned the American 2-6-0s, then barely 6 months old. Running costs were deemed to be high with coal consumption at 10lbs.per mile. Repair costs were some 33% higher than a Beyer,Peacock engine for the same period. He observed that the American Engines were not built for a long life; doubtless, the manufacturers could have told him the same thing!

Again, the situation regarding the Great Central's locomotive stock was at crisis level. Borrowings from neighbouring companies were now in the region of 50 locomotives per day and very high rates were being charged to the company for this dubious privilege. Of the G.C's own stock, only 643 out of 965 engines could be expected to be available for the ordinary train services. As an example of the direful nature of the situation Robinson reported that, during August of 1900, the Locomotive Department was being called upon to provide power for as many as 751 regular turns per day-yielding a deficiency of 108 engines which could only be made up by both the borrowings mentioned and overworking the existing locos. Some engines, it was reported, were in steam for days, boiler washouts were suffering because of inferior water with the result that spaces in fireboxes were choked solid with encrustation-thus ruining many copper fireboxes. No less than 50% of

engines then at Gorton required new inside copper fireboxes and 25% also required new Tubeplates and other extensive firebox repairs. Reports from outstation locomotive depots stated that approximately 300 engines required a mixture of new boilers and fireboxes and a heavy general overhaul. Some engines were stated to be over 40 years old and a large number between 30 and 40 years old.

Robinson's report concluded that with the constant failure of fireboxes and boilers 100 boilers and fireboxes were needed from outside manufacturers. The Committee decided to invite tenders from 'leading firms' for 100 engines and that the Locomotive Engineer should prepare drawings and specifications for 100 boilers and fireboxes.

The tenders for new boilers were submitted as follows:

COMPANY	WORKS	PRICE
Yorkshire Engine Co.	Meadow Hall	£760
Stephensons	Newcastle	£780
Vulcan Foundry	Newton-le-Willows	£780
Dubs	Glasgow	£780
Hawthorn,Leslie & Co.	Forth Bank, Newcastle	£795
Neilsons	Glasgow	£835
Kitsons	Leeds	£835
Beyer,Peacock & Co.	Gorton	£840
Sharp,Stewart & Co.	Glasgow	£850

The range of quoted prices is interesting, the difference between the lowest (Yorkshire Engine) and highest (Sharp,Stewart) is very marked. Not surprisingly, The Yorkshire Engine Company were awarded the contract. A penalty clause of 20 per month per boiler was included in the event of non-delivery.

By the end of October 1900 tenders had been invited for 75 goods and 25 passenger locomotives. Looking over their shoulder the Committee noted that the Midland Railway were also in the market for engines and that no time should be lost! Orders were to be placed right away for 40 Goods and 10 Passenger engines. The use of outside contractors once again is noteworthy; Robinson had reminded the Committee earlier that month that Gorton was unable to build new engines as extensions to the Works and the provision of new machinery was far from complete.

Firm decisions had now been made regarding the immediate supply oflocomotives. Neilson Reid of Glasgow were awarded the contract to build 40 0-6-0 goods engines, to be designated Class 9J-the famous 'Pom-Poms.' 4 were to be delivered by July 1901 and 4 more per month afterwards. The cost of each engine was

---

* *Sharp, Stewart offered a nett price of £829, a 2/99D/% discount being allowed.*

It was Robinson 'Pom-Pom' (the Class 9J 0-6-0 of 1901) no.16 that had the distinction of being the first Great Central locomotive to be superheated . Seen here at Manchester London Road on a local passenger working, no.16 was built at the Great Central's own works at Gorton, Manchester, in April 1909. By this time, Robinson had established a number of features that were to become something of design hallmarks: commodious cabs, Belpaire fireboxes, handsome boiler mountings-especially chimneys, an unmistakable smokebox front and, most importantly, a sound and rugged engineering pedigree. This engine was distinguished also by being the only one of its class to be built with both superheater and piston valves. The latter were replaced in 1927, the engine then being fitted with slide valves. Worthy of mention here too is the Ritter mechanical lubricator driven via a small crank from the front coupling rod pin. A conventional Wakefield lubricator was later fitted behind the leading splasher. No.16's piston valves carried tail rods which required a longer platform in front of the smokebox.

Collection of G.H.Platt

agreed at £3445. Perusal of the original tender document reveals very tight specifications. Engines had to be delivered to Gorton and no payment was to be made until each engine had satisfactorily run 1500 miles. Sharp,Stewart & Co.,another Glasgow builder, were contracted to build 10 4-4-0 passenger engines, 5 to be delivered each month in January and February 1902. A penalty of £50 per engine per month was to be enacted in the event of non-delivery.

Thus were completed the events that saw the start of Robinson's office. The portents were surely promising; the G.C.had a brand new line, a new century had dawned and the nation was on the brink of a new era.

Sadly, the Victorian age was almost over-Queen Victoria herself was to die early the following year. Just over twelve months later Sam Fay was to become the G.C. General Manager, an appointment of tremendous consequence for the company. Maybe the Great Central was never prosperous in the financial sense, its route mileage ranked it well below many of its neighbours and a late entry into the capital gave it the reputation of being something of an upstart.

Despite all this, it was a great railway in more ways than a mere name can suggest- Robinson's beautiful and well-engineered locomotives, passed off by many casual observers in the same way that much of F.W.Webb's work and ideas were on the the the L.N.W.R, the superbly engineered London Extension, the development of the East Coast port of Immingham. But over-exposure has, thankfully, never been the lot of the G.C. Perversely, the enthusiast knows little of the company's Gorton Works where so many of Robinson's creations first saw the light of day.

Many G.C.locomotives survived into B.R.days, hard-working veterans, past their best, but living proof of a sound engineering pedigree. Those of us who were fortunate enough to see them and travel behind them remember with affection the fine sight they presented.

In preservation, the Great Central has suffered badly. Only two of Robinson's engines are still with us today and only 'Butler-Henderson' has been restored to its original glory. Gone too are the great trunk routes plied by the locomotives within these pages. But enough of sentimentality! Who needs an excuse to admire a G.C.engine?

E.M.Johnson, Burnage, Manchester. July 1989.

ABOVE: Robinson introduced his 9K 4-4-2 suburban tank design in 1903. 40 engines appeared up to 1905 and a further 12 (Class 9L) with enlarged water capacity were built in 1907. No.20, built at Gorton in 1904, is pictured outside Manchester London Road in early G.C.days. The same setting saw the locomotives still at work over 50 years later. Robinson's engines were built to last.

BELOW: The magnificent Atlantics were Robinson's first big passenger engine and proved themselves an outstanding success from their inception in 1903. No.267 was one of 5 locomotives built by Beyer,Peacock & Co. in 1904. She is seen here at the head of a down express at Guide Bridge, a location that was a focal point of Great Central operations in the north-west.

Collection of G.H.Platt

Great Central Railway Locomotive Classifications

Throughout this book the G.C.R. system of locomotive classification is used when describing the various classes. Though this may be confusing for those hitherto only familiar with the more common LNER letter/number system, it was felt necessary to adhere to the Great Central classification on account of the use of the company's engine diagrams and the fact that we are concentrating on pictures taken, by and large, in the pre-1923 era.

The chief drawback to the Great Central system though, is its use of chronology, irrespective of engine type. Thus, we proceed from 8C, a 4-6-0 of 1903, to 8D, 2 years on and an Atlantic. 8E takes us to another Atlantic, whilst 8F brings us back to another 4-6-0! The '8' series breaks up when we arrive at 1912 with *Sir Sam Fay* which was classified '1'. Quite logically, its successor, *Glenalmond*, built in the following year, was designated '1A'. In First War days the construction of 4-6-0s was resumed with the appearance of *Lord Faringdon* in 1917 classed as '9P'!

But the system did have some consistency, as witness the relative orderliness of what might be termed the '11+' sequence-the MS&L/G.C. 4-4-0s and the classification of 0-6-0 goods tender engines from Parker through to Robinson.

For the sake of completeness the entire MS&L/G.C. class list is given. Some classes appear twice, though in most cases the engines concerned were scrapped before, or shortly after, the appearance of the succeeding locomotive. Early MS&L classifications such as '3rd' and '4th' have been omitted as have the same company's early named engines and locomotives built for the Wrexham, Mold & Connah's Quay Railway.

CLASS NO./LETTER.	WHEEL ARRGT.	YEAR FIRST BUILT.	DESCRIPTION.
1	2 - 4 - 0	1864	Well tank.
1	4 - 6 - 0	1912	*Sir Sam Fay* Class.
1A	4 - 6 - 0	1913	*Glenalmond* Class.
1B	2 - 4 - 0	1865	5'-6" Tender engine.
1B	2 - 6 - 4	1914	Robinson 'Heavy tank'.
1C	2 - 4 - 0	1864	5'-6" Tender engine.
2	2 - 4 - 0	1861	Rebuild of Sharp Bros 2 - 2 - 2.
2	4 - 4 - 0	1887	Parker Inside frame Passenger engine.
2A	4 - 4 - 0	1894	Ditto, bearing & spring diffs.
3	2 - 4 - 2	1889	Parker Suburban tank.
3 Altered	2 - 4 - 2	1892	Ditto longer bunker.
4	2 - 2 - 2	1859	Fairbairn Passenger engine.
4	Misc.	1873 on	0 - 4 - 0 & 0 - 6 - 0 Dock tanks (one extra engine taken into stock 1909)
5	0 - 6 - 0	1858	First engines built at Gorton.
5	0 - 6 - 0	1897	Pollitt Dock shunter.
5A	0 - 6 - 0	1906	Robinson Dock shunter.
6A	0 - 6 - 0	1874	Sacre Goods engine.
6A1	0 - 6 - 0	1887	5'-3" Goods engine.
6B	4 - 4 - 0	1877	Sacre Passenger tender engine.
6C	0 - 6 - 0	1880	Sacre 'Bulldog' outside frame, Goods.
6D	2 - 4 - 0	1887	Parker Passenger tender engine.
6DB	4 - 4 - 0	1888	Attrib.Parker Pass. tender engine.
7	0 - 6 - 0	1885	Sacre Side tank.
8	2 - 4 - 0	1862	5'-6" Passenger engine.
8	4 - 6 - 0	1902	First Robinson 4 - 6 - 0 (Fish).
8A	0 - 8 - 0	1902	Robinson Heavy freight engine.
8B	4 - 4 - 2	1903	Simple Atlantics.
8C	4 - 6 - 0	1903	Comparative 4 - 6 - 0 design with above.
8D	4 - 4 - 2	1905	Compound Atlantics.
8E	4 - 4 - 2	1905	Ditto, frame differences.

8F	4 - 6 - 0	1906	*Immingham* Mixed traffic loco.
8G	4 - 6 - 0	1906	5'-4" version of above.
8H	0 - 8 - 4	1907	Wath 'Hump' shunter.
8J	4 - 4 - 2	1908	3-cylinder rebuild.
8K	2 - 8 - 0	1911	Heavy freight loco.
8M	2 - 8 - 0	1918	Ditto, larger boiler.
8N	4 - 6 - 0	1918	Development of above into 4 - 6 - 0 type.
9	0 - 6 - 0	1889	Parker Inside frame Goods loco.
9A	0 - 6 - 2	1889	Parker Tank, Joy valve gear.
9A Altered	0 - 6 - 2	1892	Ditto, long bunker.
9B	0 - 6 - 0	1891	5'-1" version of Class 9.
9C	0 - 6 - 2	1891	Parker Tank, Stephenson valve gear & Belpaire firebox.
9D	0 - 6 - 0	1892	Development of 9B with Stephenson valve gear.
9E	0 - 6 - 0	1894	Pollitt version of 9B-detail differences.
9F	0 - 6 - 2	1893	Ditto, improved valve gear.
9G	2 - 4 - 2	1898	Pollitt Suburban tank.
9H	0 - 6 - 0	1896	Pollitt Goods, Belpaire firebox.
9J	0 - 6 - 0	1901	Robinson Goods ('Pom-Pom').
9K	4 - 4 - 2	1903	Small suburban tank.
9L	4 - 4 - 2	1907	Ditto, extra coal & water capacity.
9M	0 - 6 - 0	1908	Rebuild of one 9H loco with bigger boiler.
9N	4 - 6 - 2	1911	Large suburban tank.
9O	0 - 6 - 2	1915	Rebuild of one 9F tank with larger water tank & detail differences.
9P	4 - 6 - 0	1917	First 4-cylinder 4 - 6 - 0.
9Q	4 - 6 - 0	1921	5'-8" version of above.
10	2 - 4 - 0	1869	5'-6" Passenger loco.
11	0 - 4 - 2	1874	No information.
11	4 - 4 - 0	1895	Pollitt 7'-0" Express loco.
11A	4 - 4 - 0	1897	Ditto, piston valves.
11B	4 - 4 - 0	1901	First Robinson 4 - 4 - 0.
11C	4 - 4 - 0	1907	Two engines rebuilt from above.
11D	4 - 4 - 0	1909	Development of above with s/h and piston valve cylinders.
11E	4 - 4 - 0	1913	Original 'Directors'.
11F	4 - 4 - 0	1919	Improved 'Directors'.
12	2 - 4 - 0	1873	Outside frame 6'-3" Passenger engine.
12A	2 - 4 - 0	1875	Outside frame 6'-0" Passenger engine.
12AT	2 - 4 - 0	1880	Suburban tank for MSJ&A line.
12AM	2 - 4 - 0	1906	Altered version of above for motor working.
13	0 - 6 - 0	1862	5'-0" Goods engine.
13	4 - 2 - 2	1900	Pollitt Single Driver.
14	2 - 2 - 2	1882	7'-6" Single.
15	2 - 4 - 0	1865	5'-6" Passenger engine.
15	2 - 6 - 0	1899	American 'Moguls'.
16	2 - 2 - 2	1864	Rebuilds of Fairbairn locos.
18	0 - 6 - 0	1869	Sacre outside frame Goods loco.
18 Converted	0 - 6 - 0	1902	Rebuilds of above with saddletanks.
18T	0 - 6 - 0	1871	Sacre Saddletank.
18 Altered	0 - 6 - 0	1903	Robinson altered version of above.
19	2 - 4 - 0	1876	Rebuilds of Hawthorn 2 - 2 - 2.
20	2 - 4 - 0	1860	Rebuilds of Hawthorn 2 - 4 - 0.
22	0 - 6 - 0	1864	Rebuild of Sharp, Stewart 0 - 6 - 0.
23	0 - 6 - 0	1865	5'-3" Outside frame Goods engine.

24	2 - 4 - 0	1866	6'-0" Passenger engine.
25	2 - 4 - 0	1859	6'-0" Passenger engine.
A*	0 - 6 - 2	1895	Kitson 4'-9" tanks built for L.D.&.E.C.R.
B*	0 - 6 - 0	1897	Kitson 4'-7" tanks built for L.D.&.E.C.R.
C*	0 - 4 - 4	1897	Kitson 5'-6" tanks built for L.D.&.E.C.R.
D*	0 - 6 - 4	1904	Kitson 4'-9" tanks built for L.D.&.E.C.R.

All absorbed by G.C.R. 5th August 1891.

8A no. 86 outside Guide Bridge in a somewhat 'workaday' condition in later G.C.days. No.86 was built by Kitsons of Leeds who turned out the impressive number of 15 8As between September and December 1903. The 2 cylinders-size 19ins. X 26ins. were fed by balanced slide valves driven, as with (almost) all Robinson's engines by Stephenson valve gear-modellers please note the balance weights on the reversing shaft behind the front sandbox. A well-coaled tender of 3250 gallons capacity is attached behind no.86. Later engines, built from 1907 onwards had the larger, 4000 gallon pattern tender; after the Grouping, the earlier locos too were so fitted, though the process took until 1930 to complete. No.86 remained in saturated condition all her life. She was withdrawn by the LNER in April 1937.
Collection of G.H.Platt

THE GREAT CENTRAL LOCOMOTIVE STOCK-A SYNOPSIS APRIL 25TH 1899

Mention was made in the introduction of the condition of the Great Central locomotives on Robinson's arrival in 1900. To give the reader a broader, more detailed picture, there follows a copy of a report produced by Pollitt for the Locomotive Committee in 1899. Dated April 21st, it paints an interesting picture of the company's locomotive fleet at the time and gives a good impression of the task facing Robinson upon his arrival in Manchester.

Gentlemen,

I beg to lay before you a report on the present general condition of the Company's Locomotive Stock.
There are at present 893 Engines, which may be classified as follows:-

246 Passenger Engines
474 Goods Engines
65 Shunting Engines (Large & Small)
39 Passenger Engines belonging to the Rolling Stock Trust Limited
69 Goods Engines

893 total

Taking these classes in the order named, I may say that of the Passenger Engines, only 250 are what may be termed Engines of good design as regards their capacity for dealing with modern requirements: the remainder being either altogether worn out, or obsolete.
In like manner, the Goods Engines may be briefly summarized thus:-
516 Goods Engines of good type.
27 Goods Engines worn out or requiring renewal.

Generally speaking the Shunting Engines cannot be improved upon, excepting in the way of increased Repairs, and the Engines belonging to the Rolling Stock Trust Limited, are, of course, in good condition. Having thus sketched the position, I beg to give details as under:-

PASSENGER ENGINES STANDING AT GORTON

ENGINE	CLASS	BUILT	AT	CONDITION
47	1	1868	Gorton	Cylinders thin: left hand outside frame broken: coupled tyres worn out: boiler and firebox worn out.
76	8	1863	Gorton	Boiler and firebox worn out: and other parts require renewing.
79	1	1866	Gorton	As above.
80	1	1868	Gorton	Cylinders thin: tyres worn out: boiler and firebox worn out.
81	1	1868	Gorton	Cylinders thin: boiler and firebox worn out.
82	19	1876	Sheffield	Both outside frames broken: tyres worn out: boiler and firebox worn out.
83	19	1862	Sheffield	Cylinders worn out: both outside frames cracked: boiler and firebox worn out.
90	10	1870	Gorton	Firebox and boiler worn out: cylinders and other parts need renewing.
96	8	1869	Gorton	Firebox and boiler worn out: cylinders and other parts need renewing.
99	16	1869	Gorton	Firebox and shell require renewing: inside frame and tyres worn out: cylinders require renewing.
101	16	1869	Gorton	Cylinders thin: boiler and firebox worn out.
151	1	1864	Newcastle	Cylinders worn out: frames light: firebox and boiler worn out.
212	15	1865	Gorton. B.P.& Co.	Cylinders worn out: defective crank axle: boiler and firebox worn out.
213	15	1863	Gorton. B.P.& Co.	Cylinders worn out: coupled wheel tyres worn down: crank axle condemned: boiler and firebox very bad.
214	15	1865	Gorton. B.P.& Co.	Cylinders worn out: frames cracked: tyres worn out: boiler and firebox bad.
215	15	1865	Gorton. B.P.& Co.	Tyres worn out: boiler and firebox worn out.
406	11	1877	Sheffield	Everything thoroughly run down and in bad condition: boiler and firebox worn out.

The last engine on Pollitt's list was this 0-6-0 goods tender engine built by Kitsons of Leeds in 1866 for the Mid-Wales Railway at a cost of 1250. When built it carried the number 10. Along with two 0-4-2s, it was bought by the MS&L in 1868 who re-numbered it 270. The engine had two inside cylinders 16 ins. x 24 ins. and was fitted with coupled wheels 4ft.6ins. in diameter. In this very early view, no.270 is standing just outside the train shed at Manchester London Road, a station shared, almost from its inception, by the MS&L with the LNWR, a partnership that had been far from harmonious to say the least. The raised firebox with polished brass throatplate beading was a feature possessed by many MS&L engines of the period along with the correspondingly high safety valve seating. Protection on the footplate was provided by the bent 'weatherboard', a mere 'port in a storm' for the engine crews who needed a tough disposition to survive such rigours as the passage over Woodhead.

Collection of G.H.Platt

PASSENGER ENGINES WORKING BUT REQUIRING RENEWAL

There are 18 Engines, which are employed at various points on the Line, and are with great difficulty kept in condition for doing even light work,such as 'Banking' etc. I beg to submit particulars as follows viz:-

Engine No.2 : This is an engine built at Gorton in 1868. It requires new cylinders, and boiler and firebox etc.

Engines Nos.65, 68, 71, 77, 86, 87, 146B, 147B,

148, 149, 150. The whole of these are small four coupled Passenger Engines. They are at work on various parts of the System, but are getting very far worn, and, at best, are only fit for 'Banking' or other light work.

Engines Nos.74, 75, 94, 97 & 98. These are also Engines of light construction. They are doing 'Banking' service in the South Yorkshire District.

Engine No.67. This a small four coupled Engine of No.25 Class and is working locally at Mexbro. The boiler and firebox are nearly 20 years old, and need extensive repairs.

GOODS ENGINES STANDING AT GORTON

ENGINE	CLASS	BUILT	AT	CONDITION
21	13	1863	Gorton	Cylinders patched: right hand inside frame cracked: tyres worn out: boiler and firebox worn out.
25	23	1861	Leeds	Both inside and outside frames broken: wheels worn out: boiler and firebox require renewing.
27	23	1861	Leeds	Firebox and casing and iron tubeplate worn out: outside frames broken: cylinders require renewing.
35	18	1870	Gorton	Now cut up.
51	13	1863	Gorton	Cylinders thin: left hand outside frame broken: boiler and firebox worn out.
54	13	1864	Gorton	Cylinders thin: right hand inside frame broken: boiler and firebox worn out.
84	23	1861	Leeds	Cylinders worn out: both frames cracked: boiler and firebox worn out.
95				Bought from South Yorkshire Co. Firebox and shell already cut up: other parts worn out.
103	22	1861	Gorton	Boiler and firebox require renewing: new cylinders required: frames are too light and require to be renewed.
116		1864		Bought from S. Y. Co. Boiler and firebox worn out: frames and tyres worn out: cylinders require renewing.
119		1864		Bought from S. Y. Co. Firebox and casing worn out: frames broken.
122	23	1860	Leeds	Cylinders very bad: both frames cracked: wheels and axles bad: boiler and firebox worn out.
127	23	1860	Leeds	Cylinders worn out: frames broken: crank axle condemned: boiler and firebox worn out.
130	23	1860	Leeds	New firebox and shell required: tyres worn out: new cylinders required.
131	23	1860	Leeds	Cylinders, boiler and firebox worn out: crank axle flawed: inside frames patched: outside frames cracked (too light).
132	13	1865	Leeds	Cylinders worn out: both frames broken: cast iron wheels: tyres worn out: boiler and firebox worn out.
134	23	1863	Leeds	Boiler and firebox worn out: frames broken: cylinders require renewing: all box brackets require renewing.
141	23	1863	Leeds	Inside frames broken: cylinders worn out: boiler and firebox worn out.
175	23	1864	Gorton. B.P.& Co.	Boiler and firebox worn out: cylinders require renewing: inside and outside frames broken: wheels require truing up.
189	23	1865	Glasgow	Now cut up
191	23	1865	Glasgow	Firebox worn out: tyres wheels and cylinders worn out: motion too light.

Locomotives with double frames were very popular with Charles Sacre, Thomas Parker's predecessor in charge of the Locomotive Department on the MS&L. The double frame arrangement provided two sets of journals on each of the coupled axles and gave extra security in the case of crank axle failure–a thing the MS&L had had more than their fair share of. No.169 (of 1885) was the last surviving member of Sacre's 12A 6ft. 2-4-0 express engines built over the decade from 1875 onwards. Standing outside Manchester Central's 'A' signalbox, the engine exhibits features typical onSacre's designs; amongst these were the double frame arrangement with springs above the footplate, 'a rather sparse cab with oval side window and round-topped firebox with safety valves mounted on a polished brass base. The picture is made more interesting by the fact that Robinson has had a hand in rebuilding the engine. His elegant chimney is a notable trademark complete with new smokebox, the earlier wingplates being done away with. Other alterations included a new boiler (added in 1902) with a flush-topped firebox and an altered profile to the lower cab panel. 169 had been built as no.549 and was re-numbered in 1893. The 'B' suffix was added in 1911 when the engine was placed on the duplicate list. Working throughout the Great Central era, no.169B survived, just, into LNER days and was withdrawn in June 1923.

Collection of G.H.Platt

193	23	1865	Glasgow	Cylinders heavily patched: inside frames condemned: outside frames broken.
197	23	1865	Glasgow	New boiler and firebox required: cylinders (old type) require renewing: both inside and outside frames broken, also buffer beam: crank axle badly worn.
199	23	1865	Glasgow	Boiler and firebox worn out: outside frames broken (too light): tyres worn out.
251	23	1867	Gorton. B.P.& Co.	Now cut up.
270	27	1866		Bought from Mid Wales Rly. Now cut up.

Goods Engine No.100, which was purchased from the South Yorkshire Company, is doing light work in the Mexbro District, but the boiler, firebox, and other parts, are so far worn that it would not be worth while spending money upon it.

For the most part, the Engines just mentioned, have been standing at Gorton for some considerable time, without turning a wheel, and although many of them are only fit for scrap, I have hesitated to cut them up because of leaving gaps in the Stock.

I beg to recommend that the whole of them be at once replaced by Goods Tender Engines of the same type as those built on the London Extension Account, and as we have already the necessary drawings, and patterns, by us, this could, I estimate, be accomplished for a sum, not exceeding £2,300 per Engine and Tender complete, after allowing scrap price for the old ones, and taking materials at their present prices.

It must not be for one moment assumed that the Engines just mentioned, are the only ones needing money spending upon them, as a considerable portion of those already in Service, are, more or less, in need of repairs, but cannot be withdrawn from Traffic because we are not in a position to spare them, and, even though we could withdraw them, our accomodation and appliances, as explained in another Report, are inadequate for getting the jobs through, with anything like reasonable expedition. I might also mention that a further large number of the Engines built by Messrs. Neilson & Co.,Messrs.Beyer,Peacock & Co., and Messrs. Sharp, Stewart & Co. about 1865-6-7 and known as No.23 Class, are now becoming very far worn, and their replacement, in the not very far distant future, needs to be taken into consideration.'

I have the honour to be, Gentlemen,
Your obedient servant,
Harry Pollitt.

Locomotive Engineers of the MS&L and GC Companies

Richard Peacock* 1841-1854
Peacock's official title was Locomotive Superintendent, a title passed on to his successor.

William Grindley Craig.......................1854-1859

Charles Reboul Sacre...................................1859-1886
Sacre's designation was Engineer and Superintendent of Locomotive and Stores Department.
Thomas Parker 1886-1893
Parker was designated Locomotive, Carriage and Wagon

Superintendent.
Harry Pollitt 1893-1899
Locomotive Engineer.
John George Robinson 1900-1922
Appointed as Locomotive Superintendent but designated Chief Mechanical Engineer, incorporating Locomotive, Carriage & Wagon departments, from May 1st 1902.

* Richard Peacock was in office with the Sheffield, Ashton-under-Lyne & Manchester Railway prior to this company's incorporation into the Manchester, Sheffield & Lincolnshire Railway from July 27th 1846.

No.889 in its original state at a location believed to be Birkenhead Docks. The engine is in 'as built' condition with warning bell on top of the cab and Pollitt stovepipe chimney. Steam sanding was fitted to these engines from new with sandboxes, as seen here, either side of the centre coupled wheels. The paintwork around the cab is set out in lined panels; lining is applied too, to the sandboxes. The ensemble is completed by polished motion and cylinder covers with those splendid loco lamps carried fore and aft. Notice that the driver, mirabile dictu, wears a collar and tie!

Collection of G.H.Platt

Class 5 0-6-0 Saddle Tank

The Great Central Railway Company was formally established on August 1st.1897. Hitherto a provincial, cross-country line, under the Chairmanship of Edward Watkin (later Sir Edward) the Manchester, Sheffield & Lincolnshire, the 'money sunk and lost' empire of the Victorian lampooners and cartoonists, had set its sights on London. Watkin, with incredible foresight, envisaged the day when through trains might be run from the North of England to Paris via a channel tunnel.

Such a lofty plane might seem an odd point to introduce a diminutive and somewhat insignificant-looking tank engine. Indeed, though most readers could readily identify a Robinson 4-4-0 or 4-6-0, Director or Atlantic as a 'typically' Great Central design-relatively few would associate the humble engines in these accompanying illustrations as being part of the G.C.motive power stud. Yet a railway company with large dock complexes needs small, short-wheelbase engines as much as it needs a passenger design with large coupled wheels when it is contemplating a lengthy main line. So it may surprise some enthusiasts to realise that the first design to be built under true Great Central auspisces was *not* a large-wheeled 4-4-0 or a Single driver but a somewhat unprepossessing tank engine.

Harry Pollitt produced his 0-6-0 tank in 1897 on the eve of the demise of the MS&L. Intended for use on the Grimsby dock lines and other areas where curvature tended to be tight, the Class 5 saddle tank had coupled wheels of only 3'-6" diameter-just about the size of a bogie wheel on a 4-4-0 passenger engine. With a wheelbase of only 12' in total, here was indeed a charming little engine. A 'horse for a course' if ever there was one.

MAIN DIMENSIONS

CYLINDERS: (2 Outside).13" x 20"
MOTION: Stephenson with slide valves
BOILER: Max. outside diameter 3'-6 15/16"

Barrel length: 9'-3"
Firebox length outside: 4'-6"
Pitch above rail level: 6'-0"
Heating surface: Firebox 60sq.ft.
Heating surface: Tubes (124 x 1¾")-530 sq.ft.
Total heating surface: 590 sq.ft.

GRATE AREA: 11.43 sq.ft.
BOILER PRESSURE: 150 p.s.i.
COUPLED WHEEL DIAMETER: 3'-6"
TRACTIVE EFFORT: (at 85% b.p.) 10,260 lbs.
LENGTH OVER BUFFERS: 26'-11½"
COUPLED WHEELBASE: 6'-0" + 6'-0"
                           (12'-0" total)
WEIGHT IN WORKING ORDER: 30 tons 17 cwt
MAXIMUM AXLE LOADING: 11 tons 10 cwt
WATER CAPACITY: 600 gallons
COAL CAPACITY: 1½ tons

Note.Withdrawal dates given in each Class Summary represent the first and last loco withdrawals, except where indicated.

Away from dock areas, we return inland to Gorton to view no.885-probably returned there for a heavy repair. The Pollitt stovepipe chimney is still carried, though steam sanding has given way to dry sanding with the front sandbox prominently mounted alongside the smokebox. After Grouping, transfer away from previous 'home' areas took place. Ipswich and Neasden, Chester, Trafford Park and Ardsley were all recorded as playing host to members of the class. First of the class 5 saddletanks to be withdrawn was no.892 (then 5892) in April 1935. The last one, no.883 of 1897 soldiered bravely on at Wrexham (as B.R.no.68200) until November 1951.

Collection of G.H.Platt

In 1903 Robinson rebuilt no.889 as an 0-6-2 complete with a crane mounted on its rearward extension. Vulcan Foundry of Newton-le-Willows, Lancs. supplied the crane of 4 tons lifting capacity which boosted the weight of the engine by just over 5½ tons. An odd-looking machine, it apparently rejoiced in the popular sobriquets of *Little Dick* and *Fat Dan*. Differences from no.884 are obvious, but the warning bell in front of the cab - normally fitted to engines of this class working in dock areas where foot traffic would be expected - is a feature of interest. 889 was rebuilt back into its original state in January 1918 after damage to its rear end in a collision. This quite remarkable little engine gave its three respective owners excellent service. It was withdrawn on the eve of the B.R. era, just 6 months on top of a life of 50 years.

Collection of G.H.Platt

Class 5. Type 0.6.0. No. of Engines ... 12.

Makers	Year Built	No. of Engines	Makers	Year Built	No. of Engines	Makers	Year Built	No. of Engines
G. C. R.	1897	12						

CYLINDERS.
Diameter .... 13"
Stroke .... 20"
Centres .... 6'-6¾"

BOILER.
Class 5
Working Pressure .... 150 ...Lbs. per ☐"
Barrel Dia. Outs. Max. .... 3'-6⁹⁄₁₆"
Barrel Length .... 9'-3"
Barrel Thickness of Plates .... ¹⁵⁄₃₂

TUBES.
Large No. .... Dia. Outs. ......
Small No. 124 Dia. Outs. 1¾"
Length between Tubeplates .... 9'-7⁹⁄₁₆"

SUPERHEATER.
Kind of Header ....
Elements { Dia. Outs. ....
Dia. Ins. ....
Number ....

IF FITTED WITH
Draft Retarder ....
Circulating Valve ....
Header Discharge Valve ....
Pressure Release Valves ....
Combined Pressure Release } ....
and Piston Valves }

FIREBOX SHELL.
Length Outs. at Bottom .... 4'-6"
Width ,, ,, ,, ... 3'-7⅞"
,, ,, ,, Top .... 3'-7⅞"
Thickness of Plates—
Back ½" ..Casing ¹⁵⁄₃₂ ..Throat ⁹⁄₁₆"

COPPER FIREBOX.
Length of Grate .... 3'-9¹³⁄₁₆"
Width ,, ,, ... 3'-0"
Depth to Top of Ring, Front .... 4'-5⅞"
,, ,, ,, Back .... 4'-0⅝"

Width of Ring.
Back and Front .... 3" Sides .... 3"
Thickness of Plates—
Back ⁹⁄₁₆" ..Casing ¹⁵⁄₃₂ ..Tube { ¾"
{ ⁹⁄₁₆"

HEATING SURFACE.
Firebox Outside .... 60 ..Sq. ft.
Large Tubes .... -- ,,
Small Tubes .... 530 ,,
Superheater Inside .... ,,
Total .... 590 ,,

GRATE AREA. .... 11 .. Sq. ft.

WHEELS. Diameter. See Diagram.
Tyres Thickness .... 3"
JOURNALS. Dia. Length.
Leading Bogie or Truck ....
Leading Coupled .... 6" 7"
Driving .... 6" 7"
Intermediate ....
Trailing Coupled .... 6" 7"
Trailing Bogie or Truck ....
Tractive Power at { Lbs. 10,218
85% Boiler Pressure { Tons .... 4·5
Adhesion Coefficient. Lbs. per Ton 343
Height. Rail to Top of Chimney .... 11'-0"
,, ,, Centre of Boiler .... 6'-0"

VALVES. Kind .... Unbalanced Slide

CYLINDER LUBRICATOR. Kind .... "Roscoe"
If Fitted with Steam Sanding Apparatus .... Yes
,, ,, Train Warming .... No

BRAKE. .... Steam
TANK ~~TENDER~~. Capacity. Water, Gallons 600
,, Coal, Tons 1½
WHEELS. Diameter .... --
JOURNALS. Dia. .... -- Length .... --

Pollitt Class 5 0-6-0 no.884. 12 of these little engines were built over a fairly even span from January to December 1897. Numbered consecutively from 882 to 893, no.891 was the last engine to be built for the MS&L, no.892 being the first to appear in the G.C. era proper. The saddle tank was somewhat reminiscent of the Sacr'e class 18 and 18T of the same wheel arrangement which had first appeared some 28 years earlier. 884 carries the original Pollitt stovepipe chimney. Steam sanding, equipped from new, has given way to dry sanding; the front sandbox is clearly discernible whilst that for the rear wheels is situated under the cab, behind the footstep. The saddle tank itself held just 600 gallons of water, the coal-railed bunker having just a mere 1½ tons coal capacity. Notice the absence of vacuum pipes, the engines being fitted only with steam brake and no vacuum ejector. Original MS&L taper-shank buffers have given way to the parallel-cased G.C.variety. Round-head buffers, as seen here, were the exception for the class, oval heads being the apparent norm for most engines. Cylinder lubrication is carried out by means of a drip-feed pattern lubricator fixed to each side of the smokebox.

Collection of G.H.Platt

SUMMARY OF CLASS 5 0-6-0 SADDLE TANK (LNER J62)

NUMBER	BUILDER	DATE BUILT	WITHDRAWN
882 - 893	Gorton Works	January to December 1897	Apr 1935-Nov 1952

Another look at these most attractive little engines shows some distinctive variations from the rest of the class. Though the engine in question is not identifiable by any marking we may well be looking at no.890. The original steam sanding gear (as opposed to dry sanding) is carried and Pollitt's neat stovepipe chimney has been substituted by one of Robinson's own design as fitted to his 5A tank (see later). A bucket or basket-type spark arrester is rivetted to the rim of the chimney, a device carried by several members of the class at various times. Buffers are, again, of the Great Central variety carried on a buffer plank which is literally that a wooden beam backed either side by a steel flitch plate. This engine, together with no.884 and 891 carry twin smokebox door handles compared to the wheel and dart carried by the crane loco-no.889.

Collection of G.H.Platt

Class 9F 0-6-2 tank no.775 as built by Beyer,Peacock & Co.in August 1898. Both Pollitt and Robinson continued to build this powerful and useful design, the latter up until 1901. 775 appears as she emerged in the first full year of the Great Central's existence: i.e. with stovepipe chimney, tall twin-pillar safety valves mounted on a high base on top of the original Belpaire firebox, two whistles-one for warning, the other for signalling purposes, hook and chain coupling with adjacent side chains, taper-shank buffers and double brake hangers with brake block between. A displacement lubricator is fitted to the left-hand side of the smokebox, a fitting removed fairly early on in the engines' life and the coal rails display an outward curve. By the look of the enormous heap of coal the engine has been saddled with, the three rails are barely adequate!No.775 was amongst the last of the class to be withdrawn. She was taken out of service in January 1960.

Author's collection

Class 9C. Type 0.6.2. Nº of Engines ... 3.

Maker	Year Built	Nº of Engines	Maker	Year Built	Nº of Engines	Maker	Year Built	Nº of Engines
G C R	1891	1						
"	1892	2						

CYLINDERS.
Diameter .... 18"
Stroke .... 26"
Centres .... 2.0"

BOILER.
Class .... Nº 1 Standard
Working Pressure .... 160 Lbs. per □"
Barrel Dia. Outs. Max. .... 4'-4"
Barrel Length .... 10'-8⅛"
Barrel Thickness of Plates .... ½"

TUBES.
Large No. .... —   Dia. Outs. .... —
Small No. 190   Dia. Outs. .... 1¾"
Length between Tubeplates .... 11'-0²⁹⁄₃₂"

SUPERHEATER.
Kind of Header .... —
Elements { Dia. Outs. .... —
Dia. Ins. .... —
Number .... —

IF FITTED WITH
Draft Retarder .... —
Circulating Valve .... —
Header Discharge Valve .... —
Pressure Release Valves .... —
Combined Pressure Release and Piston Valves } .... —

FIREBOX SHELL.
Length Outs. at Bottom .... 6'-0"
Width „ „ „ .... 4'-1"
 „ „ „ Top .... 4'-6¼"
Thickness of Plates—
Back ⁷⁄₃₂" Casing ½" Throat ⁵⁄₈"

COPPER FIREBOX.
Length of Grate .... 5'-4²⁹⁄₃₂"
Width „ „ .... 3'-5"
Depth to Top of Ring, Front .... 5'-6"
 „ „ „ Back .... 4'-8½"

Width of Ring.
Back and Front .... 7½" Sides 3"
Thickness of Plates—
Back ½" Casing ½" Tube { ⅞"
½"

HEATING SURFACE.
Firebox Outside .... 99 Sq. ft.
Large Tubes .... — „
Small Tubes .... 964 „
Superheater Inside .... — „
Total .... 1063 „

GRATE AREA. .... 18.3 Sq. ft.

WHEELS.   Diameter.   See Diagram.
Tyres   Thickness .... 3"

JOURNALS.   Dia.   Length.
Leading Bogie or Truck .... —   —
Leading Coupled .... 7½"   9"
Driving .... 7½"   9"
Intermediate .... —   —
Trailing Coupled .... 7½"   9"
Trailing Bogie or Truck radial .... 7"   11"
Tractive Power at 85% Boiler Pressure { Lbs. 18,781
Tons 9.4
Adhesion Coefficient. Lbs. per Ton 401
Height.   Rail to Top of Chimney .... 13'-3"
 „   „   Centre of Boiler .... 7'-4½"

VALVES.   Kind .... Balanced Slide

CYLINDER LUBRICATOR.   Kind .... Sight Feed
If Fitted with Steam Sanding Apparatus .... Yes
 „   „ Train Warning   „ .... No

BRAKE. .... Auto Vacuum
TANK TENDER.   Capacity. Water, Gallons 1360
 „   Coal, Tons 3

WHEELS.   Diameter. .... —

JOURNALS.   Dia. .... —   Length. .... —

0-6-2 Tanks Built for the MS&L and GC Railways

Classes 9C/9F/9O

It is something of a paradox that of all the volumes of words written about railway locomotives and trains in general and of all the countless pictures taken of them, the least has been said and recorded of goods train operations and their associated motive power. A paradox because it was freight operations that earned the railways the bulk of their revenues. Indeed, railways had been born to move goods.

Statistics, it is said, can prove anything but these figures for the Great Central's traffic movements for the year ended December 31st 1913 should speak for themselves:

Gross Receipts
Passenger train traffic: £1,307,514
Goods train traffic: £3,589,047

To create this income 31,013,332 passengers were carried at an average fare of 6.75d.

Goods and livestock traffic broke down as follows:
Merchandise: 6,158,742 tons
Coal, coke and patent fuels: 23,728,437 tons
Other minerals: 5,120,155 tons
Head of livestock: 666,933

Mention is made elsewhere of the difficulties that faced railway photographers in the pre-Group era. Passenger engines because of their size, livery, nature and status did, in the main, tend to steal the limelight. In any case, yards were 'off limits' as far as photographers were concerned and the seemingly humble goods trains never looked as attractive as their passenger counterparts, adorned as they were in often splendid liveries and with overtones of romance and far-away destinations.

Nevertheless, a good many pictures of goods engines and their work exist and we should be thankful to those photographers who were thoughtful enough to provide them for later generations. On to the 0-6-2 tanks of the MS&L.

Thomas Parker, Locomotive Superintendent of the company from 1886 to 1893 had introduced the 0-6-2 tank desgn to that railway in 1889. This particular wheel arrangement was quite popular one with the companies that made up the LNER group, athough other railways, notably the Midland and the GWR (until absorption of the South Wales companies) eschewed its use almost entirely.

Parker made a cautious start with his 9A design, building just three examples at the end of 1889 and the beginning of 1890. With 5ft 1in coupled wheels, Joy valve gear (favoured by him for goods work) and a weight in working order of just over 61 tons they represented a massive advance over any goods tank design on the

MS&L up to that date. The 9A tank was a big engine - larger certainly than anything comparable on neighbouring railways such as the LNWR who had some good 0-6-2 tanks of their own. A successful and useful design ensued; 55 examples were built between the aforementioned date and 1892.

The last batch of 9A tanks were turned out with a slightly longer coal bunker causing them to be reclassified 9A Altered. This later series, somewhat perversely, was modelled on the second class of MS&L 0-6-2 tanks, Class 9C with its 9F and 9O variants; these were introduced by Thomas Parker from September 1891 onwards.

The 9C was a logical development of the 9A engine and it was this later design that was to prove the most successful and numerous of the Great Central's tank engine stud. Built up to 1901 the 9C/9F design was multiplied under both Pollitt and Robinson to eventually total 131 locomotives.

As with his first 0-6-2 tanks, Parker trod carefully before embarking on any degree of large-scale production. The 9C incorporated two radical changes to the initial design, these were: the use of Stephenson valve gear as opposed to the Joy gear employed in the 9As and secondly, the application of a Belpaire firebox - the first to an engine built for use on a British railway - in lieu of the round-topped design hitherto used. This latter development had never really been given the credit it deserved; Beyer, Peacock had first used the Belpaire firebox on a rather obscure locomotive, a 2-4-0 tender engine they had built for the Melnes and Terneuzen Railway (Belgium and Netherlands) in 1871. Given the close proximity of Beyer, Peacock to the MS&Ls own Gorton Locomotive works it is not surprising that ideas were transmitted, particularly in view of the company's work for the MS&L; though it has to be said that a gap of 20 years for the idea to be applied could hardly be described as catching on like wildfire!

So successful was the Belpaire firebox that it was applied eventually to all the 9A tanks, used almost exclusively by Robinson for all his work on the GC and became practically 'standard issue' for the GWR and LMS in later years

The three Class 9C engines were, as stated, built with Stephenson valve gear. Some experimentation was made in respect of the layout of the drive to the slide valves. Once this had been resolved the new layout was used for all future engines - then classified 9F.

Initially the cylinder diameter was set at 18½ins; this was later bored out to 19ins but by Grouping a size of 18ins was in use; this bore will be observed on the accompanying GC engine diagram.

Though the whole class had been fitted with Belpaire fireboxes on building, alterations had been made to the

Reference is made elsewhere in the text of this book to Guide Bridge, an important focal point on the Great Central's Manchester-Sheffield line. North-east of the station were the company's Brookside sidings which ran parallel to the G.C's line to Dukinfield, Ashton and Stalybridge. The Guide Bridge area was closely associated with cotton spinning and possessed a variety of other industries-coal mining, hat manufacture and rope making, to name a few. The 0-6-2 tanks inhabited this typical goods environment: rows of ash-ballasted siding roads, a not too pristine-looking locomotive with open wagons to the fore. Brookside sidings were bordered by the Manchester & Ashton-under-Lyne canal. The building to the left is part of Gartside's Brookside Brewery; in the background can be seen the Oxford Cotton mills, one of many such mills in the vicinity. This photograph of 9F no.542 typifies the general outlines of the early series of 0-6-2 tank engines and gives a good general impression of the MS&L/GC 0-6-2 varieties as a whole. Gorton 542 was one of a batch of 30 engines built by Beyer, Peacock & Co.in 1893-94. The company constructed 81 of the class total including the final 2 batches built under Robinson's jurisdiction in 1900-1901. Gorton works completed the remaining 50 up to 1900. Robinson has applied his own elegant pattern of chimney to no. 542, replacing the stovepipe version favoured by Parker. It might be argued that these engines lost something of their original character by being 're-chimneyed' as it were. Though Robinson's own chimneys had a definite elegance, the stovepipe was a characteristic MS&L feature-lost on rebuilding.MS&L taper-shank buffers feature on the engine, substituted later by the standard G.C.R parallel pattern. These locomotives as originally built had side hooks and chain-type couplings, removed fairly quickly and replaced, as seen here, by the 3-link pattern. After Grouping, screw couplings became the norm. Note that no.542 is vacuum fitted-a standard for all the class. Coal bunkers on the 9C/9F engines held 3 tons of fuel and had been altered in shape as building progressed: those engines built prior to December 1895 had bunkers with curved backs-as shown here-those built after this date had straight backed bunkers. The coal rails were a later addition. A study of Great Central engines in their later years reveals a curious anomaly in respect of smokebox door handles. The various MS&L/GC 0-6-2 tanks all received twin smokebox door handles when built; these reverted fairly quickly to the wheel and single handle-a more or less standard Robinson fitting. This somewhat reversed the treatment meted out to other classes, though twin handles became a standard for the engines in later LNER days and through to the B.R.era.

Collection of G.H.Platt

boilers, particularly in respect of the number of firetubes - from 233 originally to 190 in the 1901 engines. This improved boiler was to be designated the GC Standard No.1 boiler and was used on a wide variety of classes. Boiler pressure was standardized at 160lbs p.s.i. on the first engines of the class. Those built after 1894 had their safety valves set to blow off at the higher pressure of 170lbs p.s.i. By Grouping the original pressure had been restored as standard for the whole class. It is interesting to note that when Robinson took up his appointment as Locomotive Engineer in 1900 one of his first acts had been to seek approval for the purchase of spare boilers from outside contractors. Thus the advantages of standardisation in such a crucial area were obvious to him and, as has been observed, many of his designs showed a wide interchangeability of component parts.

SUMMARY OF CLASSES 9C/9F/9O 0-6-2 TANKS (LNER N5)

NUMBER	BUILDER	DATE BUILT	WITHDRAWN
515 - 517	Gorton	September to November 1892	Jul 1949-Aug 1956
518 - 535/537 -548	Beyer Peacock & Co.	August 1893 to March 1894	Nov 1936-Nov 1960
744 - 755*	Beyer Peacock & Co.	August to November 1894	Jan 1954-Nov 1960
536	Gorton	May 1895	Nov 1960
200	Gorton	September 1895	Jan 1960
21/25,54,756 - 762	Gorton	December 1895 to December 1896	Nov 1937-Dec 1960
754/755	Beyer Peacock & Co.	January 1896	Dec 1938-Dec 1957
409/410**	Beyer Peacock & Co.	1896	Feb 1936-Oct 1956
763 - 775	Beyer Peacock & Co.	March to August 1898	Jan 1939-Dec 1960
51,173/189,251	Gorton	February to May 1898	Mar 1943-Jun 1958
894 - 924	Gorton	March 1899 to December 1900	Nov 1954-Jan 1960
925 - 940	Beyer Peacock & Co.	April to July 1900	Jun 1955-Mar 1960
941 - 946	Beyer Peacock & Co.	February to March 1901	Nov 1955-Sep 1960

Notes:
1) Some renumbering of engines had taken place between 1893 and 1903. Insofar as this affects this number series, No.538 had become No.127 in 1903
*2) * Nos.754 & 755 had been sold to the West Lancashire Railway in 1895 and were replaced in 1896 by two new engines with the same numbers.*
*3) ** These two engines had been built for the Wrexham, Mold & Connah's Quay Railway in 1896 (Nos. 17 & 18) and were taken into G.C.stock in 1905.*

The next two photographs show the final development of the MS&L 9F 0-6-2 tank design in the Great Central era under two different Locomotive Engineers. 9F no.901 built at Gorton in August 1899 under Pollitt's jurisdiction is on Gorton shed around the turn of the century. The engine displays nicely most of its original features, showing stovepipe chimney-as mentioned, a strong MS&L characteristic and tall, uncased Ramsbottom safety valves; these were later replaced by a shorter pattern enclosed in a cast iron casing. Hook and chain couplings are fitted, side chains having now been abandoned. Notice that two whistles are carried here, later reduced throughout the class to just one. Below the pillars of the safety valves, the smooth contours of the now standard Belpaire firebox appear-compare this with the other pictures in the sequence showing the 'blisters' of the Robinson G.C.standard no.1 boiler. Final MS&L touches are the taper shank buffers, giving way later to the standard G.C.parallel-cased pattern. No photographs have come to light of this later series of 9F tanks running without coal rails. Given the early condition of no.901 it is possible that the engines carried these from new. The straight-backed bunker was carried by all the post-1895 engines, the earlier ones having bunkers with curved backs (q.v.). Inexplicably, three 9Fs built at Gorton in 1898 (nos.51/173/189) reverted to the curved shape. Livery here appears to be plain black with unshaded letters and numerals. An altogether very interesting and appealing study.

Collection of G.H.Platt

Robinson experimented with superheating with the 9C/9F tanks, treating just seven of them in 1915/16. The apparatus was removed from all but one engine in LNER days and it may have been thought that the initial first cost and maintenance of the superheater could not be recouped from locomotives with relatively low daily mileages. This picture of 9F no.127, seen shunting alongside the goods warehouse at Huddersfield, shows the engine carrying the longer smokebox (with necessary front frame extensions) required to accommodate the superheating fitments-wet and dry headers and requisite pipework. Notice again the curved back to the bunker with coal rails on top and the substitution of parallel-cased buffers for the earlier taper-shank variety. Wheel and handle fastening have been substituted on the smokebox door in lieu of the twin handles carried by no.542.

Collection of G.H.Platt

Class 9F. Type 0.6.2. No. of Engines ... 125.

Maker	Year Built	No. of Engines	Maker	Year Built	No. of Engines	Maker	Year Built	No. of Engines
Beyer Peacock	1893	17	Beyer Peacock	1896	2	G.C.R.	1900	15
"	1894	25	" "	1898	12	Beyer Peacock	1900	16
G.C.R.	1895	3	G.C.R.	1899	4	" "	1901	6
"	1896	9	"	1899	16			

Figures in red refer to superheated engines only. Total Superheated 7.

CYLINDERS.
Diameter .... 18"
Stroke .... 26"
Centres .... 2'0"

BOILER.
Class .... No 1 Standard
Working Pressure .... 160 Lbs. per ☐"
Barrel Dia. Outs. Max. .... 4'.4"
Barrel Length .... 10'.8½"
Barrel Thickness of Plates .... ½"

TUBES.
Large No. .... 15 .... Dia. Outs. .... 5¼"
Small No. 190. 167 Dia. Outs. 1¾" 1⅞"
Length between Tubeplates .... 11'.0⅞/32"

SUPERHEATER. Robinson
Kind of Header .... New Cover —
Elements { Dia. Outs. .... 1⅜"
Dia. Ins. .... 1⅛"
Number 15

IF FITTED WITH
Draft Retarder .... No —
Circulating Valve .... No —
Header Discharge Valve .... No —
Pressure Release Valves .... No —
Combined Pressure Release and Piston Valves } .... No —

FIREBOX SHELL.
Length Outs. at Bottom .... 6'.0"
Width " " " .... 4'.1"
" " " Top .... 4'.6¼"
Thickness of Plates—
Back 7/32" Casing ½" Throat ⅝"

COPPER FIREBOX.
Length of Grate .... 5'.4²⁷/₃₂"
Width " " .... 3'.5"
Depth to Top of Ring, Front .... 5'.6"
" " " Back .... 4'.8½"

Width of Ring.
Back and Front .... 2½" Sides .... 3"
Thickness of Plates—
Back ½" Casing ½" Tube { ⅞"
{ ½"

HEATING SURFACE.
Firebox Outside .... 99 99 Sq. ft.
Large Tubes .... 277 "
Small Tubes .... 884 964 "
Superheater Inside .... 113 — "
Total 995 1063 "

GRATE AREA. .... 18·3 Sq. ft.

WHEELS. Diameter. See Diagram.
Tyres Thickness .... 3"
JOURNALS. Dia. Length.
Leading Bogie or Truck .... — —
Leading Coupled .... 8" 9"
Driving .... 8" 9"
Intermediate .... — —
Trailing Coupled .... 8" 9"
Trailing Bogie or Truck radial .... 7" 11"
Tractive Power at 85% Boiler Pressure { Lbs. 18,781
{ Tons 8.4
Adhesion Coefficient. Lbs. per Ton 383
Height. Rail to Top of Chimney .... 13'.3"
" " Centre of Boiler .... 7'.4½"
VALVES. Kind .... Balanced Slide
CYLINDER LUBRICATOR. Kind Sight Feed
If Fitted with Steam Sanding Apparatus .... No
" " Train Warming " .... Yes & No
BRAKE. .... Auto Vacuum
TANK TENDER. Capacity. Water, Gallons 1360
" " Coal, Tons 3
WHEELS. Diameter .... —
JOURNALS. Dia. .... — Length .... —

We move forward in time, well and truly into the Robinson era to stand outside Manchester London Road station for this next view. On show here is 9F no.942-the second of the last six of the class turned out from Beyer,Peacock's Gorton Foundry in February and March 1901. Before plunging into the details of the last of these locomotives notice the church spires reaching loftily into the beyond. Seen on a good many views outside London Road, St.Andrews, smoke- blackened like so much Manchester architecture in those days, stood in a square of that name at the end of 'Travis Street. And it was from 'Travis Street in November 1841 that the very first trains ventured forth on the Sheffield, Ashton-under-Lyne and Manchester Railway as far as Godley Toll Bar. Thus, a little piece of history was made; the earliest beginnings of the Great Central's forerunners.No.942 appears to be on empty coaching stock duties; the G.C.brake-ended corridor coach (running no.1873) is one of the 60 ft.vehicles built by the company at the Dukinfield carriage and wagon works. Activities were transferred to Dukinfield, east of Guide Bridge, in 1910, Gorton having simply become too small and congested for operations to continue. Robinson had been appointed Chief Mechanical Engineer in 1902, his remit widened to include such matters. This final batch of 9F's bore detail differences from the earlier engines. The omni-present Robinson chimney is fairly obvious, but safety valves also differ; though of the Ramsbottom variety, the pillars are mounted directly on top of the firebox, lacking the circular base carried by no.901.Locomotives built under Parker and Pollitt displayed rows of snap-head rivets (modellers must curse here!) Robinson appears to have disliked their use as none of his designs show anything like the same preponderance of such fastenings. Tenders, particularly, are a case in point. Significantly, the last six engines-built in 1901-had countersunk rivets to hold their side tanks and bunkers together, giving a smoother side profile and making them quickly recognisable from the rest of the class.

Collection of G.H.Platt

Class 9O.   Type 0.6.2.   N° of Engines ... 1.

Maker	Year Built	N° of Engines	Maker	Year Built	N° of Engines	Maker	Year Built	N° of Engines
Beyer Peacock & C°.	1898	1						

— Rebuilt from 9F Class. —

CYLINDERS.
Diameter .... 18½"
Stroke .... 26"
Centres .... 2'.0"

BOILER.
Class .... N° 1 Standard
Working Pressure .... 180 Lbs. per □"
Barrel Dia. Outs. Max .... 4'.4"
Barrel Length .... 10'.8½"
Barrel Thickness of Plates .... ½"

TUBES.
Large No. 15   Dia. Outs. .... 5¼"
Small No. 102   Dia. Outs. .... 1⅛"
Length between Tubeplates .... 11'.0 ⁹⁄₃₂"

SUPERHEATER. *'Robinson'*
Kind of Header .... Front Cover
Elements { Dia. Outs. .... 1⅜"
Dia. Ins. .... 1¹⁄₁₆"
Number 15

IF FITTED WITH
Draft Retarder ....
Circulating Valve .... No.
Header Discharge Valve .... Yes.
Pressure Release Valve .... No.
Combined Pressure Release and Piston Valves } .... No.

FIREBOX SHELL.
Length Outs. at Bottom .... 6'.0"
Width " " " .... 4'.1"
" " " Top .... 4'.6¼"
Thickness of Plates—
Back ⁷⁄₃₂". Casing ½". Throat ⅝"

COPPER FIREBOX.
Length of Grate .... 5'.4 ²⁹⁄₃₂"
Width " " .... 3'.5"
Depth to Top of Ring, Front .... 5'.6"
" " " Back .... 4'.8½"
Width of Ring.
Back and Front 2½". Sides 3"
Thickness of Plates—
Back ½". Casing ½". Tube { ⅞" ½"

HEATING SURFACE.
Firebox Outside .... 99 Sq. ft.
Large Tubes .... 227 "
Small Tubes .... 554 "
Superheater Inside .... 113 "
Total .... 993 "

GRATE AREA. .... 18.3 Sq. ft.

WHEELS. Diameter. See Diagram.
Tyres Thickness .... 3"
JOURNALS. Dia.   Length.
Leading Bogie or Truck ....
Leading Coupled .... 8"   9"
Driving .... 8"   9"
Intermediate ....
Trailing Coupled .... 8"   9"
Trailing Radial as Truck .... 7"   11"
Tractive Power at 85% Boiler Pressure { Lbs. 19,583 Tons 8.7
Adhesion Coefficient. Lbs. per Ton. 365
Height. Rail to Top of Chimney .... 13'.3"
" " Centre of Boiler .... 7'.4½"

VALVES. Kind .... Balanced Slide

CYLINDER LUBRICATOR. Kind .... Intensifore
If Fitted with Steam Sanding Apparatus .... Yes
" " Train Warming " .... Yes
BRAKE. .... Steam + Auto Ejector
TANK TENDER. Capacity. Water, Gallons 2,000
" Coal, Tons 4

WHEELS. Diameter ....
JOURNALS. Dia. ....   Length ....

This rather grotesque and certainly un-Robinson-esque locomotive was a rebuild of 9F no.771, carried out in November 1915. Re-classified 9O by the G.C., this almost monstrous-looking specimen had been given a standard no.1 boiler (with superheater), extended side tanks and bunker. This had increased the water capacity by 480 gallons and the coal capacity by 17cwt., raising the weight in working order to some 66 tons.

Wheels, cylinders and motion were unaltered save for amending the design of the trailing axle from that of radial pattern to a pony truck in order to ease the locomotive's passage round tight radius curves.

The purpose of the rebuilding was reputedly to enable the engine to work passenger trains from Chester Northgate to Connah's Quay and Shotton. The G.C. had territory here, including the lines of the former WM&CQ Rly absorbed by the company in 1905. (Incidentally two 9F engines had been built by Beyer, Peacock & Co. in 1896 for the WM&CQ). No watering facilities existed at Shotton, hence the provision of no.771 with its enhanced water capacity. A particular

hazard in this area was the 4 mile bank on a gradient of 1 in 53 between Hawarden and Hope. It is reported, however, that the engine worked in the Chester district for only 14 months before returning to Gorton and its subsequent removal from passenger duties.

The caged-in bunker is reminiscent of that carried by the 9L and 9N tanks, whilst the side cab profile matches exactly that carried by the Robinson L1 2-6-4 tanks of 1914 and 1917,

No further examples of 9F rebuilds were made; the very ugly but essentially functional long side tanks remind one of the Great Northern's J23 (LNER J50) tanks, although lacking the latters sloping tops. 771 survived into the LNER period, classified N5/2, later N5/3. The mandatory 'flowerpot' chimney was fitted and her superheater was removed in 1930. Becoming B.R. no.69311, she was withdrawn in early 1952.

Note: The engine diagram for this singular class gives the weight in working order as 62 tons 18 cwts. This is thought to be incorrect, a weight of some 66 tons being more accurate.

This broadside view of no.771 reveals the slab-sided appearance of this rather ungainly-looking locomotive.

The neat, yet sturdy, outlines of the 9G 2-4-2 tank are faithfully captured here in this study of no.777 standing on the siding roads adjacent to the turntable outside Manchester Central station-an area referred to in the section dealing with the Class 1 4-6-0s. Though reference to the engines' predecessors, the Class 3 2-4-2 tanks, will be made in a subsequent volume, the basic outline of the two types was very similar. The boiler was pitched 5in. higher on the 9G and they shared the longer bunker of the Class 3 Altered design, though lacking the latter's outwardly curved top. As mentioned, Stephenson's Link Motion was fitted to the later engines, in preference to Joy's valve gear and the piston stroke was increased from the previous 24in. to 26in. Slide valves were retained, operated by rocking shafts from the Stephenson gear.

Collection of G.H.Platt

A magnificent study of 9G 2-4-2 tank no.782 resplendent in Great Central green livery outside Manchester Central 'A' signalbox, just beyond the main station. These natty little engines, 10 in all, were built by Beyer-,Peacock & Co. between March and June in 1898. As with the 9F tanks, the 9G's were fitted with Belpaire fireboxes from new. Their predecessors, the Class 3 2-4-2 tanks, carried round-topped fireboxes when built and were subsequently re-boilered. Similarly, Joy valve gear, favoured by Parker, had been abandoned by Pollitt in favour of the ubiquitous Stephenson's link motion for this (and other designs.) Though built with stovepipe chimneys in true MS&L style, Robinson fitted his own pattern, instantly recognisable with its curvaceous, elegant outlines. The location of Manchester Central would appear to be appropriate, for 782 spent at least the latter part of its working life based on Gorton shed. *Collection of G.H.Platt*

Class 9G 2-4-2 Tanks

Three Classic MS&L designs were selectively enlarged and developed to provide 'workhorse' locomotives for duty in the early years of the Great central. They were: the Parker 9A 0-6-2 tank of 1889, developed into the 9F series, the 9H 0-6-0 goods engine, another Parker design originating in 1892 and itself a throwback to an earlier engine of the late 1880s. This formed the basis for the celebrated 'Pom-Pom' of the early Robinson years. Finally, in like manner, Pollitt took the Class 3 (Altered version with extended bunker) 2-4-2 tank built by Parker for the MS&L between 1889 and 1893 and produced the design described here, the 9G 2-4-2 tank engines - all built in 1898.

SUMMARY OF CLASS 9G 2 - 4 - 2 TANKS (LNER F2)

NUMBER	BUILDER	DATE BUILT	WITHDRAWN
776 - 785	Beyer Peacock & Co.	March to June 1898	Oct 1947-Dec 1950

Note: All the class were fitted with push and pull gear for Auto-Train working. Although this was not done until LNER days, the dates are given below.

776	*February 1937*	781	*November 1936*
777	*July 1937*	782	*October 1937*
778	*November 1936*	783	*November 1936*
779	*May 1943*	784	*November 1936*
780	*May 1943*	785	*May 1943*

Class 9G. Type 2.4.2. No. of Engines ... 10.

Maker	Year Built	No of Engines	Maker	Year Built	No of Engines	Maker	Year Built	No of Engines
Beyer Peacock	1898	10						

CYLINDERS.
Diameter .... 18"
Stroke .... 26"
Centres .... 2'.0"

BOILER.
Class .... *No 2 Standard*
Working Pressure ......160. Lbs. per □"
Barrel Dia. Outs. Max. ......4'.4"
Barrel Length ......10'.8⅛"
Barrel Thickness of Plates ......½"

TUBES.
Large No. ...... — Dia. Outs. ......
Small No. ......190. Dia. Outs. 1¾"
Length between Tubeplates ......11'.0²/₃²

SUPERHEATER.
Kind of Header .... —
Elements { Dia. Outs. .... —
Dia. Ins. .... —
Number .... —

IF FITTED WITH
Draft Retarder .... —
Circulating Valve .... —
Header Discharge Valve .... —
Pressure Release Valves .... —
Combined Pressure Release and Piston Valves } .... —

FIREBOX SHELL.
Length Outs. at Bottom ......6'.0"
Width ,, ,, ,, ...4'.1"
,, ,, ,, Top ......4'.6¼"
Thickness of Plates—
Back ⁷/₃₂ Casing ½" Throat. ⅝"

COPPER FIREBOX.
Length of Grate ......5'.4²⁷/₃₂"
Width ,, ,, ...3'.5"
Depth to Top of Ring, Front ......5'.6"
,, ,, ,, Back ......4'.8½"

Width of Ring.
Back and Front 2½" Sides ......3"
Thickness of Plates—
Back ½" Casing ½" Tube { ⁷/₈"
½"

HEATING SURFACE.
Firebox Outside ......99. Sq. ft.
Large Tubes .... ,,
Small Tubes ......964 ,,
Superheater Inside ......— ,,
Total ......1063 ,,

GRATE AREA. ......18.3 Sq. ft.

WHEELS. Diameter. See Diagram.
Tyres Thickness ......3"

JOURNALS. Dia. Length.
Leading Bogie or Truck *radial* ......7" 11"
Leading Coupled ......
Driving ......8" 9"
Intermediate ......
Trailing Coupled ......8" 9"
Trailing Bogie or Truck *radial* ......7" 11"

Tractive Power at { Lbs. 17.099
85% Boiler Pressure { Tons 7.6
Adhesion Coefficient. Lbs. per Ton. 1199
Height. Rail to Top of Chimney 13'.1½"
,, ,, Centre of Boiler ......7'.9½"

VALVES. Kind *Balanced Slide*

CYLINDER LUBRICATOR. Kind *Sight Feed*
If Fitted with Steam Sanding Apparatus *Yes*
,, ,, Train Warming ,, *Yes*

BRAKE. *Auto Vacuum*

TANK TENDER. Capacity. Water, Gallons 1360
,, Coal, Tons 2½

WHEELS. Diameter. ......—

JOURNALS. Dia. ...... Length ......—

A look at Class 11 no.695. Taken on Trafford Park shed in pre-First War days, this picture shows the Class 11 as evolved under Robinson with extended cab, a feature applied from around 1912 onwards to the original, rather sparse, Parker/Pollitt version. The Robinson chimney has arrived on no.695 and the smokebox carries his ash ejector, a fitting applied to all the class with the exception of no.699. The original boiler is still carried, the twin pillar safety valves very much a feature of later MS&L locomotive practice.

Collection of G.H.Platt

Class 11 4-4-0

Though nominally outside the scope of this volume, it was thought necessary to include a reference to both the Class 11 and the 2/2A 4-4-0s to show the development of the whole MS&L/GC 4-4-0 family.

Beginning with the 2/2A series back in 1887, the double frame-so reminiscent of the Sacre era-had been abandoned. The Class 11s, built in 1895, marked another step forward with the introduction of the Belpaire firebox to a passenger engine, allied to the use of 7'-0" coupled wheels. Development continued in 1897 when the 11A locmotives emerged, this time evolving the use of piston valves instead of the ubiquitous slide valves hitherto applied.

The history can be neatly summed up in diagramatic form via the 'family tree' set out below.

MS&L / G.C.R. 4 - 4 - 0 CLASSES.

Class 2/2A of 1887 (Parker)

(6'-9" wheels-first use of inside frames on an express engine)

Class 11 of 1895 (Pollitt)

(7'-0" wheels-first use of Belpaire firebox on express engine)

Class 11A of 1897 (Pollitt)

(above refinements + use of piston valves)

Class 11B of 1901 (Robinson)

(reversion to 6'-9" coupled wheels and slide valves but retaining Belpaire firebox)

Class 11C
rebuild of 11B in 1907

(larger boiler diameter + longer firebox, two engines only)

Class 11D
rebuild of both 11C and then 11B (1909 onwards)

(superheater boiler and piston valves with outside admission)

Class 11E 'Director' of 1913

(cylinder block and valves from 11D + shortened *Sir Sam Fay* boiler)

Class 11F 'Improved Director' built 1919-22 and 1924

(inside admission piston valves and boiler from Class 11E)

End of the 4-4-0 type on the G.C.R. Development of express locomotive design now shifts to the 4-6-0

A full three-quarter view of no.695, again at Trafford Park in the Robinson era. A strong resemblance to the earlier, somewhat similar 2/2A 4-4-0 design of Parker is noticeable. The later class used a boiler barrel of the same diameter as the 2/2A but with a slightly longer barrel and a 3in. higher pitch. Both designs carried slide valve cylinders, the valves driven by the ubiquitous Stephenson link motion. 695 retains its original boiler, the tell-tale 'blisters' of the no.3 Standard Belpaire yet to appear. The engine was re-boilered in 1911 and was superheated in 1926, this and no.694 being the only members of the class to be so dealt with. She was withdrawn as LNER no.5695 in July 1931.

Collection of G.H.Platt

The introduction of the MS&L's Class 11 4-4-0, built at Gorton in 1895, was something of a landmark in that company's locomotive history. For it was on this class of six 7'-0" passenger engines that the Belpaire firebox, developed by Beyer, Peacock & Co. was used for the first time on an express engine built for service in this country. So was established a feature which became for the Great Central and others a *sine qua non* in the evolution of their boiler practice.

Pollitt had taken the 2/2A 4-4-0 of Parker, increased the cylinder diameter by ½" and slightly enlarged the boiler proportions. These alterations, together with the use of coupled wheels 3 inches bigger in diameter, were of only minor consequence; the real item of any significance was, as descibed, the Belpaire firebox. Like other MS&L 4-4-0 classes, these engines were put to work on the Manchester-Kings Cross expresses to and from Grantham. Rapidly eclipsed by the piston-valved 11As, the Class 11s were based at Sheffield working stopping trains to Leicester and Grimsby. Before Grouping, all six engines were sent to Trafford Park to work trains over the C.L.C. system to Chester, ending their days on duties in the Liverpool and Southport areas.

No.694 at Gorton in re-boilered form and sporting a full-length smokebox. Other modifications from the original emerge in the form of safety valves mounted directly on the firebox top (no round base) and altered front frame profile to carry the extra length of the new smokebox. A 4000 gallon tender is coupled behind no.694, these replaced the earlier 3080 gallon version carried when built. Later changes resulted in the smaller tenders appearing once again, though two engines retained the larger type. 694 was re-boilered in 1913 and superheated by the LNER, in November 1925. Withdrawal of the Class 11s had begun in 1930 with no.696. No.694 was one of the last engines to be withdrawn, both it and no.697 going in October 1932.

Collection of Brian Hilton

Class 11. Type 4.4.0. Nº of Engines ... 6.

Maker	Year Built	Nº of Engines	Maker	Year Built	Nº of Engines	Maker	Year Built	Nº of Engines
Great Central Railway	1895	6						

CYLINDERS.
Diameter .... 18½"
Stroke .... 26"
Centres .... 2'-0½"

BOILER.
Class .... Nº 3 Standard
Working Pressure .... 160 Lbs. per □"
Barrel Dia. Outs. Max. ...... 4'-4"
Barrel Length .... 11'-0"
Barrel Thickness of Plates .... ½"

TUBES.
Large No. ..... — Dia. Outs. ..... —
Small No. ..... 190 Dia. Outs. ..... 1¾"
Length between Tubeplates .... 11'-4¾"

SUPERHEATER.
Kind of Header .... —
Elements { Dia. Outs. .... —
Dia. Ins. .... —
Number .... — }

IF FITTED WITH
Draft Retarder .... —
Circulating Valve .... —
Header Discharge Valve .... —
Pressure Release Valves .... —
Combined Pressure Release } .... —
and Piston Valves }

FIREBOX SHELL.
Length Outs. at Bottom ...... 6'-4"
Width " " " ...... 4'-1"
" " " Top ...... 4'-6½"
Thickness of Plates—
Back 17/32" Casing ½" Throat ⅝"

COPPER FIREBOX.
Length of Grate ...... 5'-8²⁷/₃₂"
Width " " ...... 3'-5"
Depth to Top of Ring, Front .. 5'-5⅝"
" " " Back .. 4'-11⅞"

Width of Ring.
Back and Front .... 2½" Sides .. 3"
Thickness of Plates—
Back ½" Casing ½" Tube { ⅞" / ½" }

HEATING SURFACE.
Firebox Outside .... 108 Sq. ft.
Large Tubes .... — "
Small Tubes .... 993 "
Superheater Inside .... — "
Total .... 1.101 "

GRATE AREA. .... 19.4 Sq. ft.

WHEELS. Diameter. See Diagram.
Tyres Thickness .... 3"
JOURNALS. Dia. Length.
Leading Bogie as Truck ...... 5¾" 9"
Leading Coupled .... — —
Driving .... 8" 9"
Intermediate .... — —
Trailing Coupled .... 8" 9"
Trailing Bogie or Truck .... — —
Tractive Power at { Lbs. 14.400
85% Boiler Pressure { Tons 6.43
Adhesion Coefficient. Lbs. per Ton... 427
Height. Rail to Top of Chimney .. 13'-3"
" " Centre of Boiler .. 7'-11"
VALVES. Kind Unbalanced Slide

CYLINDER LUBRICATOR. Kind Sight Feed
If Fitted with Steam Sanding Apparatus .... Yes
" " Train Warning " .... Yes

BRAKE. .... Automatic Vacuum
TENDER. Capacity. Water, Gallons .. 3.080
" " Coal, Tons 5
WHEELS. Diameter .... 3'-9"
JOURNALS. Dia. 5½" Length .. 9"

Alongside Manchester Central's platform 4, no.711, a Kitson engine of the 1892 series, is in what might be termed 'intermediate' condition and should be compared with no.687. Although the engine has a long smokebox, none of the class were ever fitted with superheaters. The Robinson chimney confirms the post-1900 period, while the cab has been extended rearwards over the footplate. Later modifications would provide the class with Belpaire fireboxes and weatherboards were fitted to the tender in LNER days. A particularly unfortunate alteration in this period was the infamous 'Flowerpot' chimney, used as a substitute forthe Robinson pattern which, apparently, was prone to cracking.

Collection of G.H.Platt

Class 2 & 2A 4-4-0

The Class 2 4-4-0 engines emerged between 1887 and 1894 to a design by Parker with construction shared between Kitsons of Leeds and Gorton Works. Built for the MS&L's Manchester to King's Cross expresses which they worked to and from Grantham, they had a fairly brief reign on these crack turns before being replaced by the later Pollitt Class 11 7-footers.

With single inside frames for the coupled wheels and a sweeping splasher panel, the Class 2s were something of a flag-bearer for the next generation of MS&L/G.C.4-4-0s. Hitherto, MS&L express passenger designs had had double frames, a throwback to the Sacre era and a feature perpetuated in light of the severe problems encountered with crank axles.

The pioneer engine, no.561, remained as a lone example for almost three years before the class was multiplied. These subsequent engines had a slightly different frame pattern and sandbox arrangement. In 1894, a final 6 engines were built at Gorton with a bigger coupled wheel journal and different springing to the coupled axles; this final derivation was classed as 2A.

In the Robinson era the class became a much changed animal. Principal amongst these changes was the fitting of new boilers with Belpaire fireboxes. The particular configuration becoming known as the standard G.C.no.1 boiler.

Quickly displaced from their top-link duties, the Class 2s were concentrated over the northern half of the Great Central system. Prior to the end of the First War, a goodly proportion of the class were based at Sheffield from where they worked stopping trains as far south as Leicester. None appear to have been based at sheds on the London Extension in this period.

Towards the end of the Great Central era the greater part of the 2/2A engines were split between Lincoln and Immingham sheds with 10 locomotives apiece. The remaining 11 were split between Retford, Mexborough and Northwich. The latter 4 worked trains over the C.L.C. system from Manchester Central to Northwich and Chester as well as filling in on local services out of Manchester as far as Irlam.

Those at Immingham were used on local services in that district, taking in trains to and from Cleethorpes, Grimsby, Immingham Dock, New Holland and Barton-on-Humber. It is with services in this area together with those around Lincoln that the class seem particularly associated in their final days.

The outbreak of the Second War saw all but two members of the class extinct, No.704 of 1892 being the final engine to succumb, broken-up in April 1940.

Robinson systematically re-boilered the Class 2 and 2A 4-4-0s from 1909 with his Standard no.1 Belpaire, a process completed in 1918. The new boilers altered the look of the class slightly being pitched 3½in. higher, the shoulders of the Belpaire firebox giving the engines a slightly 'beefier' look. In consequence, the cab spectacles had to be altered from a round profile to something of a flattened 'D' shape.Complete with her new boiler, fitted in June 1909, no.707 stands outside Manchester London Road, St.Andrew's Church, Ancoats forming a now familiar backdrop. 707 is coupled to a Parker 3080 gallon tender with 5 ton coal capacity. From around 1910, solid coal plates were fitted to these tenders, bringing them into line with those built for Robinson's engines.No.707 was one of the batch transferred to the C.L.C. system for duties on the Manchester/Northwich/Chester line, the 1921 allocation showing Northwich as her home shed. Re-numbered 5707 under LNER Class D7, she was withdrawn in May 1933.

Collection of G.H.Platt

Class 2 no.687 in original condition in the early years of the G.C. at Macclesfield Central. Great Central trains reached this south Cheshire market town via the G.C & North Staffs. Joint line from Marple Wharf Junction. The headcode, conforming to an MS&L standard of 1896, tells us the engine is in charge of a slow passenger working. Comparison with no.711 shows many subtle differences. The engine has Parker's rather plain stovepipe chimney and twin lubricators on the smokebox centreline. Notice the tender carries no coalguard while the cab roof bears both the small 'organ pipe' and conventional domed whistle.

Collection of G.H.Platt

SUMMARY OF CLASS 2/2A 4-4-0 (LNER D7)

NUMBER	BUILDER	DATE BUILT	WITHDRAWN
561	Kitson & Co.	November 1887	September 1928
562 - 567	Gorton	April to December 1890	Dec 1926-Aug 1935
682 - 687	Gorton	November 1891 to May 1892	Jul 1930-Apr 1937
700 - 711	Kitson & Co.	October to December 1892	Jan 1930-December 1939
688 - 693	Gorton	April to September 1894	Feb 1930-May 1937

Class 2. Type 4.4.0. No of Engines ... 25.

Maker	Year Built	No of Engines	-	Maker	Year Built	No of Engines	Maker	Year Built	No of Engines
Kitson & Co.	1887	1		G. C. R.	1892	3			
G. C. R.	1890	6		Kitson & Co.	1892	12			
	1891	3							

CYLINDERS.
Diameter .... 18"
Stroke .... 26"
Centres .... 2' 4½"

BOILER.
Class .... No 1 Standard
Working Pressure .... 160 Lbs. per □"
Barrel Dia. Outs. Max. .... 4'-4"
Barrel Length .... 10'-8⅛"
Barrel Thickness of Plates .... ½"

TUBES.
Large No .... — Dia. Outs. .... —
Small No .... 190 Dia. Outs. 1¾"
Length between Tubeplates .... 11'-0"⁹⁄₃₂

SUPERHEATER.
Kind of Header .... —
Elements {
Dia. Outs. .... —
Dia. Ins. .... —
Number .... —
}

IF FITTED WITH
Draft Retarder .... —
Circulating Valve .... —
Header Discharge Valve .... —
Pressure Release Valves .... —
Combined Pressure Release and Piston Valves } .... —

FIREBOX SHELL.
Length Outs. at Bottom .... 6'-0"
Width ,, ,, ,, ... 4'-1"
,, ,, ,, Top .... 4'-4¼"
Thickness of Plates—
Back ⁷⁄₃₂" Casing ½" Throat ½"

COPPER FIREBOX.
Length of Grate .... 5'-4⁷⁄₃₂"
Width ,, ,, ... 3'-5"
Depth to Top of Ring, Front .... 5'-6"
,, ,, ,, Back .... 4'-8½"

Width of Ring.
Back and Front .... 2½" Sides .... 3"
Thickness of Plates—
Back ½" Casing ½" Tube ½" .... ⁷⁄₈"

HEATING SURFACE.
Firebox Outside .... 99 Sq. ft.
Large Tubes .... — ,,
Small Tubes .... 964 ,,
Superheater Inside .... — ,,
Total .... 1063 ,,

GRATE AREA. .... 18.3 Sq. ft.

WHEELS. Diameter. See Diagram.
Tyres Thickness .... 3"
JOURNALS. Dia. Length.
Leading Bogie or Truck .... 5¾" 9"
Leading Coupled ....
Driving .... 7½" 7"
Intermediate ....
Trailing Coupled .... 7½" 7"
Trailing Bogie or Truck ....
Tractive Power at 85% Boiler Pressure {
Lbs. 14,140
Tons 6.32
}
Adhesion Coefficient. Lbs. per Ton 447
Height. Rail to Top of Chimney .... 13'-0"
,, ,, Centre of Boiler .... 7'-8"

VALVES. Kind Unbalanced Slide
CYLINDER LUBRICATOR. Kind Sight Feed
If Fitted with Steam Sanding Apparatus .... Yes
,, ,, Train Warning .... Yes
BRAKE. Auto Vacuum or { R Vacuum, Westinghouse }
TENDER. Capacity. Water, Gallons 3,080
,, ,, Coal, Tons 5
WHEELS. Diameter .... 3'-9"
JOURNALS. Dia. .... 5½" Length .... 9"

Maker	Year Built	N⁰ of Engines	Maker	Year Built	N⁰ of Engines	Maker	Year Built	N⁰ of Engines
			Class 2A. Type 4.4.0 N⁰ of Engines ... 6					
G.C.R.	1894	6						

CYLINDERS.
Diameter .... 18"
Stroke .... 26"
Centres .... 2'-4½"

BOILER.
Class .... N⁰ 1 Standard
Working Pressure .... 160 Lbs. per □"
Barrel Dia. Outs. Max. .... 4'-4"
Barrel Length .... 10'-8⅛"
Barrel Thickness of Plates .... ½"

TUBES.
Large No. .... — .... Dia. Outs. .... —
Small No. .... 190 .... Dia. Outs. .... 1¾"
Length between Tubeplates ...... 11'-0⁹⁄₃₂"

SUPERHEATER.
Kind of Header .... :
Elements { Dia. Outs. .... :
          { Dia. Ins. .... :
          { Number .... :

IF FITTED WITH
Draft Retarder .... :
Circulating Valve .... :
Header Discharge Valve .... :
Pressure Release Valves .... :
Combined Pressure Release } .... :
and Piston Valves }

FIREBOX SHELL.
Length Outs. at Bottom ...... 6'-0"
Width „ „ „ .... 4'-1"
  „ „ „ Top ...... 4'-6¼"
Thickness of Plates—
Back ⁷⁄₃₂" Casing ½" Throat ⅝"

COPPER FIREBOX.
Length of Grate .... 5'-4⁹⁄₁₆"
Width „ „ .... 3'-5"
Depth to Top of Ring, Front .... 5'-6"
  „ „ „ Back ..... 4'-8½"

Width of Ring.
Back and Front .. 2½" Sides .. 3"
Thickness of Plates—
Back ½" Casing ½" Tube { ⅞"
                       { ½"

HEATING SURFACE.
Firebox Outside .... 99 Sq. ft.
Large Tubes .... — „
Small Tubes .... 964 „
Superheater Inside .... — „
Total .... 1,063 „

GRATE AREA. .... Sq. ft.

WHEELS.   Diameter.   See Diagram.
Tyres   Thickness .... 3"

JOURNALS.   Dia.   Length.
Leading Bogie or Truck ...... 5¾"   9"
Leading Coupled ....
Driving .... 8"   7"
Intermediate ....
Trailing Coupled .... 8"   7"
Trailing Bogie or Truck ......
Tractive Power at { Lbs. 14,140
85% Boiler Pressure { Tons 6.32
Adhesion Coefficient. Lbs. per Ton ... 447
Height.   Rail to Top of Chimney ... 13'-0"
  „   „ Centre of Boiler ...... 7'-8"

VALVES. Kind .... Unbalanced Slide

CYLINDER LUBRICATOR. Kind Sight Feed
If Fitted with Steam Sanding Apparatus ... Yes
  „ „ Train Warming „ ...... Yes

BRAKE. .... Auto Vacuum

TENDER. Capacity. Water, Gallons .. 3,080
  „ Coal, Tons 5

WHEELS. Diameter .... 3'-9"

JOURNALS. Dia. .... 5½" Length ...... 9"

No.691 was one of the 6 of the series classified 2A. Differences were minor, a coil spring being used on the driving axle and an increase of a half inch in the diameter of the coupled wheel journals-from 7½ ins. to 8 ins. 691 appears at Penistone on a stopping train complete with Belpaire firebox. All 31 engines were rebuilt with Belpaires between 1909 and 1918, 691 being one of the last 2 to be so treated, in June of the latter year. The elegant Robinson chimney is carried on an extended smokebox, a fitting applied when the original stovepipe chimneys were removed. The rearward extension to the cab, applied to the class from 1912 onwards, is identical to that fitted to no.711 while the tender, of 3080 gallon capacity, carries a coal guard with scalloped or rounded ends. 691 was withdrawn in 1933.

Collection of G.H.Platt

No.881, the last of the class, built by Beyer, Peacock in the Spring of 1899, stands, spotlessly groomed in G.C. dark green livery, on the turntable outside Manchester Central. 881 appears in re-boilered and superheated form (post-December 1912) with consequent full-length smokebox, and extended cab. The fitting of longer smokeboxes required a parallel increase in the length of the front mainframes, compare the profile here with that of previous members of the class. The 'blisters' on the shoulders of the Belpaire firebox were a feature of the standard no.3 boiler. A seemingly insignificant feature of the engines, they covered a vital component of their anatomy-the boiler washout plugs.

Collection of G.H.Platt

Class 11A 4-4-0

Pollitt's Class 11A 4-4-0s were built for services on the London Extension for the fast, lightweight trains that were anticipated. Prior to the opening of the Great Central's new line, some of the class had been at work, like their Sacre , Parker and Pollitt predecessors, on the Manchester-King's Cross expresses to and from Grantham. They were completed between 1897 and 1899. Although not a new design in the original sense, the 11A incorporated a similar boiler, firebox and coupled wheel size (7'-0") as the previous Class 11 engines, this particular 4-4-0 design did incorporate one radical departure from Parker's engines-the provision of piston valves for the two inside cylinders. 33 engines were built altogether, the first 13 at Gorton with Beyer, Peacock & Co. contracted to build the last 20. However, at the end of 1897, Beyer,Peacock were embroiled in a strike and the Great Central was desperately short of locomotives, anxiously awaiting the delivery of new passenger engines to cope with the traffic on the forthcoming London Extension. Meeting at London Road Station, Manchester, the G.C. Board viewed the matter as something of a crisis. A meeting on December 17th.1897 expressed the

view that....'a serious question it would be if, after expending so much Capital, the Line (the London Extension) could not be opened for want of engines....' The following minute, taken from their next meeting records succinctly the plans put in hand to rectify the situation. The Earl of Wharncliffe was in the Chair on January 12th.1898.....'Mr.Pollitt (the General Manager, William Pollitt-not to be confused with Harry, the Locomotive Engineer) reminded the Board that he had brought before them at the last Meeting the question of the Engines required for the London Extension Line, and the position of Messrs. Beyer Peacock & Company owing to the strike. Mr.Pollitt had seen Colonel Peacock again and had a very long discussion with him. Colonel Peacock saw the seriousness of the matter and sympathised with the Company, but he could do no more, and so long as the strike continues he is willing that the Company shall construct in their own shops ten passenger engines. It would be remembered that the Company originally intended to build the Engines themselves, the material being ordered, and certain of the work carried out when the Rolling Stock Trust was formed. It was

11A no.880 has backed down alongside platform 5 at Manchester Central in readiness for its train, probably a Manchester to Liverpool express. This view shows the altered cab, its rearward extension supported by pillars connecting at waist-level with the side sheet-a feature applied to the class from 1912 onwards. No.880 carries the (almost) G.C.standard oval brass numberplate on the cabside, a nice touch of permanence compared to the painted numbers of earlier years.Despite the engine's three-quarter length smokebox, added when the engines received their Robinson chimneys, it remains in saturated form, still retaining the original boiler and high, twin-pillar safety valves.No.880 remained as a 'wet one', throughout her G.C.existence. She was not superheated until April 1923 and survived for another sixteen years-although one engine was withdrawn as early as 1930.

Collection of G.H.Platt

then arranged for these unfinished Engines to be transferred to Messrs Beyer Peacock and Company for completion. Two or three shifts of men could be put onto the work at Gorton, and would turn out three or four Engines per month. Although it is a breach of Contract, Colonel Peacock will not object, and he merely expressed the hope that when the Company require more Engines his firm should be given the preference. Mr. Pollitt had at once instructed the Locomotive Engineer (Harry Pollitt) to commence building these Engines, on the understanding that when Messrs Beyer Peacok & Company resume work, they should be allowed to complete the engines not then under construction.' 'The Locomotive Engineer afterwards pointed out that it would be more economical and convenient to commence with ten Engines than with three, and he was accordingly instructed to take the larger number in hand , at once which the Board approved........' How far Gorton Works got with the 10 engines is not certain, all had Beyer,Peacock works numbers, so it is reasonable to assume that the company got to finish at least part of their contracted obligations and the story serves to reinforce the chronic locomtive shortages then extant.

Changes began to appear in the outline of the 11A Class from around 1900-inevitable progressions in a series of locomotives that spanned just over half a century. Robinson chimneys-reminiscent of those on Johnson's Midland 4-4-0s-replaced the austere Pollitt stovepipes fairly early on in the locomotives' lives.

MS&L taper-shank buffers gave way to a standardised G.C.parallel pattern. Extra protection was now afforded for footplate crews with a cab that had been extended rearwards and supported by two stanchions, a process we know, had begun in 1912. The earlier light green livery with chocolate frames and yellow lining gave way to a darker green similar to the 'Brunswick' shade described previously. Cab and splashers were seen to have a black border edged with white, while the tender sides wore the beautifully simple, but very neat, black line double-edged in white. The whole livery ensemble was complemented by claret for the tender frames, footsteps and mainframes above the footplate. Coal plates were now fitted to the tender sides although Robinson appears to have disliked the use of snap-head rivets on engines and tenders built in his regime.

Aside from livery changes, alterations to chimneys and cab, the only performance-related alterations made to the class in G.C.days centred around re-boilering. Robinson developed his own saturated boiler which differed slightly from the original pattern in having a marginally higher heating surface and a lower working pressure. (160 lbs.p.s.i compared to 170 lbs.p.s.i.) The replacement boilers also differed in having a smaller grate area, the result of a decrease in the width of the water space between the inner and outer fireboxes (3″ on the original boiler, 2½″on the Robinson version). Designated No.3 standard, the new saturated boilers do not appear to have been carried by all the class, total re-boilering not being carried out until superheating com-

Mention is made elsewhere of the G.C's joint involvement at Manchester London Road with the LNWR. Though primarily thought of as a terminus, London Road had 2 through platforms on its south side belonging to the former Manchester, South Junction and Altrincham Railway. Before Grouping, the MSJ&A was in the joint hands of the G.C. and the LNWR, the two companies taking turns for the responsibility of the line in 3-year blocks. In the years prior to 1909, no.878 rests at the end of the up MSJ&A platform with a special express working. The engine is known to have been fitted with a no.3 saturated boiler in 1909. She remained in this condition until 1934 when she was superheated. Withdrawal took place in 1938.

Collection of G.H.Platt

Few trunk lines had opened with such optimism and high hopes as the Great Central's London Extension. Whereas other companies had begun their services with almost monopoly power, the G.C. would have to fight tooth and nail for their traffic. That they achieved this is no small tribute to the verve and flair displayed by both management and men alike. Decked with Union Flags, the chimney ornamented with winged devices and a crest mounted in front of her smokebox 11A no.269 has been coaled from Neasden's stage. The purpose of this finery and ornamentation was the working of one of the special trains up to Marylebone to celebrate the opening of the London Extension in March 1899. no.269 was the second engine of the class to built; one of a pair constructed by the company themselves in September and December 1897. Temporarily numbered 269A, the engine was re-numbered in February 1898. Superheated in 1927, 269 was withdrawn as LNER no.5269 in November 1932.

Collection of Dave Banks

Class 11A. Type 4.4.0. N° of Engines ... 33.

Maker	Year Built	N° of Engines	Maker	Year Built	N° of Engines	Maker	Year Built	N° of Engines
Great Central Railway	1897	2	Beyer Peacock & C°	1899	18			
" "	1898	11						
Beyer Peacock & C°	1898	2						

Particulars in red refer to superheated engines only   Total N° Superheated ... 28.

CYLINDERS.
Diameter ... 18½"
Stroke ... 26"
Centres ... 7'.0½"

BOILER.
Class ... No 3 Standard
Working Pressure ... 180 Lbs. per ☐"
Barrel Dia. Outs. Max. ... 4'-4"
Barrel Length ... 11'.0"
Barrel Thickness of Plates ... ½"

TUBES.
Large No. ... Dia. Outs. 5¼"
Small No. 190 46 Dia. Outs. 1¾" 1⅞"
Length between Tubeplates ... 11'. 4¾"

SUPERHEATER.
Kind of Header ...
Elements { Dia. Outs. ...
Dia. Ins. ... 1⅛"
Number ...

IF FITTED WITH
Draft Retarder ... No
Circulating Valve ... No
Header Discharge Valve ... No
Pressure Release Valves ... Yes
Combined Pressure Release and Piston Valves } —

FIREBOX SHELL.
Length Outs. at Bottom ... 6'- 4"
Width " " " ... 4'-1"
" " " Top ... 4'- 6¼"
Thickness of Plates—
Back ¹⁷/₃₂" Casing ½" Throat ⅝"

COPPER FIREBOX.
Length of Grate ... 5'. 8⁷/₃₂"
Width " " ... 3'- 5"
Depth to Top of Ring, Front 5'- 5⅞"
" " " Back 4'- 11⅜"

Width of Ring.
Back and Front 2½" Sides 3"
Thickness of Plates—
Back ½" Casing ½" Tube { ⅞" , ½"

HEATING SURFACE.
Firebox Outside ... 108 108 Sq. ft.
Large Tubes ... 252 "
Small Tubes ... 993 503 "
Superheater Inside ... 138 "
Total 1101 1031 "

GRATE AREA. 19.4 Sq. ft.

WHEELS.
Diameter. See Diagram.
Tyres Thickness ... 3"

JOURNALS.
	Dia.	Length.
Leading Bogie or Truck	5¾"	9"
Leading Coupled		
Driving	8"	9"
Intermediate		
Trailing Coupled	8"	9"
Trailing Bogie or Truck		

Tractive Power at 85% Boiler Pressure { Lbs. 14,400 , Tons 6.43
Adhesion Coefficient. Lbs. per Ton. 427
Height. Rail to Top of Chimney 13'. 3"
" " Centre of Boiler 7'. 11"

VALVES.
Kind Piston Outs. adm.

CYLINDER LUBRICATOR.
Kind Sight Feed Mechanical
If Fitted with Steam Sanding Apparatus ... Yes
" " Train Warming ... Yes

BRAKE.
Auto Vacuum or { Auto Vacuum and Westinghouse

TENDER.
Capacity. Water, Gallons ... 4,000
" Coal, Tons ... 6

WHEELS.
Diameter ... 4'- 3"

JOURNALS.
Dia. 6" Length 11"

menced.

Superheating of the 11A 4-4-0s began in 1912. Largely complete in Great Central days, it was not until 1934, almost three years after the first engine had been withdrawn, that the process was finished. Superheating involved fitting the locomotives with longer smokeboxes to accommodate the superheater headers, a feature which completely altered the appearance of the engines, with the attendant loss of the elegant flowing curve to the front mainframes. It is relevant at this point, though, to record that some engines were fitted with renewed smokeboxes of a longer pattern whilst retaining the original saturated boilers.

At this point, Robinson was getting into his stride with the development of superheating. His highly successful pattern of header, developed into numerous varieties, with the attendant element pipes expanded directly into the block, doing away with troublesome pipe fittings and unions, became a standard G.C.fitting and was used extensively on engines of other companies both at home and abroad. A 15-element superheater was tried out at first on the 11As-this giving way to the 18-

No.861 seen in an earlier period alongside the water tower outside Manchester Central. The engine (in saturated condition) displays short smokebox, cup lubricators, a Robinson chimney and original length cab. Notice the transfer numerals, yet to be replaced by the later oval brass plate with raised figures. 861 has a special place in Great Central history; on March 9th 1899, sent on its way by the Rt.Hon.C.T.Ritchie, M.P., President of the Board of Trade, it hauled a special train out of Marylebone to mark the official opening of the London Extension.861 was superheated in February 1916 and withdrawn in April 1931.

Collection of G.H.Platt

SUMMARY OF CLASS 11A 4-4-0 (LNER D6)

NUMBER	BUILDER	DATE BUILT	WITHDRAWN
268 & 269*	Gorton	September & December 1897	
268		Jul 1933, 269-Nov 1932	
852 - 861 + 270	Gorton	April to November 1898	Apr 1931-Dec 1947
862 - 881	Beyer Peacock & Co.**	December 1898 to April 1899	Jun 1930-Dec 1947

Nos.268 and 269 originally numbered 268A and 269A (i.e. on the Duplicate list) to distinguish them from earlier locomotives then still working. The A suffix was dropped in February 1898 when the earlier engines were withdrawn.
** See text.*

We pause on Neasden shed in early Great Central days to observe 11A no.872 posing with footplate staff and an inspector. The gleaming condition of the locomtive and the presence of three lamps suggests a special working, probably another one related to the opening of the London Extension.

Collection of R.P.Hepner

element version which became standard for the class, though some of the 15-element superheater boilers lasted until as late as 1935. Something of a 'one-off' had been tried with 11A no.268 in January 1915 when it was fitted with Robinson's 'small tube' superheater. One of the designer's many experiments with differing patterns and numbers of elements and types of superheater header, the 'small tube' version consisted of no less than 78 elements inserted into flues that were, as the name suggested, smaller than the conventional pattern. No.268 remained the only 11A to carry this superheater and six of the elements were later removed. The rather congested apparatus was also tried on an 8A 0-8-0 (Q.V.) and several large boilered Class 8M 2-8-0. No.268 received a conventional boiler in 1927.

As detailed in the previous historical notes, these locomotives were built for working express trains over the newly-opened London Extension. Prior to this historic event, they worked between Manchester London Road and Grantham on the joint MS&L/G.N. expresses from Manchester to Kings Cross. Displaced from the London line by Robinson's 11B 4-4-0s, the 11As were dispatched northwards to power the Manchester-Liverpool expresses over the C.L.C., their allocation split between Manchester's Trafford Park

and Liverpool's Brunswick sheds. Before the First War, 4 Westinghouse-fitted engines were based at Lincoln to work trains composed of Great Eastern stock emanating from East Anglia, notably the Harwich-Liverpool Boat expresses.

A year before Grouping, the allocation of the 11As was divided almost evenly between Trafford Park and Brunswick sheds, their duties now being almost exclusively the working of expresses between Manchester and Liverpool with occasional forays over the line from Glazebrook to Godley Junction via Northenden, Cheadle and Stockport Tiviot Dale.

In their latter years, as superheated engines, the 11As did their best work, ironically, well away from their intended home ground. None of the class quite made it to Nationalisation, as withdrawal had been completed by the end of 1947 with nos. 855 and 874 (numbered as LNER 2101 and 2106 under Class D6).

So passed away the first of the Great Central's express engines and one that had stood as something of a watershed-appearing at the end of one era and the start of another; the demise of Pollitt and the age of Victoria and the ascendency of the company's London Extension which looked to the twentieth century and the beginning of the Robinson regime.

No.969, the third of the 6 engines built standing outside the shed at Trafford Park, Manchester complete with bowler-hatted inspector and cloth-capped driver posing for the camera. The engine presents an 'as-built' condition mechanically with stovepipe chimney, tall uncased safety valves and no coal plates on the tender. Again, distinguishing marks from the Pollitt era-the liberal use of snaphead rivets on the platework-are present, a feature eschewed by Robinson. Rectangular cast brass numberplates are fitted, a throwback to Robinson's Irish days on the Waterford & Limerick Railway. The 2 previous Class 13 s had borne transfer numerals when built which marked them from their successors, although the standard G.C.oval plate was applied later on.Livery here is Robinson's standard dark green with black and white lining carried by the last 4 of the class , although all would have been repainted in this standard company livery by the Grouping.In 1911 no.969 was fitted with a boiler of the 11B pattern as fitted to Robinson's first 4-4-0 s. As this was 6 inches wider than the original it was necessary to raise the centre line by 7 inches. A new cab was required in consequence and was fitted with a rearward extension. The resulting ensemble gave the engine an altogether enormous appearance. This however, belied reality, as the new boiler had a firebox 1 foot shorter with a corresponding reduction in grate area. When the engine was superheated, in 1915, a boiler of the original dimensions was fitted. Three others of the six Class 13 s were also superheated between 1916 and 1919.

Collection of G.H.Platt

Class 13 4-2-2

Towards the end of the Nineteenth Century, the single-driver express engine was enjoying something of a Renaissance. Johnson on the Midland had resumed construction of the type in 1887 culminating in the celebrated 'Princess of Wales' of 1900. 1892, the year of the demise of the Broad Gauge on the Great Western, had seen the arrival of another 'Single' classic-the superbly proportioned Dean 7'-8" engines numbering 80 in all.

It was on December 22nd.1898 that Harry Pollitt wrote to the General Manager thus:

Dear Sir,

I beg to submit a design for a new type of Bogie Passenger engine that I have got out for working the southern portion of the New Line, London to Leicester as the ruling gradient on that section is a fairly easy one and the wear and tear on a Single engine would be so much less than in the case of one with 4 wheels coupled that an engine of this character can be run easily at very high speeds. The engine is in every respect larger and would be more powerful than our present type of bogie express passenger engine and, with the exception of the boiler and driving wheels, the bulk of the parts of the engine are interchangeable with those of the 4-coupled express engines, the tenders being exactly the same which would be an advantage to ease in maintenance. The cost per engine would, I estimate, be about the same as for those we are now building viz £2,900 each and I would suggest that in the first instance we build, say, half a dozen at Gorton as a trial. I have got out all the necessary detailed drawings and could commence building at once. You can only favour me with your instructions.

Yours truly,

Harry Pollitt

The archive reference carries the footnote:'Sanctioned by the Board, 13th January 1899.'

Pollitt sounds as though he was in a hurry; although the original G.C.express traffic was light and well within the capacity of a single-wheeler on the section mentioned, he

Though Pollitt had designed his Singles for the London Extension they were soon displaced by Robinson's 11B 4-4-0 s. Consequently the class migrated northwards in 1904 to CLC territory where they were put into useful harness on Manchester-Liverpool express trains until their withdrawal from 1923 onwards.It would have been whilst working trains such as these that no.972 was photographed, like her sister no.969, on Trafford Park shed, Manchester. The last of this small group of engines, she is in superheated form which dates the photograph as post-September 1919. Superheater boilers were fitted to four of the six Class 13s from 1915 to 1919. This required the use of an extended smokebox and a consequent lengthening of the front mainframes-compare no.972's front profile to that of the original on no.969. Robinson's elegant chimney has also made its mark and the wheel and handle fastening for the smokebox door has replaced the earlier twin handles. A Wakefield mechanical lubricator with rather untidy pipework and cased safety valves of reduced height are also worthy of study. A solitary whistle now appears on the cab roof and the engine is something removed from the pristine condition so readily displayed by other G.C.engines in these pages.

Collection of G.H.Platt

must have known that the writing was well and truly on the wall for this type of locomotive when he wrote the letter.

In the event, the Class 13 engines were built- at a cost of £2,900 each. Construction commenced one year after Pollitt had stated his intentions. The initial target was for one engine to be completed by Christmas 1899 with two further engines to be delivered each month until March 1900. However, only 2 locomotives were constructed at Gorton during his term of office-Robinson having arrived on the scene in the interim. The remainder were turned out as planned during 1900 which made up the 6 referred to above. As will be seen, Robinson had

radically different ideas on engine design from his predecessor and responded in a very positive way to the chronic motive power shortages prevalent on the G.C.when he entered office. Not that this diminished the usefulness of the Class 13 s which survived en bloc into the LNER era.

With the demise of no.972 in August 1927 the Class 13 (then LNER X4) became extinct. The single- wheeled locomotive was, by then, almost at an end as a working type. But this was not just the passing of another engine class, rather the eclipse of a locomotive type that had literally seen the railway born.

SUMMARY OF CLASS 13 4-2-2 (LNER X4)

NUMBER	BUILDER	DATE BUILT	WITHDRAWN
967 - 972	Gorton	January to December 1900	Dec 1923-Jul 1926

Note: Four engines superheated as follows:-

No.967   *July 1916*
No.969   *December 1915 (after removal of Class 11B boiler)*
No.970   *September 1919*
No.972   *September 1919*

Another Manchester Central picture, this time showing no.971 alongside platform 4 with a good head of steam and ready for the 'off' with the 12.30 p.m.express for Liverpool Central. The picture is dated April 21st.1923; at this time, the engine working this train would return from Liverpool with the 2.00pm non-stop express back to Manchester.No.971 was one of the two Pollitt Singles that remained in saturated form throughout its life. Though the engine has acquired a new smokebox, it retains the two displacement lubricators either side of the smokebox door. This engine was the first of the Class 13s to be withdrawn, departing in the December of 1923.

H.A.White, courtesy of W.A.Brown

The reboilered no.969 at Manchester Central in its saturated form. The upper part of the locomotive is virtually an 11B 4-4-0 which boiler type it carried for 4 years. The cab front , too, is reminiscent of the later versions of this class, its split spectacles replacing the original plain round variety. Notice too, the 'waisted' appearance of the Belpaire firebox in contrast to the straight sides of Pollitt's original version.

Collection of G.H.Platt

Class 13. Type 4.2.2. N° of Engines ... 6.

Maker	Year Built	N° of Engines	Maker	Year Built	N° of Engines	Maker	Year Built	N° of Engines
G C Rly	1900	6						

Particulars in red refer to Superheated Engines only.   Total Engines Superheated ... 4

CYLINDERS.
Diameter ...... 19½"
Stroke ...... 26"
Centres ...... 2'-1½"

BOILER.
Class 13
Working Pressure ...... 100 Lbs. per □"
Barrel Dia. Outs. Max. ...... 4'-3"
Barrel Length ...... 11'-2"
Barrel Thickness of Plates ...... 9/16"

TUBES.
Large No. — 18 Dia. Outs. — 5¼"
Small No. 190 76 Dia. Outs. 1¾" 1⅞"
Length between Tubeplates ...... 11'-7⅛"

SUPERHEATER. "Robinson"
Kind of Header ...... Twin Cover
Elements { Dia. Outs. ...... 1⅜"
Dia. Ins. ...... 1⅛"
Number 18

IF FITTED WITH
Draft Retarder ......
Circulating Valve ......
Header Discharge Valve ......
Pressure Release Valves ......
Combined Pressure Release and Piston Valves } ...... No

FIREBOX SHELL.
Length Outs. at Bottom ...... 8'-0"
Width „ „ „ ...... 4'-1"
„ „ „ Top ...... 4'-5 7/16"
Thickness of Plates—
Back 9/16" Casing 9/16" Throat 2/32"

COPPER FIREBOX.
Length of Grate ...... 7'-3 21/32"
Width „ ...... 3'-4¾"
Depth to Top of Ring, Front 5'-10¾"
„ „ „ Back 5'-2¼"

Width of Ring.
Back and Front 3" Sides 3"
Thickness of Plates—
Back 9/16" Casing 9/16" Tube { 7/6" 9/16"

HEATING SURFACE.
Firebox Outside ...... 128 128 Sq. ft.
Large Tubes ...... — 287 „
Small Tubes ...... 956 490 „
Superheater Inside ...... — 138 „
Total 1084 1043 „

GRATE AREA. ...... 24·5 Sq. ft.

WHEELS.   Diameter.   See Diagram.
Tyres   Thickness ...... 3"

JOURNALS.   Dia.   Length.
Leading Bogie or Truck ...... 5¾" 9"
Leading Coupled ......
Driving ...... 8" 9"
Intermediate ......
Trailing Coupled ...... 7" 9"
Trailing Bogie or Truck ......

Tractive Power at 85% Boiler Pressure { Lbs. 14,280
Tons 6.37

Adhesion Coefficient.   Lbs. per Ton ...... 75!
Height.   Rail to Top of Chimney ...... 13'-3"
„   „ Centre of Boiler ...... 8'-2"

VALVES.   Kind Piston Rotary Cuts Valve

CYLINDER LUBRICATOR.   Kind Mechanical
If Fitted with Steam Sanding Apparatus ...... Yes
„   „ Train Warming „ ...... Yes

BRAKE.   Auto Vacuum

TENDER.   Capacity.   Water, Gallons 4,000
„   Coal, Tons 6

WHEELS.   Diameter ...... 4'-3"

JOURNALS.   Dia. ...... 6"   Length ...... 11"

One of the 20 American-built *Moguls* supplied by Messrs. Burnham Williams and built at their Baldwin Works in Philadelphia for the G.C. between 1899 and 1900. The use of locomotives built overseas is a measure of the desperate plight of the Great Central for engine power around the turn of the Century. Builders at home were unable to supply the company's needs and the Great Central themselves lacked facilities to produce extra locomotives, with a shortage of both sufficient machine tools and workshop space. The 20 Moguls replaced an equal number of Pollitt's 9H 0-6-0 goods engines then on order; the American engines appeared to be a poor substitute. Robinson spoke disparagingly of the engines, quoting coal consumption and repair costs well above contemporary home-built locomotives. The 'Yankees' had 2 cylinders 18 ins. x 24 ins. with 5 foot coupled wheels. Classed '15' by the G.C., they cost the company £2,600 each. Number 963 was built in December 1899, became 963B in 1910 and was withdrawn in January 1915. All the Baldwin engines had gone by the end of 1915, the last survivor being no.948-withdrawn in the September of that year.

Collection of G.H.Platt

'Mogul'
Class 15 2-6-0

Looking more like a scene in an early Western, Mogul no.956 stands at an unidentified engine shed. The appearance of such a locomotive must have come as a profound shock to G.C. enginemen in an age that lacked the instant worldwide communications that we take for granted nowadays. 956 became 956B in 1910-the suffix indicating a number on the duplicate list. She was withdrawn from service in May 1913.

Author's collection

Brocklesby Junction, between Barnetby and Grimsby, was the scene of an accident on March 27th.1907 when two goods trains collided. One train was drawn by Mogul no.966 which was severely damaged. In charge of two youthful guardians, the engine presents an opportunity for inspection of some details not otherwise visible. Not surprisingly, 966 did not run again and was cut up in July 1907.

Collection of G.H.Platt

ROBINSON ELEGANCE: Early and middle period Robinson locomotives are seen in this view at Gorton shed in very early LNER days. No.1024, first built in 1902, represents the designer's first study in express power. The result of empirical work in boiler, superheating and front end design, she was rebuilt to Class 11D in 1915. To the right of the picture, from Robinson's pre-First War period is Class 1 no.426 *City of Chester* built at Gorton in 1913. The 'C' suffix was an early form of LNER designation for Great Central area locomotives. Behind no.426 is the tower of the coal pulverising plant.

Collection of G.H.Platt

J.G.Robinson
A Thumbnail Sketch

John George Robinson was born in Newcastle-on-Tyne in 1856. His father, Matthew Robinson, was District Locomotive Superintendent of the Bristol and Exeter Railway, a post he retained after the company merged with the Great Western (in 1875) until his retirement in 1897.

Robinson served his apprenticeship on the G.W.R. under Joseph Armstrong and William Dean at Swindon where he rubbed shoulders with the young George Jackson Churchward. The Great Western had further connections with the Robinson family: J.G.'s elder brother, James Armstrong Robinson, also worked for the company for over fifty years, retiring in 1920. Family connections with the railway generally were augmented by Robinson's son, Matthew, who became District Locomotive Superintendent at (appropriately) Neasden during the Second World War.

After obtaining his indentures at Swindon, Robinson took a post on the Great Western at Bristol in the Running Department. In 1884, at the age of only 28 he was appointed as Assistant Locomotive Superintendent under Henry Appleby on the Warterford, Limerick & Western Railway in Ireland. Appleby resigned in 1888 whereupon Robinson took over the post of Chief of the Locomotive, Carriage & Wagon Department. His work in Ireland is largely unknown but he produced 35 locomotives of 8 different classes in the 12 years of his tenure. Included in these were 4-4-0 passenger engines, 4-4-2 tanks and 0-6-0 goods tender engines which bore some 'family' features passed on to his English designs.

The Great Central Board had obviously heard of Robinson's prowess in Ireland and accordingly 'head-hunted' him following Pollitt's resignation in 1900. It has been suggested that S.W. Johnson of the Midland had a hand in the appointment, certainly Johnson cannot have been unsympathetic to the G.C. cause having worked at Gorton under Sacre from 1859 to 1864.

Robinson left Ireland in June 1900 and took up office as Locomotive Superintendent at Gorton. Manchester from July 2nd. Finding the G.C. locomotive fleet in something of a shambles (viz. Pollitt's report of April 1899), he set in motion a modernisation programme, building on existing sound designs, then carefully enlarging them. Working on many occasions with Beyer, Peacock & Co. then probably the most experienced locomotive builders in the world. Robinson produced some superb designs; he did make some mistakes but these were not always the monumental catastrophes they have been painted as. Underpinning his work was a basic ruggedness and soundness of construction interwoven with beauty and a finely-flowing line. Empirical methods of building and development manifested themselves in his Atlantics, 9N 4-6-2 tanks, 8K 2-8-0 freight engines and the superb 'Directors' of 1913.

Away from locomotives in the direct sense, Robinson had done a great deal of work in connection with superheating. Impressed with trials conducted with Schmidt's apparatus in 1909, he had gone on to develop his own version with elements expanded directly into the superheater header itself, of which more anon. Refining and developing his ideas in this field, Robinson obtained patents for his numerous superheater innovations. Locomotives not only for the Great Central but for other railways both home and abroad were fitted with his superheaters; he even extended his system into the realm of marine engineering.

Lubrication was another Robinson speciality. His 'Intensifore' system with sight-feeds was successfully used on many of his engines taking preference on occasions to the well-established 'Wakefield' mechanical lubricator. In post-First War days a shortage of locomotive coal both in quality and quantity led him to pursue alternative fuels. Experiments with pulverised coal and oil, though something of a success, were not pursued for any length of time - the cost of grinding the coal out-weighing any savings.

Experiments with automatic train control, anti-collision devices for coaching stock, locomotive compounding and various sundry devices to aid locomotive efficiency such as ash ejectors and automatic water release valves for cylinders - all flowed from his fertile and productive mind.

Awarded a CBE for his services to the War effort in 1914/18 Robinson was in a strong position in the last months of the Great Central's existence. The new Board of the LNER selected him for the post of CME of the new group, but though no doubt flattered by this selection, he was then 66 years of age and turned the post down. His recommendation of Gresley for the new appointment has been told before, but its significance has, perhaps, been overlooked.

Following Robinson's retirement, he retained an interest in locomotive matters via a directorship of Beyer, Peacock & Co. Links with his old seniors were also maintained in the shape of Sir Sam Fay as Beyer, Peacock's Chairman. John G. Robinson C.B.E., M. Inst.C.E. M.I. Mech.E, 'The Blacksmith' from Gorton Tank, retired to Bournemouth. He died there on December 7th 1943 aged 87.

Superheated engine no.307 at Guide Bridge. She was so fitted in 1916 which narrows down the date of the photograph to around the time of the First War–probably accounting for the somewhat grimy appearance of the engine in a period when labour had become scarce. Generally, superheating caused three visual changes to the 9J Class: a lengthened smokebox to accommodate the headers coupled with an altered front mainframe profile and the fitting, on the locomotive's left-hand side of a mechanical lubricator. Like no. 293, 307 is coupled to a 4000 gallon tender. This version consists of short swivel links bolted through the frames. 293's tender (and no.16's) have longer hangers which pass through angled brackets rivetted to the frames and held underneath by square blocks of steel and nuts. Information of practical use, perhaps, only to modellers who like to 'get it right.' Another subtlety in Robinson tender design lies in his provision of a centre spring 6ins. longer than the outer two compared to 3ft.0ins.

Collection of G.H.Platt

Class 9H & 9J 0-6-0

When Robinson took over the helm of Locomotive Engineer in 1900 he had had to act promptly to deal with the company's chronic motive power shortages. As mentioned in the Introduction, one of the first designs to leave his drawing board was the 9J 0-6-0 goods engine. Using the already numerous Parker/Pollitt 9H design, Robinson selectively enlarged the key features of cylinders, coupled wheelbase, boiler and firebox-the latter retaining its Belpaire form introduced by Pollitt in the previous decade. Reference to this earlier design of 0-6-0 at this point in G.C. locomotive history is timely, as the 9H design, with origins going back to 1889, continued to be built by both Pollitt and Robinson-forty examples appearing under the latter's regime at Gorton Works between February 1901 and October 1902.

Having established that the 9J goods engine had its genesis in earlier locomotive designs, it is worthwhile taking a sidestep to study the relationship between Robinson's 9J and the, albeit smaller and slightly less sophisticated, goods tender engines of his predecessors. As with the 4-4-0 passenger classes, we can do this simply by means of the 'family tree' diagram.

9J no.293 coupled to a solitary G.C.single-verandah 15 ton brake van stands at ease in the MSJ&A platforms at Manchester London Road. The engine carries the G.C. standard goods livery of all-over black lined red and edged in white. Although not in absolutely pristine conditiion, 293's splasher beading has been polished and the single white line edging the footplate valance and buffer beam is clearly visible. The tender carried is a 4000 gallon version fitted with 4 coal rails and water pickup-notice the characteristic 'ship's wheel'; as the G.C. main line was not built with water troughs (the first were laid down at Charwelton in 1903) and earlier engines did not carry this feature.No. 293 was built at Gorton Works in April 1907. She appears here in saturated condition, not receiving a superheater until 1934. 293 was withdrawn by British Railways in 1956 as no. 64408.

Collection of G.H.Platt

EVOLUTION OF MS&L/G.C. 0 - 6 - 0 GOODS TENDER ENGINES

Parker **Class 9** of 1889 (6 engines only)

Inside frames, loco wheelbase of 7'-11" + 8'-7" used for next four designs. Built with round-topped fireboxes and 18" cylinders. 4'-10" coupled wheels. Rebuilt with standard No.1 Belpaire boilers (0-6-2 tanks *et al*) 1910-1920.

Class 9B (Parker) & **Class 9E** (Pollitt) of 1891-1895.

(Development of above, but using 5'-1" coupled wheels.)

Class 9E variant used Stephenson valve gear in preference to Joy's on previous goods engines. Both 9B & 9E built with round-topped fireboxes but rebuilt with No.1 Belpaire 1910-1921.

Class 9D (Parker) & **Class 9H** (Pollitt and Robinson) 1892-1902.

9D was a variation by Parker of his 9B class using Stephenson's valve gear, but retaining a round-topped firebox. Class 9H was a development of the 9D but used a Belpaire firebox from new. Both classes used 18" cylinders and 5'-1" coupled wheels. 9D engines rebuilt 1910-1923 with standard No.1 Belpaire boilers.

Class 9J ('Pom-Pom'- Robinson 1901-1910).

Development of 9H with longer coupled wheelbase (8'-1" + 9'-0"), cylinders enlarged to 18½" and bigger boiler used. Belpaire firebox adopted as standard and superheating applied from 1909 onwards.

Parker 9H class 0-6-0 no.815 standing outside Guide Bridge on the sidings known locally as 'The Park.' The 9H represented the final style of goods tender engine in MS&L days using the Belpaire firebox and Stephenson valve gear. Appearing under both Pollitt and Robinson, the engines had been built over the years 1896 to 1902. Robinson used the 9H design as the basis for his 9J 0-6-0 or 'Pom-Pom' goods engine, arguably one of the best medium-sized freight engines ever to run on a British railway. No.815 carries a Robinson chimney but still retains the high-pillar safety valves and extensions to the rear of the cab, features added in later years which brought them into something of a visual line with the 9Js. 815 was built by Beyer, Peacock & Co. in November 1896 and was withdrawn as British Railways no.65419 in March 1953.

Collection of G.H.Platt

The first forty engines of the 9J Class were built by Neilson, Reid & Co. of Glasgow and appeared between September 1901 and May 1902. A further nine were also turned out by Neilsons later in that year. Construction continued unabated up to May 1910 by which time no less than 174 examples of the class had appeared.

As with his first 4-4-0 (Class 11B), Robinson opted for slide valves for all but one of the 9Js. This solitary exception was engine No.16 built with piston vaives and Schmidt superheater in 1909. Footplate crews quickly dubbed the 9Js 'Pom-Poms' as the noisy bark of their exhaust was likened to a certain type of rapid-firing gun deployed in the recent Boer War.

Robinson had selected the Schmidt superheater for this first venture into the field. He reported to the Chairman and Directors on October 7th 1909 thus: *No.16....has been at work for some weeks with most favourable results....have made an experiment over 12 days....in order to test the merits of the Superheater-....working goods trains between Manchester and Grimsby and Fish trains between Grimsby and Manchester....and for comparison, a sister engine, which is practically new, on the same trains.* The engine selected for comparative trials was 9J no.207 which had come out of the shops in February of that year, having been built in 1904.

The Locomotive Inspectors, in turn, had reported to Robinson: *Both engines have been supplied with similar coal and the boilers of each make steam freely. Therefore the trial has been as fair as it is possible to get, under the circumstances.*

No.16 had covered 1476 miles, returning a coal consumption of 48.31 lbs/mile.
No.207 had covered 1491¼ (sic) miles, returning a coal consumption of 59.75 lbs/mile.

Robinson concluded: *Taking reasonable supposition, engines on fast goods trains doing, say, 40,000 miles in a year, coal being at 8/6d per ton, would effect a saving of over £85 per annum in the cost of coal alone and the same ratio could be applied in the saving of water. Against this however, must be taken into account the extra consumption of oil of the superheater, also the upkeep of the latter in repairs etc. over the non-superheated engine. With the superheater there is little, or no, priming, owing to the dryness of the steam, less condensation and also a reduced strain on the firebox-brought about by carrying only 150 lbs. pressure to the square inch.....no experience yet of maintenance costs.....no trouble reported by the Lancashire & Yorkshire or the Great Northern.....they are*

Class 9H. Type 0.6.0. № of Engines ... 105.

Maker	Year Built	№ of Engines	Maker	Year Built	№ of Engines	Maker	Year Built	№ of Engines
Beyer Peacock	1896	39	G.C.R.	1902	17			
" "	1897	27						
G.C.R.	1901	22						

... ... to superheated engines only. Total Superheated - 1.

CYLINDERS.		
Diameter		19"
Stroke		26"
Centres		2'0"

BOILER.
Class ... No 1 Standard
Working Pressure ... 160 Lbs. per □"
Barrel Dia. Outs. Max. ... 4' 4"
Barrel Length ... 10' 8⅛"
Barrel Thickness of Plates ... ½"

TUBES.
Large No. ... 5¼ Dia. Outs.
Small No. ... 190 Dia. Outs. 1¾" 1⅞"
Length between Tubeplates ... 11' 0 ²⁹⁄₃₂"

SUPERHEATER.
Kind of Header ... Schmidt
Elements { Dia. Outs. ... 1⅜"
Dia. Ins. ... 1¼"
Number ... 18

IF FITTED WITH
Draft Retarder ... No
Circulating Valve ... Yes
Header Discharge Valve ... Yes
Pressure Release Valves ... 3
Combined Pressure Release and Piston Valves } ... No

FIREBOX SHELL.
Length Outs. at Bottom ... 6'0"
Width ,, ,, ,, ... 4'1"
,, ,, ,, Top ... 4'6¼"
Thickness of Plates—
Back ... ¹⁷⁄₃₂" Casing ... ½" Throat ... ⅝"

COPPER FIREBOX.
Length of Grate ... 5' 4²⁄₃₂"
Width ,, ,, ... 3'5"
Depth to Top of Ring, Front ... 5'6"
,, ,, ,, Back ... 4'8½"

Width of Ring.
Back and Front ... 2½" Sides ... 3"
Thickness of Plates—
Back ... ½" Casing ... ½" Tube { ⅞"
½"

HEATING SURFACE.
Firebox Outside ... 99.99 Sq. ft.
Large Tubes ... ,,
Small Tubes ... 964 ,,
Superheater Inside ... 115 ,,
Total ... 1063 ,,

GRATE AREA. ... 18.3 Sq. ft.

WHEELS. Diameter. See Diagram.
Tyres Thickness ... 3"
JOURNALS. Dia. Length.
Leading Bogie or Truck ...
Leading Coupled ... 8" 9"
Driving ... 8" 9"
Intermediate ...
Trailing Coupled ... 8" 9"
Trailing Bogie or Truck ...

Tractive Power at 85% Boiler Pressure { Lbs. ... 19,781
Tons ... 8.4
Adhesion Coefficient. Lbs. per Ton ... 432
Height. Rail to Top of Chimney ... 13'3"
,, ,, Centre of Boiler ... 7'4½"

VALVES. Kind ... Balanced Slide
CYLINDER LUBRICATOR. Kind ... Sight Feed
If Fitted with Steam Sanding Apparatus ... Yes
,, ,, Train Warming ,, ... No
BRAKE. Auto Vacuum or Steam + Auto
TENDER. Capacity. Water, Gallons ... 3080 or 4000
,, Coal, Tons ... 5 or 6
WHEELS. Diameter ... 3'-9" or 4'3"
JOURNALS. Dia. ... 5½" or 6" Length ... 9" or 11"

satisfied with the Schmidt superheater.....can fit the last of the 8-wheel goods (Class 8A) *if the Committee decides.....cost approximately £170, which includes £50 royalty to the patentee.*

The Committee evidently did not feel inclined to foot the bill as the engines in question, the last batch of Class 8A 0-8-0s were not built with superheaters, this process being deferred until 1914.

Although four years were to elapse before the next 9J was given the superheater treatment, the process and its ramifications had obviously made their mark. Robinson's next class, the 8K 2-8-0, were all superheated from new and superheating was applied to all new construction thereafter. Retrospective application was also made to the Atlantics from 1912 onwards. Robinson devised his own variation of the Schmidt apparatus which did away with the need for the copper jointing rings and packings for fitting the steam pipes into the superheater header. This was overcome by expanding the pipes themselves directly into the headers; this Robinson patented, as well as inventing a type of hydrostatic sight-feed lubrication system patented in turn, under the name 'Intensifore'.

A general-purpose medium duty goods engine had ample work to do on virtually any part of the railway network and, in consequence, the 9J Class was found all over the Great Central system, with most sheds on the railway having some examples. Immingham possessed, at Grouping, the largest number-32, marginally ahead of Gorton with 31. The former L.D.& E.C.R. sheds at Tuxford and Langwith had 1 and 4 'Pom-Poms' respectively. The engines were also busy on the London Extension, as we will see, with 4 at Annesley, 16 at Leicester, 7 at Neasden and no less than 29 at Woodford.

An interesting dispersal took place in LNER days with some engines finding themselves on former 'foreign territory'-on ex G.E.R. lines and on parts of the M & G.N. system. An even broader front for the locomotives was opened up in post-Nationalisation days, with workings over the lines of the former C.L.C. It was this system that proved to be something of a happy hunting ground for so many former G.C. engines. Like their 4-4-0 brethren, 'Pom-Poms' worked Manchester-Chester trains and had even been pressed into service on the Manchester-Liverpool expresses. Duties of a more humdrum nature included local trains out of Manchester over former G.C. routes, with forays as far afield as Sheffield on stopping services from Manchester.

Class 9J.　Type 0.6.0　Nº of Engines ... 174

Maker	Date Built	Nº of Engines	Maker	Year Built	Nº of Engines	Maker	Year Built	Nº of Engines
Neilson	1901	22	Vulcan Fdy	1904	15	G.C.R.	1906	2
"	1902	27	Yorks. Eng. Cº	1904	5	"	1907	35
Beyer Peacock	1903	10	Beyer Peacock	1904	15	"	1908	11
G.C.R.	1903	3	Yorks. Eng. Cº	1905	5	"	1909	1
"	1904	9	" " "	1906	5	"	1910	9

Particulars in ... refer to Superheated engines only.　Total Superheated　30

CYLINDERS.	
Diameter	18½"
Stroke	26"
Centres	2'-0"
BOILER.	
Class	9J.
Working Pressure	160 Lbs. per □"
Barrel Dia. Outs. Max.	5'-0"
Barrel Length	11'-0"
Barrel Thickness of Plates	5/8"
TUBES.	
Large No. ... Dia. Outs.	5¼"
Small No. 254 Dia. Outs.	1¾"
Length between Tubeplates	11'-4⅞"
SUPERHEATER.	
Kind of Header	Coil
Elements { Dia. Outs. / Dia. Ins. / Number	18
IF FITTED WITH	
Draft Retarder	
Circulating Valve	
Header Discharge Valve	
Pressure Release Valves	
Combined Pressure Release and Piston Valves	

FIREBOX SHELL.	
Length Outs. at Bottom	6'-4"
Width " " "	4'-1"
" " " Top	5'-2¾"
Thickness of Plates—	
Back ⅝" Casing ⅝" Throat ¾"	
COPPER FIREBOX.	
Length of Grate	5'-7 15/16"
Width " "	3'-4 5/8"
Depth to Top of Ring, Front	6'-3⅛"
" " " Back	5'-9"
Width of Ring.	
Back and Front 3" Sides 3"	
Thickness of Plates—	
Back 9/16" Casing 9/16" Tube { ⅞" / 9/16"	
HEATING SURFACE.	
Firebox Outside	130 Sq. ft.
Large Tubes	"
Small Tubes	1322 "
Superheater Inside	"
Total	1452 "
GRATE AREA.	19 Sq. ft.

WHEELS. Diameter. See Diagram.		
Tyres Thickness		3½"
JOURNALS.	Dia.	Length.
Leading Bogie or Truck		
Leading Coupled	8"	9"
Driving	8"	9"
Intermediate		
Trailing Coupled	8"	12"
Trailing Bogie or Truck		
Tractive Power at 85% Boiler Pressure { Lbs. / Tons	21,975 / 9.8	
Adhesion Coefficient. Lbs. per Ton.	425	
Height. Rail to Top of Chimney	13'-2½"	
" " Centre of Boiler	7'-11½"	
VALVES. Kind Balanced or unbalanced Slide		
CYLINDER LUBRICATOR. Kind Sight Feed		
If Fitted with Steam Sanding Apparatus	No	
" " Train Warming "	No & Yes	
BRAKE. Steam & Auto Ejector		
TENDER. Capacity. Water, Gallons	3250 or 4000	
" Coal, Tons	6	
WHEELS. Diameter	4'-3" or 4'-4"	
JOURNALS. Dia. 6" Length 11"		

No. 316 was built at Gorton Works in December 1907. The later batches of 'Pom-Poms', were all built there, from the end of 1906 to the May of 1910. At the west end of Guide Bridge station, 316 takes water into a rather empty-looking tender whilst working 'light engine.' This locomotive was superheated in May 1915, a move which caused the vacuum ejector pipe of the engines so treated to be moved outside the boiler and above the handrail-compare with no. 293.

Collection of G.H.Platt

SUMMARY OF CLASS 9J 0-6-0 (LNER J11)

NUMBER	BUILDER	DATE BUILT	WITHDRAWN
973 - 1012	Neilson Reid & Co.	September 1901 to May 1902	Apr 1955-Sep 1962
1043 - 1051	Neilson Reid & Co.	October and November 1902	Aug 1955-Sep 1962
198,201/203/205/206/	Beyer Peacock & Co.	September to November 1903	Sep 1954-Sep 1962
209/210/211/214/215			
216/218/219/221-231/234	Beyer Peacock & Co.	February to April 1904	Oct 1954-Sep 1962
177/197,202/204/207/208/	Gorton	November 1903 to July 1904	jul 1955-Oct 1962
217/220/232/233/240/241			
235-239/242-250/252	Vulcan Foundry	June to August 1904	Jan 1954-Sep 1962
253 - 257	Yorkshire Engine Co.	March and April 1904	Mar 1959-Oct 1961
1078 - 1082	Yorkshire Engine Co.	August and September 1904	May 1955-Sep 1962
1115 - 1119	Yorkshire Engine Co.	June to August 1906	Jan 1955-Jul 1962
281-309/311-320/322-330	Gorton	December 1906 to November 1908	Oct 1955-Sep 1962
16	Gorton	April 1909	May 1961
947 - 955	Gorton	January to May 1910	Oct 1956-Aug 1962

Notes:
1) Only one engine, No.16, built with superheater from new. The rest were progressively dealt with by the G.G. and LNER up until 1946 (G.C.no.1119).
2) No.1009 rebuilt with cylinders and piston valves of J39 pattern but with an 18½" cylinder bore.

A work-stained no. 134 at Gorton. An immediate likeness to the 'Pom-Pom' design is detected, a boiler carrying an extra 8 ins. girth making an obvious difference . When rebuilt, the engine was provided with a cab to suit the bigger boiler which, again, altered its looks. The new boiler lasted until 1924 when a no.1 Standard, as carried by the 9H, was again fitted, the cab regaining a lowered profile to suit.

Collection of W.A.Brown

Class 9M 0-6-0 Goods Engine

A 'four-square' view of no.134, a Gorton picture again. This side-on photograph reflects the resemblance to the 'Pom-Pom' profile, the safety valves are of the four pillar variety carried also by the 9J. A noticeable difference in tender size will be apparent, the rebuilt engine carrying the smaller 3080 gallon tender with 5 ton coal capacity compared to the 3250 or 4000 gallon/6 ton coupled to the 'Pom-Pom'. As British Railways 65204 the erstwhile no.134 was withdrawn in November 1952, something of a 'two-timer' in the locomotive world and a creditable half-centenarian.

Collection of W.A.Brown

Class 9M. Type 0.6.0. Nº of Engines ... 1.

Maker	Year Built	Nº of Engines	Maker	Year Built	Nº of Engines	Maker	Year Built	Nº of Engines
Great Central Railway	1902	1						

— Rebuilt from 9H Class —

CYLINDERS.
Diameter .... 18"
Stroke .... 26"
Centres .... 2' 0"

BOILER.
Class 9M
Working Pressure .... 180 Lbs. per □"
Barrel Dia. Outs. Max. .... 5' 0"
Barrel Length .... 10'-8"
Barrel Thickness of Plates .... 9/16"

TUBES.
Large No. .... ¯ Dia. Outs. .... ¯
Small No. 254 Dia. Outs. 1¾"
Length between Tubeplates .... 11' 0¾"

SUPERHEATER.
Kind of Header .... ¯
Elements { Dia. Outs. .... ¯
Dia. Ins. .... ¯
Number .... ¯

IF FITTED WITH
Draft Retarder .... ¯
Circulating Valve .... ¯
Header Discharge Valve .... ¯
Pressure Release Valves .... ¯
Combined Pressure Release and Piston Valves } .... ¯

FIREBOX SHELL.
Length Outs. at Bottom .... 7'-0"
Width „ „ „ .... 4'-1"
„ „ „ Top .... 5'-2¾"
Thickness of Plates—
Back 21/32 Casing 5/8 Throat ¾"

COPPER FIREBOX.
Length of Grate .... 6'-3¹¹/₃₂
Width „ „ .... 3'-4⅛"
Depth to Top of Ring, Front .... 6'-3"
„ „ „ Back .... 4'-9½"

Width of Ring.
Back and Front 3" Sides 3"
Thickness of Plates—
Back ⅝" Casing ⅝" Tube ⅞"/5/8"

HEATING SURFACE.
Firebox Outside .... 130 Sq. ft.
Large Tubes .... ¯ „
Small Tubes .... 1282 „
Superheater Inside .... ¯ „
Total 1412 „

GRATE AREA. .... 21½ Sq. ft.

WHEELS. Diameter. See Diagram.
Tyres Thickness .... 3"

JOURNALS. Dia. Length.
Leading Bogie or Truck ....
Leading Coupled .... 8" 9"
Driving .... 8" 9"
Intermediate ....
Trailing Coupled .... 8" 9"
Trailing Bogie or Truck ....

Tractive Power at 85% Boiler Pressure { Lbs. 21,129
Tons 9.4
Adhesion Coefficient. Lbs. per Ton 425
Height. Rail to Top of Chimney .... 13'.3"
„ „ Centre of Boiler .... 7'.4½"

VALVES. Kind .... Balanced Slide

CYLINDER LUBRICATOR. Kind .... Sight Feed
If Fitted with Steam Sanding Apparatus .... no
„ „ Train Warming „ .... no

BRAKE. .... Steam + Auto Ejector

TENDER. Capacity. Water, Gallons 3,080
„ „ Coal, Tons 5

WHEELS. Diameter .... 3'- 10"

JOURNALS. Dia. 5½" Length 9"

Into the superheater era with no. 1026 typifying the final modifications to this most interesting class. Running tender-first at the east end of Guide Bridge station the engine looks ready for business with a good heap of coal piled high on the tender, albeit of a somewhat small size. As proof of her rebuilt condition, 1026 carries beneath her (extended) smokebox a works plate stating: 'Great Central Ry. Rebuilt Gorton Works 1914 Manchester.' To the right of the smokebox can be seen the Wakefield mechanical lubricator, a pre-requisite for a superheated engine, with oil feed pipes to the cylinder block. Notice the lifting arms of the Stephenson valve gear in the 'ten to' position indicating reverse running. Front main frames above the footplate now have a steeper rake in front of the smokebox and the cab side sheets retain their original length.

Collection of G.H.Platt

Class 11B/11C/11D 4-4-0

Robinson's first 4-4-0 design, his second essay for the G.C.R, was the handsome and powerful-looking 11B Class introduced in the October of 1901. As mentioned in the Introduction, the first engines were ordered with some urgency in the Autumn of 1900, Sharp, Stewart & Co. of Glasgow constructing the first 30 of the class between 1901 and 1903. Vulcan Foundry, of Newton-le-Willows in Lancashire, built the last 10 locomotives, between March and June 1904.

The engines were put to work right away on the G.C's Manchester-Marylebone expresses, duties they took over from the last of the Pollitt 4-4-0s, the Class 11A. As our pictures will show, trains on the London Extension were of a lightweight nature. But they were, nevertheless, subject to tight timings, a matter made no easier by the difficult nature of the line between Manchester and Sheffield. Although a speeded-up service, introduced by Fay in 1905, drew the 11Bs away from the fastest of the expresses, they remained in active service on the Extension trains at least up to the First War. By Grouping the class had largely migrated away from the London

services and were concentrated on cross-country workings, principally from Sheffield over the company's Woodhead Route to Manchester and Liverpool and eastwards as far as Cleethorpes and Hull. In 1921 the bulk of the fleet were stationed at Sheffield (18) with Mexborough and Immingham having 5 and 8 engines respectively. 9 were at Annesley working out their time there on stopping trains between Sheffield, Nottingham and Leicester. The Sheffield engines at this time worked trains to York, Hull and Cleethorpes and across to Manchester and Liverpool and also as far south as Leicester. In the 1930s, two main concentrations of the class (now LNER D9) came about, although odd engines were housed at Staveley, Langwith and Barnsley. The greater part of the class were housed at the C.L.C. bases of Trafford Park (Manchester) and Brunswick (Liverpool) and to various sheds in the eastern half of the country. Allocations here included March, Ipswich and Peterborough with incursions into M&G.N. territory after the LNER took over responsibility for working the line from 1936. The Cheshire

11B no.1042 outside the grimy environs of Mexborough shed in late G.C.days. The slim boiler and handsome long chimney of the original 1900 design can be clearly discerned. The Ross 'Pop' safety valves-fitted to no.1042 in 1920 were not typical of the 11B class, neither was the 3250 gallon tender with 4 coal rails, the latter suggests an exchange of tenders with another loco as the original 3250 gallon tenders with only 2 coal rails are thought to have been only short-lived. As a complement to the original tall chimney, the handsome dome cover does nicely; this should be compared to the later, squatter versions applied to the 11C and 11D variants of the class. Notice the single cab spectacle, altered to a split pattern when the larger, higher-pitched boilers were provided.

Collection of G.H.Platt

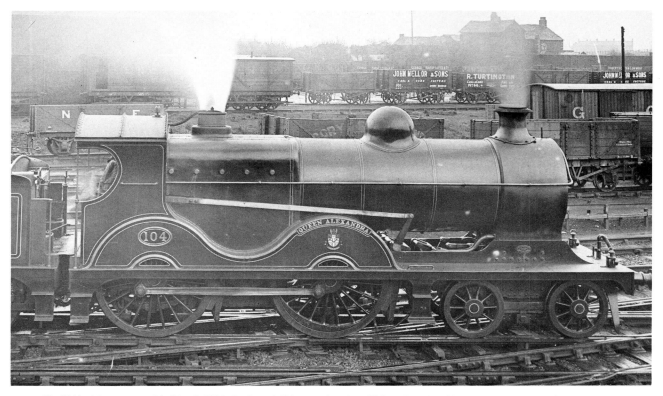

No.104 had first appeared in March 1904, the first of 10 locomotives from Vulcan Foundry. She was named *Queen Alexandra* when rebuilt to Class 11C in March 1907. This superb broadside view at the west end of Guide Bridge station shows many details visible only from a raised elevation. *Queen Alexandra* faces towards Manchester with a down express astride the crossings of the LNW line from Denton Junction. A fine selection of pre-Group rolling stock fills Cock Lane Sidings in the background; in particular, P.O.coal wagons are well to the fore. The engine's motion is revealed quite clearly and although the expansion links of the Stephenson valve gear are hidden in her skirts so to speak, the ends of the rocking shafts and levers for the valves on top of the cylinders stand out clearly. The pipe extending in an 'S' shape from the top of the cylinder block takes exhaust steam for an injector, although no records are available to show if any other members of the class carried this fitting. The plate under the smokebox reads: 'Great Central RY. Rebuilt 1907-Gorton Works.' Besides this small detail, much else is discerned. Modellers should note the rivetted angle iron bracing the cab roof-a future standard for many Robinson locos, the split cladding on top of the boiler and firebox lagging plates and the wealth of tender front detail. The curved boxes just inside the tender are sand boxes. Fitted for reverse running, a gravity feed dropped sand down a vertical pipe behind the front tender footstep.

Collection of G.H.Platt

Lines engines supplanted the Pollitt 11A 4-4-0s (then approaching retirement) on the Manchester-Liverpool services. In 1943 Trafford Park and Brunswick sheds had 13 of the class (D9) between them for the Liverpool trains. This was strengthened to 23 engines by 1947 with only four others surviving: 1 at Heaton Mersey, 1 at Walton (Liverpool) and 2 at Northwich. Run-down after the war years and approaching a fifty year life span, the last engine, G.C.R. no.1018, then British Railways no.62305 was withdrawn in July 1950.

Something of late MS&L/early G.C. practice could be detected in the outline of the design, although mechanically, Robinson reverted to the use of slide valves working on inclined Vee faces-possibly because of problems with the piston valves fitted to the Pollitt 11A 4-4-0s.

Great Central locomotive history is characterised in the main by small batches of engines, and in many of Robinson's locomotive designs, succeeding batches incorporate detail differences in an endeavour to increase performance or to fulfill a specific need. Rebuilding was undertaken only on a fairly limited scale in the light of such improvements as superheating and piston valves. This resulted in many locomotives retaining the bulk of their identity over a long period of time; witness the outlines of the Parker, Pollitt and Sacre' designs that were still active in the first decade of the LNER. We can compare this to locomotive practice on, for example, the Midland Railway where Johnson, Deeley and Fowler rebuilt their respective predecessor's designs almost, it seemed, as a matter of course.

Perhaps uncharacteristically then, the 11B design was rebuilt not once, but twice within a fairly short space of time. Though the first 4-4-0s were successful in that they improved upon previous engines and hauled heavier loads, it is thought that, having introduced his famous 'Atlantics' in 1903, Robinson felt he had room for manoeuvre with the layout and proportions of the 11B boiler.

In 1907 nos.104 and 110 were fitted with larger boilers of 5'-0" diameter (the originals were 4'-9" diameter). Together with a longer firebox-increased from 7'-0" to 8'-6"-and cylinders of slightly wider bore (18 ½" to 19") better things could reasonably have been expected of the engines, now re-classified 11C. Unfortunately, the results did not match the anticipated effect. This may have been due to a cramped ashpan layout and a reduction in the firebox heating surface, owing to the

A plentiful exhaust suggests hard work from 11D no.1015 as she passes Whetstone with an up express composed of 6 clerestory coaches. The date is unknown but no.1015 was rebuilt to Class 11D in June 1913; becoming LNER no.6015 in July 1924, the engine had a long innings. It lasted until March 1950 before withdrawal as British Railways no.62302.
G.M.Shoults

Class ... 11B   Type ... 4 4 0   N° of Engines   5.

Maker	Year Built	N° of Engines	Maker	Year Built	N° of Engines	Maker	Year Built	N° of Engines
Sharp Stewart	1903	1						
Vulcan Fdy	1904	4						

For 11B rebuilt to 11D Class see Page

CYLINDERS.
Diameter .... 18½"
Stroke .... 26"
Centres .... 2'-0½"

BOILER.
Class 11B
Working Pressure ......180.....Lbs. per □"
Barrel Dia. Outs. Max. .... 4'-9"
Barrel Length .... 11'-6"
Barrel Thickness of Plates .... ⅝"

TUBES.
Large No. ......—...... Dia. Outs. ......—......
Small No. ...230... Dia. Outs. ...1¾"
Length between Tubeplates ...11'-10⁹⁄₁₆"

SUPERHEATER.
Kind of Header .... —
Elements { Dia. Outs. .... —
          { Dia. Ins. .... —
          { Number .... —

IF FITTED WITH
Draft Retarder .... —
Circulating Valve .... —
Header Discharge Valve .... —
Pressure Release Valves .... —
Combined Pressure Release } .... —
and Piston Valves }

FIREBOX SHELL.
Length Outs. at Bottom ...... 7'-0"
Width ,, ,, ,, ... 4'-1"
,, ,, ,, Top ...... 4'-11⅝"
Thickness of Plates—
Back ...²⁹⁄₃₂".Casing... ⅝" .Throat... ¾"

COPPER FIREBOX.
Length of Grate ...... 6'-3¹⁵⁄₃₂"
Width ,, ,, ... 3'-4⅝"
Depth to Top of Ring, Front ...6'-1¼"
,, ,, ,, Back ...5'-4¾"

Width of Ring.
Back and Front 3" Sides 3"
Thickness of Plates—
Back ...⁹⁄₁₆".Casing... ⁹⁄₁₆".Tube { ⅞"
                                    { ½"

HEATING SURFACE.
Firebox Outside ...... 130 ....Sq. ft.
Large Tubes ...... — ,,
Small Tubes ...... 1248 ,,
Superheater Inside ...... — ,,
                        Total   1378 ,,

GRATE AREA. ...... 21 ....Sq. ft.

WHEELS. Diameter. See Diagram.
Tyres Thickness ...... 3"
JOURNALS.   Dia.   Length.
Leading Bogie or Truck ...... 6" ...... 9"
Leading Coupled ......
Driving ...... 8" ...... 9"
Intermediate ......
Trailing Coupled ...... 8" ...... 12"
Trailing Bogie or Truck ......

Tractive Power at { Lbs. 16850
85% Boiler Pressure { Tons 7.53
Adhesion Coefficient. Lbs. per Ton ... 456
Height. Rail to Top of Chimney ...13'-3"
,, ,, Centre of Boiler ... 8'-1½"

VALVES. Kind ... Unbalanced Slide

CYLINDER LUBRICATOR. Kind ...Sight Feed
If Fitted with Steam Sanding Apparatus ...... Yes
,, ,, Train Warming ,, ... Yes
BRAKE. ...... Steam & Auto Ejector
TENDER. Capacity. Water, Gallons ...4.000
,, ,, Coal, Tons 6
WHEELS. Diameter ...... 4'-4"
JOURNALS. Dia. ... 6" Length ...... 11"

These two pictures of no.110, named *King George V* in 1911, illustrate clearly the details of the 11C rebuilding applied to this engine and compatriot no.104 *Queen Alexandra* The first picture, taken on Gorton shed, shows the rebuilding of May 1907 with the 5ft.0ins. diameter boiler set at the higher pitch of 8ft.6ins. above rail level, longer firebox and shortened cab side sheets to gain access to the washout plugs. Both chimney and dome are of an immediately identifiable squatter pattern.In August 1918 *King George V* lost its larger boiler and was re-fitted with an original 4ft.9ins. diameter saturated version. Strangely enough, the larger boiler was transferred to no.113 along with the cut-back cab. To complete the ensemble, Robinson-ever meticulous with such details-reinstated the original chimney and dome; the longer cab side sheets too, carried when first built were replaced. The lower cab spectacles were also done away with. A fascinating, if somewhat cumbersome, operation.

Collection of G.H.Platt

Class ... 11C Type ... 4.4.0. No. of Engines ... 2.

Vulcan Fdy	1904	2						

CYLINDERS.
- Diameter ... 19"
- Stroke ... 26"
- Centres ... 2'-0½"

BOILER.
- Class ... 11C
- Working Pressure ... 180 Lbs. per □"
- Barrel Dia. Outs. Max. ... 5'-0"
- Barrel Length ... 11'-6"
- Barrel Thickness of Plates ... 5/8"

TUBES.
- Large No. ... – Dia. Outs. ... –
- Small No. ... 254 Dia. Outs. ... 1⅞"
- Length between Tubeplates ... 11'-10⅜"

SUPERHEATER.
- Kind of Header ... –
- Elements: Dia. Outs. ... –; Dia. Ins. ... –; Number ... –

IF FITTED WITH
- Draft Retarder ... –
- Circulating Valve ... –
- Header Discharge Valve ... –
- Pressure Release Valves ... –
- Combined Pressure Release and Piston Valves ... –

FIREBOX SHELL.
- Length Outs. at Bottom ... 8'-6"
- Width " " " ... 4'-0½"
- " " " Top ... 5'-2¾"
- Thickness of Plates— Back ... 21/32" Casing ... 5/8" Throat ... 3/4"

COPPER FIREBOX.
- Length of Grate ... 7'-9 15/32"
- Width " " ... 3'-4⅛"
- Depth to Top of Ring, Front ... 5'-11½"
- " " " Back ... 4'-5½"

Width of Ring.
- Back and Front ... 3" Sides ... 3"
- Thickness of Plates— Back ... 9/16" Casing ... 9/16" Tube ... 7/8" / 9/16"

HEATING SURFACE.
- Firebox Outside ... 148 Sq. ft.
- Large Tubes ... – "
- Small Tubes ... 1478 "
- Superheater Inside ... – "
- Total ... 1626 "

GRATE AREA. ... 26 Sq. ft.

WHEELS. Diameter. See Diagram.
- Tyres Thickness ... 3"

JOURNALS.

	Dia.	Length.
Leading Bogie ~~or Truck~~	6"	9"
Leading Coupled		
Driving	8"	9"
Intermediate		
Trailing Coupled	8"	12"
Trailing Bogie or Truck		

- Tractive Power at 85% Boiler Pressure: Lbs. ... 17584; Tons ... 7.8
- Adhesion Coefficient. Lbs. per Ton ... 467
- Height. Rail to Top of Chimney ... 13'-3"
- " " Centre of Boiler ... 8'-6"

VALVES. Kind ... Balanced Slide

CYLINDER LUBRICATOR. Kind ... Sight Feed
- If Fitted with Steam Sanding Apparatus ... Yes
- " " Train Warming " ... Yes

BRAKE. ... Steam & Auto Ejector

TENDER. Capacity. Water, Gallons ... 4000
- " Coal, Tons ... 6

WHEELS. Diameter ... 4'-4"

JOURNALS. Dia. ... 6" Length ... 11"

Class ... 11D Type ... 4.4.0 No. of Engines ... 33.

Maker	Year Built	No. of Engines	Maker	Year Built	No. of Engines	Maker	Year Built	No. of Engines
Sharp Stewart	1901	5	Vulcan Fdy.	1904	4			
"	1902	20						
"	1903	4						

Converted from 11B Class.

CYLINDERS.
- Diameter ... 19"
- Stroke ... 26"
- Centres ... 2'-0½"

BOILER.
- Class ... No 4 Standard
- Working Pressure ... 180 Lbs. per □"
- Barrel Dia. Outs. Max. ... 5'-0"
- Barrel Length ... 11'-6"
- Barrel Thickness of Plates ... 5/8"

TUBES.
- Large No. ... 22 Dia. Outs. ... 5¼"
- Small No. ... 134 Dia. Outs. ... 1⅞"
- Length between Tubeplates ... 11'-10⅜"

SUPERHEATER.
- Kind of Header ... Front Cover
- Elements: Dia. Outs. ... 1⅜"; Dia. Ins. ... 1 1/16"; Number ... 22

IF FITTED WITH
- Draft Retarder ...
- Circulating Valve ... Yes
- Header Discharge Valve ... Yes
- Pressure Release Valves ...
- Combined Pressure Release and Piston Valves ... Yes

FIREBOX SHELL.
- Length Outs. at Bottom ... 7'-0"
- Width " " " ... 4'-0½"
- " " " Top ... 5'-2¾"
- Thickness of Plates— Back ... 21/32" Casing ... 5/8" Throat ... 3/4"

COPPER FIREBOX.
- Length of Grate ... 6'-4 15/32"
- Width " " ... 3'-4⅛"
- Depth to Top of Ring, Front ... 6'-7¼"
- " " " Back ... 5'-10¼"

Width of Ring.
- Back and Front ... 3" Sides ... 3"
- Thickness of Plates— Back ... 9/16" Casing ... 9/16" Tube ... 7/8" / 9/16"

HEATING SURFACE.
- Firebox Outside ... 136 Sq. ft.
- Large Tubes ... 359 "
- Small Tubes ... 780 "
- Superheater Inside ... 178 "
- Total ... 1453 "

GRATE AREA. ... 21 Sq. ft.

WHEELS. Diameter. See Diagram.
- Tyres Thickness ... 3"

JOURNALS.

	Dia.	Length.
Leading Bogie ~~or Truck~~	6"	9"
Leading Coupled		
Driving	8"	9"
Intermediate		
Trailing Coupled	8"	12"
Trailing Bogie or Truck		

- Tractive Power at 85% Boiler Pressure: Lbs. ... 17584; Tons ... 7.8
- Adhesion Coefficient. Lbs. per Ton ... 520
- Height. Rail to Top of Chimney ... 13'-3"
- " " Centre of Boiler ... 8'-6"

VALVES. Kind ... Piston (Outs. Adm.)

CYLINDER LUBRICATOR. Kind ... Mechanical
- If Fitted with Steam Sanding Apparatus ... Yes
- " " Train Warming " ... Yes

BRAKE. ... Steam & Auto Ejector

TENDER. Capacity. Water, Gallons ... 4000
- " Coal, Tons ... 6

WHEELS. Diameter ... 4'-4"

JOURNALS. Dia. ... 6" Length ... 11"

SUMMARY OF CLASS 11B/C/D 4-4-0 (LNER D9)

NUMBER	BUILDER	DATE BUILT	WITHDRAWN
1013 - 1017	Sharp,Stewart & Co.	October 1901	Aug 1949-Jan 1950
1018 - 1037	Sharp,Stewart & Co.	March to May 1902	May 1939-Jul 1950
1038 - 1042	Sharp,Stewart & Co.	March 1903	Jul 1939-Feb 1950
104 - 113	Vulcan Foundry	March to June 1904	Jun 1939-Dec 1949

No.104 named *Queen Alexandra* in March 1907 when rebuilt to Class 11C.
No.110 named *King George V* sometime in 1911.

No.1014 named *Sir Alexander* in 1902. Name removed in 1913.
No.1021 named *Queen Mary* in April 1913.

inclination necessary to clear the rear coupled axle. The rebuilding was not extended to any other members of the class, an indication that the boiler/firebox proportions were not entirely satisfactory.

No.104 was the first of the two 11C rebuilds, emerging in March 1907. She had originally been built in March 1904, the first of the 10 Vulcan Foundry engines. A second 11C, no.110, followed in the May of that year. Comparison with the earlier engines will reveal the longer firebox of the 11C showing clearly-notice the number of washout plugs, 5 on the longer boilered version compared with 3 on the 11B. Rebuilding caused something of an imbalance in the rearward proportions of the design as the cab sidesheets were cut back to accommodate the longer fireboxes and provide access to the washout plugs. The new boilers on the rebuilds were pitched 4½"higher than the originals to give greater firebox depth combined with a necessity to clear the rear coupled axle.

The rebuilds had balanced slide valves set in a flat plane on top of the cylinders. In the original design the slide valves had been inclined downwards at an angle of 1 in 10. Hence the necessity for rocking shafts in the later engine with retention of the original motion.

In 1909 another phase of development of Robinson's pioneer 4-4-0 class began. Engine no.1026 was selected and in this third version-now classified 11D-Robinson reverted to a smaller firebox (7'-0" in length again). This shorter firebox could be accommodated between the two coupled axles, doing away with the previous ashpan problems. The boiler was once more set at 5'-0" in diameter and the higher pitch was retained. Upon rebuilding, 1026 was given new cylinders, this time with piston valves driven directly from the Stephenson gear (no rocking shafts as on the first rebuild, no. 104.)

Having produced a satisfactory boiler for his first express engine together with an improved cylinder and valve layout, Robinson turned his attention to super-heating.

Prior to 1913 all the Class 11B 4-4-0 boilers had produced saturated steam. But in that year, commencing with no.1021, the superheater boiler, developed from that fitted to no.1026 and adopted as standard in the meantime for the 9N 4-6-2 tank design of 1911, was set as the future norm for the 11B 4-4-0s.

To sum up then, all 40 engines were given superheater boilers beween 1913 and 1927 and (not necessarily simultaneously) received new piston valve cylinders of nominal 19" bore. It is at this point that life for the student of G.C.locomotive history begins to get com-

plicated. To minimise rebuilding costs (and the Great Central was not a prosperous company whatever else it was!) the original set of Stephenson link motion was retained in conjunction with the new cylinders. Because slide valves had been swapped for piston valves it was necessary to use outside admission of steam in the new valve/cylinder layout. This same cylinder block was adopted also for the first Director 4-4-0s which appeared in 1913. An endeavour to clarify this rather tedious situation a little further has been made in the section dealing with that class in volume 2. Records suggest that the new cylinders were lined up to 19" (from a nominal 20" as per the first LNER engine diagrams), the larger bore imposing a strain on the Class 11D boiler.

A damp April morning on the platforms at Leicester in 1911 sees no.111, built at Vulcan Foundary in 1904, bark away with the 8.45 am Marylebone to Manchester express. Notice the more elegant, taller boiler mountings identifying the engine as an 11B and not yet rebuilt. Conversion to class 11D took place in November 1916 with both piston valves and superheated boiler fitted at the same time. 111 was withdrawn in October 1949 as British Railways no.62332.
G.M.Shoults

Here then were engines of noble appearance and lineage, reliable medium-duty express locomotives altered and improved by an innovative designer. During their initial career they had been the subject of empirical research and development, the results of which laid the foundations for some of Robinson's best work. Though they were pushed out of the front line of duty by more powerful engines, over half the 11Bs (as LNER Class D9) survived Nationalisation , providing almost half a century's sound and worthy service.

A picture with a human story to tell. Driver Fred Lancashire rests his oil feeder on the platform of 11D no.1026 resting between duties in the centre road at Leicester around 1912. Then aged 42, Fred Lancashire had come to Leicester in 1899. He had begun his railway career at Stockport's Tiviot Dale shed as a 'Bar Boy' in 1882 at the age of 13. Fred was firing shunting engines by the time he was 20 and graduated to Driver at the exceptionally early age of 26. In 1899 at only age 29, Fred Lancashire had become the youngest express driver on the Great Central.Fred achieved a degree of fame in 1899 when, in company with John Williams-another Leicester Driver-he worked the Daily Mail's Boer War newspaper special from Marylebone between Leicester and Manchester. He retired on June 18th 1935 and had reached the grand old age of 90 when the Railway Magazine interviewed him for the article from which this extract was taken.

G.M.Shoults

South of Leicester and through the fields and hedges near Whetstone goes no.1029, a Sharp Stewart engine of 1902 now rebuilt to class 11D with piston valves and superheater boiler.Though the photograph is undated, we know that the engine was rebuilt in October 1913. The train is the 2.15 pm Manchester London Road to Marylebone and consists of 4 bogie coaches with a van at either end. Mr.G.M.Shoults, who took this picture , was busy in the Leicester area from around 1910 to 1914. His photographs show 11B and 11D 4-4-0s still active on Manchester -London expresses as well as putting in a showing on local services. This was despite the arrival in the interim of Atlantics, Sir Sams and Directors, proof of the usefulness of these fine engines.1029 became LNER 6029 in November 1924. Renumbered 2313 in 1946, she survived Nationalisation and was withdrawn in October 1949 as British Railways no.62313.

G.M.Shoults

The handsome, yet simple lines of the Class 8 design are shown to advantage in this low-level shot of no.186 at Neasden when the engines stationed there were working expresses from Marylebone to Leicester. Three separate splashers, the rear one combined with the cab side sheet, was to become something of a classic Robinson feature-used on three other 4-6-0 classes, with a foreshortened version appearing on the celebrated 'Atlantics.' 186 was one of the second batch of class 8 engines, built in 1904 by Beyer, Peacock & Co., following their thinly-disguised threat. This brought the total for the class to 14 locomotives. How typical of the pre-First War period is the immaculate condition of the engine; well-polished adornments include the guard irons, smokebox fittings, motion and wheel tyres. Incidentally, a driving wheel diameter of 6ft.0ins. was quoted when the engines were built, increasing to 6ft.1ins. when the wheels were re-tyred in later years. This diameter was, of course, decreased again as the engines got nearer to heavy repairs. The fitting above the l.h.cylinder is a 20-ton screw jack carried on board for re-railing purposes. Jacks appear to have been carried by several Robinson classes and, although no photographs appear to show them in service, it would be of interest to know if, or how often, they were used.

Collection of G.H.Platt

Class 8 4-6-0
Fish Engine

Though Robinson used numerous wheel arrangements for his many designs, it was the 4-6-0 type that provided him with his greatest variety of outline. The first of these were the handsome Class 8 4-6-0s. Fourteen in number were built between 1902 and 1904. Construction was shared between Neilsons of Glasgow and Beyer, Peacock - Gorton's next door neighbours in Manchester.

A degree of wrangling had developed between Beyer, Peacock and the Great Central over the contract for the first six Class 8s. Their contract price was much in excess of that quoted by a 'rival Scottish firm'. This was obviously a reference to Neilsons who had tendered at £3,720 per loco. When this was put to them, Beyer, Peacock replied that 'at that price we cannot make any profit'. The company offered to split the difference but the G.C. were unimpressed; the end of the matter was not quite in sight however. Beyer, Peacock retorted by pointing out that a great quantity of their traffic passed over the G.C.'s lines. The threat was obvious - give us the job or we'll use another railway. A reply that the company would hope to offer work in the near future was duly dispatched. Beyer Peacock got the contract for the next eight engines!

An essentially straightforward 2-cylinder locomotive, the Class 8 was designed mainly to work express fish traffic - very much a Great Central speciality - from the East Coast port of Grimsby. It was their deployment on this type of traffic that earned the class the sobriquet of 'Fish Engines'.

When built, the 'Fish' engines were allocated between Gorton, Grimsby and Neasden for the express movement of not only fish but also express goods. Passenger work between Marylebone and Leicester was also on the engines' agenda at that time. Later G.C. work took the engines to Immingham and Mexborough and from the latter depot cross-country workings via Banbury were undertaken.

In early LNER days, Ardsley and Doncaster received 'Fish' engines, then classified 'B5'. Up to 1930 both Woodford and Lincoln housed members of the class, with migrations after the mid-1930s to Sheffield and Immingham.

During the Second War, the 'Fish' engines put in excellent performances between Sheffield and Doncaster with loads of up to fourteen coaches. Engines from Mexborough were then working on freight trains as well as acting as bankers between Wath and Dunford Bridge.

The traffic the Fish Engines were built for: One of the Neilson engines of 1902 at work on the London Extension. A Grimsby to Marylebone Fish Train hauled by Class 8 no. 1070 gets the 'right-away' from the platform home signal at Leicester on May 19th.1910. 9K 4-4-2 tank no.178 waits alongside at the head of a local working.

G.M.Shoults

Post-War, the engines, then over forty years old, saw service at Trafford Park, Lincoln and finally Mexborough. It was from here that the last of the class worked out their time acting again on banking duty from Wath. The last engine, the former G.C. no. 183, then numbered LNER 1686, was withdrawn in June 1950.

A 4'-9" diameter boiler (the same diameter as that used on the 11B 4-4-0) produced saturated steam fed to two outside cylinders. A cylinder bore of 19ins combined with a 26ins stroke, slide valves driven by Stephenson's link motion all pointed to a design of a perfectly conventional nature. The Belpaire firebox, still something of a novelty elsewhere, had been pioneered back in MS&L days having been used extensively by Beyer, Peacock & Co. Robinson's faith in this innovation was shared, of course, by his erstwhile Great Western contempories Dean and Churchward.

In 1923 a start was made in fitting superheater boilers of the type produced for the 8K freight engine. Because of the deeper firebox, this involved raising the pitch of the boilers and fitting a lower pattern of chimney in place of the very handsome original which measured, for the record, 2'-2¾" high. Superheating of the class was a lengthy process and was not completed until 1936, with no. 1070. The new boilers, together with alterations of a more sundry nature such as the removal of piston tail-rods, centre footsteps and Ramsbottom safety valves did much to alter the appearance of the class. Surviving through 25 years of the LNER and in seven cases into early BR days the Class 8 4-6-0s (then LNER B5) was a much changed machine. Several were fitted with larger cylinders of 21ins bore and acquired piston valves of the pattern produced for the 8K (04) 2-8-0 freight engine.

SUMMARY OF CLASS 8 4-6-0 (LNER B5)

NUMBER	BUILDER	DATE BUILT	WITHDRAWN
1067 - 1072	Neilson & Co.	November and December 1902	Mar 1939-Dec 1947
180 - 187	Beyer Peacock & Co.	January to March 1904	May 1947-Jun 1950

NOTE: Several engines were fitted with 21" cylinders and piston valves of the 8K pattern. Engines and dates of fitting were :-

180	*August 1938*
183	*June 1936*
184	*August 1924*
185	*May 1928*
187	*March 1937*
1067	*August 1930*
1072	*July 1935*

Tender-first (or should it be tail-first?) travel for a Fish engine. No.184 piloting a Midland van outside the Manchester Central . The Great Northern's goods warehouse, referred to in the feature on the Kings Cross expresses, is on the left, along with a fine CLC-pattern bracket signal. Central station, owned by the CLC had its own goods warehouse situated between the Great Northern building and the station itself and it will no doubt be to here that no.184 will be working. 184 is coupled to a 3250 gallon tender with 4 coal rails. This pattern appears to have been fitted to the class early on in their lives. Later pictures (viz.no.1070 at Leicester) show the 4000 gallon version with a solid coal guard.

Author's collection

Class ... 8 . Type 4.6.0 . N° of Engines ... 14 .

Maker	Year Built	N°. of Engines	Maker	Year Built	N°. of Engines	Maker	Year Built	N°. of Engines
Neilson	1902	6						
Beyer Peacock	1904	8						

CYLINDERS.
Diameter .... 19"
Stroke .... 26"
Centres .... 6'-8"

BOILER.
Class 8
Working Pressure ...180...Lbs. per □"
Barrel Dia. Outs. Max...........4'-9"
Barrel Length .... 15'-0"
Barrel Thickness of Plates .... 5/8"

TUBES.
Large No....—.... Dia. Outs. ....—
Small No....207... Dia. Outs. ......2"
Length between Tubeplates ...15'-4⅜"

SUPERHEATER.
Kind of Header .... —
Elements { Dia. Outs. .... —
            Dia. Ins. .... —
            Number .... —

IF FITTED WITH
Draft Retarder .... —
Circulating Valve .... —
Header Discharge Valve .... —
Pressure Release Valves .... —
Combined Pressure Release } .... —
and Piston Valves }

FIREBOX SHELL.
Length Outs. at Bottom ....7'-9"
Width „ „ „ .... 4'-0½"
   „   „   „ Top .... 4'-11¾"
Thickness of Plates—
Back...21/32..Casing...5/8"..Throat...3/4"

COPPER FIREBOX.
Length of Grate .... 7'-0 5/32"
Width „ .... 3'-4⅛"
Depth to Top of Ring, Front ...5'-5¼"
   „   „   „ Back .....4'-6¼"

Width of Ring.
Back and Front ....3"...Sides....3"
Thickness of Plates—
Back...9/16"..Casing...9/16"..Tube { 7/8"
                                      9/16"

HEATING SURFACE.
Firebox Outside .... 130...Sq. ft.
Large Tubes .... — „
Small Tubes.................... 1665 „
Superheater Inside.................. — „
                Total   1795 „

GRATE AREA. .... 23.5 Sq. ft.

WHEELS. Diameter. See Diagram.
Tyres Thickness .... 3½"
JOURNALS.   Dia.   Length.
Leading Bogie or Truck ...... 6"   9"
Leading Coupled .... 8"   9"
Driving .... 8"   9"
Intermediate ....
Trailing Coupled .... 8"   12"
Trailing Bogie or Truck ....

Tractive Power at { Lbs. 19650
85% Boiler Pressure { Tons 8.78
Adhesion Coefficient. Lbs. per Ton 386
Height. Rail to Top of Chimney .... 13'-2"
   „   „ Centre of Boiler .... 8'-3½"

VALVES. Kind .... Balanced Slide
CYLINDER LUBRICATOR. Kind ....Sight Feed
If Fitted with Steam Sanding Apparatus ....Yes
   „ „ Train Warming „ ....Yes
BRAKE. ....Steam & Auto Ejector
TENDER. Capacity. Water, Gallons 4000 or 3250
   „   „ Coal, Tons 6
WHEELS. Diameter............4'-4" or 4'-3"
JOURNALS. Dia............6" Length...... 11"

Up along the 1-117 to the western portal of the Woodhead tunnel and through the sinuous curves by Crowden goes no.185, still with coal-railed tender, with a Manchester (London Road) to Marylebone express around 1920. The seven coaches are of the so-called 'Matchboard' pattern stock built at Dukinfield from around 1910 onwards.

G.M.Shoults

Around the same time as the photograph opposite was taken, the photographer has changed position and broadened his angle to give a different view of no.1134 and present us with a bonus in the form of no.423 *Sir Sam Fay*. 'Sir Sam', with a good head of steam, has backed into the horse landing to collect a horse box. With this, the engine will draw forward prior to backing its charge onto a waiting up express. no.423 carries an oil tank on top of the tender, having been converted to oil-firing in the summer of 1921, a change of fuel that on this occasion lasted about 6 months. In the summer of 1926, no.423 carried oil-burning equipment again; the apparatus was removed for good in March 1927. Gorton men are on record referring to the 0-8-0s as 'Kitson Tinies' - a name which must have had its origins when that maker's engines entered service in 1903 and stuck thereafter. 1134 was superheated in 1916 with the 'small tube' superheater referred to earlier. The 8As when superheated had their chimneys resited in a more forward position. 1134 however was excempt from this modification owing to the layout of the headers in the 'small tube' apparatus.

Collection of G.H.Platt

Class 8A 0-8-0
'The Tinies'

Mention of heavy freight engines of the G.C. will prompt most enthusiasts to think of the Robinson 8K 2-8-0 subsequently built in large numbers for use by the R.O.D. overseas and seen at work on many parts of the British railway system.

Before studying this celebrated class however, we must turn our attention to Robinson's first essay in heavy freight design, the class 8A 0-8-0 with 4'-8" coupled wheels, built initially in 1902.

Three engines were built in that year by Neilson Reid & Co. of Glasgow who were currently engaged in the first batch of six Class 8 'Fish Engines' (Q.V.). The two classes shared the same size of boiler and cylinders, although the 0-8-0s were able to take advantage of a deeper firebox owing to their smaller coupled wheel diameter (4'-8" as opposed to 6'-1" on the 4-6-0s.)

Superheating of the 8A 0-8-0s began in 1914 and was continued through the G.C. and LNER eras. Not all the class were dealt with however, and the rather curious situation of some engines having two periods as superheated locomotives and then reverting to saturated form is found in the class history.

A 2l-element superheater was used with the usual Robinson arrangement of the ends of the elements expanded directly into the cast-iron superheater header. Mention must be made of the 'Small Tube' superheater fitted to 8A no. 1134 in January 1916. Before describing this apparatus it is necessary to focus the reader's attention on the term *The Robinson Superheater.* There is really no such thing for this ever-innovative engineer was constantly striving for perfection in the field of superheating and in other realms of locomotive engineering. Between October 1911 and March 1916 Robinson filed at least 16 patents, all of which referred to superheating-related matters. Permutations of header design transverse as opposed to side headers, number and layout of elements, even tools for removing superheater elements - all were originated by him and quite shrewdly patented.

In 1915 the Superheater Corporation Limited were recorded as the sole owners of patents under which Robinsons apparatus was constructed. At this point a number of British and Continental railway companies were using the Robinson superheater in its various

8A 0-8-0 no.1134 at Guide Bridge in the summer of 1921. The 64-ton bulk of the engine is highlighted here along with the front-end overhang which caused one writer to nickname them 'see-saws.' Scrutiny of the photograph will reveal the covers on the smokebox sides to give access to the side-pattern of superheater header. The fitting in front of the cover is the header discharge valve, another piece of Robinson superheating apparel. This device was linked to the regulator by a rod passing through the boiler handrail. When the regulator was closed, excess steam from the 'dry' side of the superheater header was discharged to the base of the blastpipe and thus to exhaust. Concurrent with its acquisition of a superheater, no.1134 was fitted with the same type of cylinders (21 ins. diameter) and piston valves as the 8K 2-8-0. The absence of a mechanical lubricator in the usual position is interesting - this was the only 8A to be fitted with Robinson's patent 'Intensifore' lubricator.

Collection of G.H.Platt

forms on their locomotives. The Railway trade press of that time carried numerous advertisements extolling the virtues of the apparatus. Railways abroad too, pursued feverishly by British locomotive manufacturers in those days, were converts to Robinson's ideas on superheating. These included the Indian State Railways, the Federated Malay States Government Railways, the Commonwealth of Australia and Queensland Government Railways.

Neither were Robinson's superheating activities confined to railways; a variation of his ideas was applied to a marine-type of superheater and used successfully. A report in 1914 records the *S.S. Nottingham* (one of the G.C. fleet) plying between Grimsby and the Continent as having received a Board of Trade certificate after six months trial with the apparatus.

Prior to 1914 Robinson had used boiler flues of around 5ins in diameter. Through these ran superheater elements of between 18 and later 36 in number. A radical departure occured in 1914 when the 'Small Tube' superheater appeared on no. 1134; in this version no less than 93 flues were used of 3ins diameter. No small tubes as such were used in the boiler, each flue carrying a looped element of its own. The headers adapted for this conversion were of the side type with access covers

abutting almost hard up against the smokebox wall. A cover for inspection and access was cut into each side of the smokebox and one of these is visible in the picture of no. 1134.

Though used on the later large-boilered 8M 2-8-0, the small tube superheater was not used on any further examples of the 8A class. Whatever thermodynamic advantages this apparatus may have been thought to possess, its practical application left a lot to be desired. With the entire boiler tube surface taken up with superheater elements the choking of at least some of them sooner or later with ash and cinders must have been encountered. The principal advantage of Robinson's various superheaters however lay in the ease of removal of a faulty or blown element; this must have been nullified on the small tube type by the very awkward disposition of the header cover plates with their stuation tight against the smokebox wrapper, with access effected from the outside. In the event, no. 1134 only carried its small tube superheater until 1924.

Thought the 8As lacked the elegance and refinement given to the later 8-coupled engines, they were a sound robust and capable machine. Built primarily for heavy freight and coal and mineral haulage in particular, the

---

Class 8A   Type 0.8.0   N of Engines ... 89.

Neilson	1902	3	Kitson	1905	5	G.C.R.	1910	17
Kitson	1903	15	"	1907	13	"	1911	3
"	1904	18	G.C.R.	1909	15			

Particulars in   refer to Superheated engines only.   Total Superheated

CYLINDERS.
Diameter ... 19"
Stroke ... 26"
Centres ... 6' 8"

BOILER.
Class ... 8A
Working Pressure ... 170 Lbs. per □"
Barrel Dia. Outs. Max. ... 4' 9"
Barrel Length ... 15' 0"
Barrel Thickness of Plates ... 5/8"

TUBES.
Large No. ... Dia. Outs. 5"
Small No. 207 ... Dia. Outs. 2"
Length between Tubeplates ... 15' 4 3/8"

SUPERHEATER.
Kind of Header ... Core
Elements { Dia. Outs.
Dia. Ins.
Number

IF FITTED WITH
Draft Retarder
Circulating Valve
Header Discharge Valve
Pressure Release Valves
Combined Pressure Release } and Piston Valves }

FIREBOX SHELL.
Length Outs. at Bottom ... 7' 9"
Width ,, ,, ,, ... 4' 0 1/2"
,, ,, ,, Top ... 4' 11 3/4"
Thickness of Plates—
Back 21/32 Casing 5/8" Throat 3/4"

COPPER FIREBOX.
Length of Grate ... 7' 0 1/32"
Width ,, ,, ... 3' 4"
Depth to Top of Ring, Front ... 6' 0 1/4"
,, ,, ,, Back ... 5' 1 1/8"

Width of Ring.
Back and Front ... 3" Sides ... 3"
Thickness of Plates—
Back 5/8" Casing 5/8" Tube { 7/8" 5/8"

HEATING SURFACE.
Firebox Outside ... 140 Sq. ft.
Large Tubes ... ,,
Small Tubes ... 1665 ,,
Superheater Inside ... — ,,
Total ... 1805 ,,

GRATE AREA. ... 23.6 Sq. ft.

WHEELS. Diameter. See Diagram.
Tyres Thickness ... 3 1/2"
JOURNALS. Dia. Length.
Leading Bogie or Truck
Leading Coupled ... 8" ... 9"
Driving ... 8 1/2" ... 9 1/4"
Intermediate ... 8" ... 9"
Trailing Coupled ... 8" ... 12"
Trailing Bogie or Truck

Tractive Power at { Lbs. ... 25644
85% Boiler Pressure { Tons ... 11.4

Adhesion Coefficient. Lbs. per Ton ... 404
Height. Rail to Top of Chimney ... 13' 2"
,, ,, Centre of Boiler ... 8' 3 1/2"

VALVES. Kind *Balanced Slide*
CYLINDER LUBRICATOR. Kind } Sight Feed
If Fitted with Steam Sanding Apparatus ... No
,, ,, Train Warming ,, ... No
BRAKE. *Steam & Auto Ejector*
TENDER. Capacity. Water, Gallons 3250 or 4000
,, Coal, Tons ... 6
WHEELS. Diameter ... 4' 3" or 4' 4"
JOURNALS. Dia. ... 6" Length ... 11"

8A no. 86 outside Guide Bridge in a somewhat 'workaday' condition in later G.C.days. No.86 was built by Kitsons of Leeds who turned out the impressive number of 15 8As between September and December 1903. The 2 cylinders-size 19ins. X 26ins. were fed by balanced slide valves driven, as with (almost) all Robinson's engines by Stephenson valve gear-modellers please note the balance weights on the reversing shaft behind the front sandbox..A well-coaled tender of 3250 gallons capacity is attached behind no.86. Later engines, built from 1907 onwards had the larger, 4000 gallon pattern tender; after the Grouping, the earlier locos too were so fitted, though the process took until 1930 to complete. No.86 remained in saturated condition all her life. She was withdrawn by the LNER in April 1937.

8A 0-8-0s were centred upon depots where such duties were prevalent. Mexborough had the biggest contingent with Annesey, Grimsby, Staveley, Sheffield, Keadby and Gorton possessing smaller numbers. After the G.C. had absorbed the Lancashire, Derbyshire and East Coast Railway in 1907, 'Tinies' were dispatched to Langwith and Tuxford sheds.

It is interesting to note that like their 2-8-0 successors they saw War service in France in the later part of the Offensive. In LNER days some were transferred away from the G.C. system, notably to Doncaster and Ardsley where they appear to have been highly regarded by the G.N. locomen - an accolade for any locomotive! Post war days saw the engines working on further foreign territory, this time over M & G.N. lines to Melton Constable and ex-N.E.R. tracks as far as Newcastle.

Finally displaced by large numbers of ex-M.O.S. 'Austerity' 2-8-0s, 34 8As (then LNER Q4) entered the service of British Railways. The last to go was B.R. 63243 (G.C. no. 1180) then an Ardsley engine, in October 1951.

As a footnote it is necessary to record the transition of 13 engines of the class in Second World War days, from 1942 to 1945. These were completely rebuilt by Edward Thompson to form Class Q1 - an 8-coupled tank engine design these rebuilds are outside the scope of this work, but will be given full coverage in a subsequent volume.

SUMMARY OF CLASS 8A 0 - 8 - 0 (LNER Q4)

NUMBER	BUILDER	DATE BUILT	WITHDRAWN
1052 - 1054	Neilson & Co.	November 1902	Feb 1939-Jan 1951
56-59/64/65/67/68/ 70/71/85/86/87/91/92, 135-140,142-153	Kitson & Co.	September 1903 to May 1904	Aug 1934-Sept 1951
1073 - 1077	Kitson & Co.	July & August 1905	Dec 1935-Dec 1950
1132 - 1144	Kitson & Co.	February to April 1904	Dec 1934-Sept 1951
39/44/48/49/62/63, 159-164,212/213,356	Gorton	February to December 1909	Jun 1936-May 1951
401,956-965,1174-1182	Gorton	June 1910 to February 1911	Apr 1936-Oct 1951

Note: Several engines were fitted with 21" cylinders and piston valves of the 8K pattern. Dates and engines concerned were:-

136   March 1928   160   June 1932
137   January 1931   1076 July 1931
153   May 1933

8A out on the line. No.1076, a Kitson engine of 1905, heads a lengthy down class B Goods on the London Extension near Whetstone. The 4-column safety valves were carried by all the class except the 3 Neilson engines which were fitted with twin pillar valves. 20-ton jacks appear on each side of the smokebox in a similar manner to other Great Central engines. the tender is the 3250 gallon variety with 4 coal rails seen earlier and later supplanted by the larger 4000 gallon design. In common with his northern colleagues, the driver sports a cloth cap, were these uniform G.C. issue one wonders? Trackside detail is plentiful, down to the platelayer's hut and wild flowers. Prominence has been given lately to aspects of Permanent Way in railway modelling circles. Perhaps those so inclined would find it useful to know that the track seen here has 12 sleepers/chairs per length between each fishplate- Creat Central practice being to use 45ft. lengths of bullhead-pattern rail weighing 95lbs. to the yard.

G.M.Shoults

8A no.1176 seen 'on shed' beweeen duties. This is an engine from a later batch-one of 17 built at the Great Central's Gorton Works in the latter half of 1910. Construction of the Type ceased early in 1911 by which time 89 engines had appeared. 1176 is distinguished by its slim chimney-notice the slight reverse taper compared to the more elegant and full-bodied Robinson design seen on other class members. the history of chimneys carried by G.C.engines and their subsequent replacement by the various LNER 'Flowerpot' varieties is, to say the least, complicated. Briefly, Robinson chimneys were prone to cracking and the version seen here was a substitute design fitted in late 1922 derived from that carried by the class 5A tank engine of 1906. A difference seen on these last 8As compared with the earlier engines is displayed by the one-piece splasher, minus beading, extending to the front of the cab. 1176 was superheated in December 1922, so this photograph could well be said to typify the 8A in its ultimate G.C.form: fitted with superheater header discharge valve on the left-hand side of the smokebox, chimney set forward (no extension to smokebox), Wakefield mechanical lubricator and, finally, 4000 gallon tender with solid coal guard.

Collection of G.H.Platt

No less than 27 shed and footplate staff have assembled themselves around 8A no.1052 for the benefit of an unknown photographer. The photograph was given to J.D.Fley Esq. by a Mr.G.King of Swinton (Yorkshire, between Sheffield and Mexborough).Mr.King was the son of one, Herbert King who was a driver at Mexborough. Mr.King senior was born on April 2nd.1877 and died in 1960. He features in the picture here and is thought to be the man standing in front of no.1052 on the far left of the group. The picture is believed to have been taken at Mexborough shed, befor ethe time of the First War. No.1052 was the first 8A to be built. One of three locomotives turned out by Neilsons in 1902, she entered service in the November of that year. 1052 was superheated in 1924, returning to saturated form at the end of 1946. As British Railways no.63200, the engine was withdrawn from service in September 1949.

L.Franks collection

Tweedledum and Tweedledee. Two generations of MS&L/G.C. suburban tank engines stand, coaled-up and ready for work outside the shed at Trafford Park, Manchester. No.588 belongs to Class 3, a design by Parker built between 1889 and 1893, the forerunner of the 9G class 2-4-2 tank. As mentioned, the Class 3 formed the basis for the 9K 4-4-2 locomotive; the latter being a perfectly logical development of the former. No.27 belonged to the second Gorton batch of engines, from the autumn of 1904. 588 was one of 15 of her class turned out by Neilsons in 1890/91. She appears with her original round-topped boiler; the Class 3 series tanks were all (bar one) rebuilt with G.C. standard no.2 Belpaires between 1909 and 1922. No.588 received hers in July 1916 which acts as a pointer to the date of our photograph.

Collection of G.H.Platt

Class 9K & 9L 4-4-2 Tank

The 9K 4-4-2 tank was an early Robinson design appearing in March 1903, the first engine of this wheel arrangement built for either the MS&L or the GC. Robinson, in his previous post in Ireland on the Waterford, Limerick & Western Railway, had produced an engine of similar outline to the 9K which must have been an inspiration for this, one of his most long-lived designs. In true Robinson tradition, the 9K was an elegant and sturdy machine, primarily constructed for suburban passenger work. It certainly owed something to the Pollitt 9G 2-4-2 tanks with cylinders and coupled wheels of the same size, albeit carrying a boiler of enlarged proportions.

Work-wise the 9K tank engines had been drafted to cover the suburban services out of Marylebone. As this traffic grew in density and weight they were supplanted by the 9N 4-6-2 tanks. Subsequently, two batches of engines found themselves transferred to Wrexham for working the difficult routes of the absorbed Wrexham, Mold & Connah's Quay Rly and to Trafford Park, Manchester where their duties included the tightly timed 45 minute Manchester-Liverpool passenger trains of the C.L.C.line for which concern the Great Central provided the motive power. Other dispersals included Mexborough, Sheffield and Retford for working stopping trains between Sheffield and Nottingham, Barnsley and Doncaster. One of our pictures reveals the series at work between Leicester and Rugby on stopping trains in April 1911 when 9N tanks had barely begun to arrive on the London suburban scene.

Construction numbered 40 engines and was spread over the period to August 1905. Vulcan Foundry built the first 12 locomotives with Gorton Works building the remainder.

SUMMARY OF CLASS 9K 4 - 4 - 2 TANK ENGINES (LNER C13)

NUMBER	BUILDER	DATE BUILT	WITHDRAWN
1055 - 1066	Vulcan Foundry	March to June 1903	Feb 1953-Dec 1956
171/178/179/188/ 190/191/193/199	Gorton	May to September 1903	May 1954-Jan 1960
2/9/18/20/27/28/ 29/47/50/55	Gorton	August to December 1904	Sept 1954-Dec 1958
114/115/310/357/ 359/453-457	Gorton	January to August 1905	Dec 1952-Nov 1958

9K No.191 stands outside Trafford Park shed in Manchester. Appearing in typically immaculate Great Central fashion, the green passenger livery decked out with black and white lining looks particularly fine. Notice the single white line extended to cover platform valance, raised mainframes, cab side and front, balance pipe, engine steps, buffer stocks and plank and even dome cover and wheel centres. Trafford Park was shared by the G.C.,G.N. and Midland; one of the latter's rebuilt Johnson 4-4-0 standing by the water column in the background.

Collection of G.H.Platt

No.50, a Gorton engine, this time from 1904, leaves Whetstone with the 3.43 p.m. Leicester to Woodford train on May 18th 1912.

G.M.Shoults

SUMMARY OF CLASS 9L 4 - 4 - 2 TANK ENGINES (LNER C14)

NUMBER	BUILDER	DATE BUILT	WITHDRAWN
1120 - 1131	Beyer Peacock & Co.	May & June 1907	Jan 1957-Jan 1960

Class *9K* Type 4.4.2 Nº of Engines ... 40.

G. C. R.	1903	8	G. C. R.	1905	10			
Vulcan Fdy	1903	12						
G. C. R.	1904	10						

Particulars in red refer to Superheated Engines only. Total Superheated 1.

CYLINDERS.
Diameter................................ 18"
Stroke .... 26.
Centres .... 2'-0"

BOILER.
Class *Nº 3 Standard*
Working Pressure ......160 Lbs. per □"
Barrel Dia. Outs. Max...............4'-4"
Barrel Length ....11'-0"
Barrel Thickness of Plates .... ½"

TUBES.
Large No. 18 Dia. Outs. 5¼"
Small No. 190. 90 Dia. Outs. 1¾" 1⅞
Length between Tubeplates 11'-4¾"

SUPERHEATER.
Kind of Header *Front Cover*
Elements { Dia. Outs. 1⅞"
Dia. Ins. 1¼"
Number 18

IF FITTED WITH
Draft Retarder ....
Circulating Valve ....
Header Discharge Valve .... 2½"
Pressure Release Valves ....
Combined Pressure Release }
  and Piston Valves } ....

FIREBOX SHELL.
Length Outs. at Bottom .... 6'-4"
Width „ „ „ .... 4'-1"
„ „ „ Top 4'-6¼"
Thickness of Plates—
Back 17/32" Casing ½" Throat ⅝"

COPPER FIREBOX.
Length of Grate .... 5'-8 27/32"
Width „ „ 3'-5"
Depth to Top of Ring, Front 5'-5⅞"
„ „ „ Back 4'-11¾"

Width of Ring.
Back and Front 2½" Sides 3"
Thickness of Plates—
Back ½" Casing ½" Tube { ⅞"
  { ½"

HEATING SURFACE.
Firebox Outside .... 108 Sq. ft.
Large Tubes .... „
Small Tubes .... 993 „
Superheater Inside........ „
Total 1101 „

GRATE AREA. 19.4 Sq. ft.

WHEELS. Diameter. See Diagram.
Tyres Thickness .... 3"
JOURNALS. Dia. Length.
Leading Bogie ~~or Truck~~ 6" 9"
Leading Coupled ....
Driving .... 8" 9"
Intermediate ....
Trailing Coupled .... 8" 9"
  radial
Trailing Bogie ~~or Truck~~ 8" 14"
Tractive Power at { Lbs. 17099
85% Boiler Pressure { Tons 7.6
Adhesion Coefficient. Lbs. per Ton 409
Height. Rail to Top of Chimney 13'-1½"
  „ „ Centre of Boiler 7'-9½"

VALVES. Kind *Balanced Slide*
CYLINDER LUBRICATOR. Kind *Sight Feed*
If Fitted with Steam Sanding Apparatus no.
  „ „ Train Warning „ yes
BRAKE. *Steam + Auto Ejector*
TANK ~~TENDER~~. Capacity. Water, Gallons 1,450.
  „ Coal, Tons 4½
WHEELS. Diameter....................
JOURNALS. Dia. .... Length .....

Class 9L Type 4-4-2 N° of Engines ... 12.

Beyer Peacock	1907	12					

CYLINDERS.
Diameter ... 18"
Stroke ... 26"
Centres ... 2'-0"

BOILER.
Class ... No 3 Standard
Working Pressure ... 160 Lbs. per □"
Barrel Dia. Outs. Max. ... 4'-4"
Barrel Length ... 11'-0"
Barrel Thickness of Plates ... 1/2"

TUBES.
Large No. 18 Dia. Outs. 5 1/4"
Small No. 190. 90 Dia. Outs. 1 3/4" 1 7/8"
Length between Tubeplates ... 11'-4 3/4"

SUPERHEATER.
Kind of Header ... Robinson Cover
Elements {
Dia. Outs. ... 1 1/2"
Dia. Ins. ... 1 1/4"
Number ... 18
}

IF FITTED WITH
Draft Retarder ....
Circulating Valve ....
Header Discharge Valve ....
Pressure Release Valves ....
Combined Pressure Release and Piston Valves } ....

FIREBOX SHELL.
Length Outs. at Bottom ... 6'-4"
Width ,, ,, ,, ... 4'-1"
,, ,, ,, Top ... 4'-6 1/4"
Thickness of Plates—
Back 7/32" Casing 1/2" Throat 5/8"

COPPER FIREBOX.
Length of Grate ... 5'-8 27/32"
Width ,, ,, ... 3'-5"
Depth to Top of Ring, Front ... 5'-5 7/8"
,, ,, ,, Back ... 4'-11 3/8"

Width of Ring.
Back and Front 2 1/2" Sides 3"
Thickness of Plates—
Back 1/2" Casing 1/2" Tube { 7/8" 1/2" }

HEATING SURFACE.
Firebox Outside ... 108 Sq. ft.
Large Tubes ... —
Small Tubes ... 993 ,,
Superheater Inside ... ,,
Total ... 1101 ,,

GRATE AREA. ... 19.4 Sq. ft.

WHEELS.
Diameter. See Diagram.
Tyres Thickness ... 3"

JOURNALS.
	Dia.	Length.
Leading Bogie or Truck	6"	9"
Leading Coupled		
Driving	8"	9"
Intermediate		
Trailing Coupled	8"	9"
Trailing Bogie or Truck radial	8"	14"

Tractive Power at 85% Boiler Pressure { Lbs. 17.099 Tons 7.6 }
Adhesion Coefficient. Lbs. per Ton ... 462
Height. Rail to Top of Chimney ... 13'-1 1/2"
,, ,, Centre of Boiler ... 7'-9 1/2"

VALVES. Kind Balanced Slide

CYLINDER LUBRICATOR. Kind Sight Feed
If Fitted with Steam Sanding Apparatus ... No
,, ,, Train Warming ,, ... Yes

BRAKE. Steam & Auto Ejector

TANK.
Capacity. Water, Gallons ... 1825
,, Coal, Tons ... 4 1/2

WHEELS. Diameter ... —

JOURNALS. Dia. — Length —

No.1120 gleams all over on Neasden shed early on in her life. Superbly polished fittings including that GC hallmark, the steel ring around the smokebox door, appear to have an almost iridescent finish. The 20-ton screwjack carried by the smokebox weighed 270 lbs. Made by Messrs.Tangye of Manchester they must have required considerable effort to manoeuvre them into place when required.
Collection of G.H.Platt

Fired by the successful experiments with the Schmidt superheater used on no.16, a 9J Class 0-6-0, Robinson pushed ahead with various designs of superheater, applying them to new major construction. Both the 9N 4-6-2 tank and the 8K 2-8-0 goods engine benefited from this development work, emerging as superheated designs from new in 1911. Attention was then focussed on a new superheated passenger engine-the *Sir Sam Fay* 4-6-0 and to the retrospective application of superheating apparatus to the already successful Atlantics.This splendid picture shows no.361, the first simple Atlantic to be rebuilt with a superheater boiler, standing outside Gorton Works freshly outshopped in March 1912.The 'Works Grey' finish, almost an off-white in fact, reproduces beautifully the crisp, clear and flowing lines of the design. No.361 was fitted with a 24-element superheater of Robinson's own pattern. Element protection was via the louvre-type flue damper. This device, for which Robinson had filed a patent application in 1911, cut off the hot gases passing through the flues by means of a series of blades or louvres worked by a steam-operated cylinder operated in conjunction with the locomotive's blower. It could also be hand-operated, the linkage passing through the boiler handrail. the whole operating apparatus can be seen clearly on the side of 361's smokebox.Concurrent with superheating, 361 also received new piston valve cylinders of the type applied to the 8K 2-8-0. This cylinder design, with its 10ins. piston valves was an outstanding success and was applied to other classes also.(Q.V.) At 21 ins. bore, the cylinders were 1½ins. larger than those used hitherto on the Atlantics. The new cylinders carried another Robinson innovation, a combined system of pressure relief valves fitted with a silencer. The device, which Robinson successfully patented in 1912, was designed to automatically relieve excess pressure caused by water condensed from steam or carried over by priming from the boiler. Doubtless something of a novelty, the valves were removed within a short space of time.Other visual features are worth looking at: a fairly obvious one is the dome cover, now replaced by a flatter, wider pattern similar to that carried by the 8K. Later superheated Atlantics kept the originalrounder cover before the flatter type became standard for the class. Lubrication for the superheated no.361 was by means of a Wakefield-pattern mechanical lubricator mounted ahead of the leading splasher. 361 received a 22-element superheater in 1919 which had been used in the interim on the 8K 2-8-0s. The flue damper was replaced by Robinson's patent steam draught retarder with header discharge valve. In LNER days Gresley's simple arrangement of a sniffing valve, fitted behind the chimney, supplanted both the retarder and valve arrangement.Further Atlantics were superheated in the years 1920-21 (see notes) but, as with other G.C. classes, it was left to the LNER to complete the process. The last engine to be superheated was no.6094 (G.C. no.1094 of November 1905).

National Railway Museum

Class 8B & 8C
Simple Atlantics

J.G. Robinson's artistry and engineering ability shone through in practically all his designs. From his early days in Ireland to the end of his career on the Great Central, there was manifest that delicate balance between beauty and machine seen in the locomotives of Dean and Johnson in their late Victorian creations. His famous remark that 'a chimney is to a locomotive as a hat is to a man' has become something of a cliche but it indicated the care and attention the man put nto the details of his designs. Somehow, the chemistry of all this seems never to have been bettered than in his various 4-4-2 tender engines - the famous and celebrated 'Atlantics'.

There seems to have been some uncertainty as to whether or not a projected 6'-9" express design should have been built as a 4-4-2 or a 4-6-0. In the event, Robinson had his cake and ate it, for there emerged in late 1903/early 1904 the first two Atlantics classified 8B and two large 4-6-0s classified 8C. All four engines were built by Beyer, Peacock to Robinson's specifications and many details of the design were based on the smaller Class 8 4-6-0 of the previous year.

Both 8B and 8C designs were built to be interchangeable to enable the Atlantics to be converted to 4-6-0s if required. A similar move was tried on the Great Western and it has been suggested that Robinson may have been influenced by Churchward's ideas on the subject. As *Albion* did not run as an Atlantic until late in 1904 this may well be conjecture. Certainly Robinson was a Swindon man having worked with both Dean and Churchward; whether he was privy to the goings on at Swindon at the time we do not know. History tells us that all the Great Western Atlantics were rebuilt to 4-6-0s in the manner of the 'Saints' while, conversely, on the G.C. the Atlantic type remained the master of all express work and was multiplied over the years to 1906 to yield a total of 3l locomotives. Not that Robinson's faith in the 4-6-0 wheel arrangement was ever diminished!

No.262 belonged to the last batch of Simple Atlantics, built by the G.C.themselves at Gorton in 1906. She is seen outside Guide Bridge piloting a Class 1 4-6-0 with an up express. Subtle alterations now manifest themselves between these and engines of earlier years. The deeper firebox of the later engines should be apparent while steam sanding gear is now applied to both driving and coupled wheels. Buffers now have parallel side casings and the safety valves are cased, compared to the open pattern of the earlier series. This later G.C.period photograph shows some of the changes applied to the Atlantics in the last years of the company. The piston tail rods have now been removed (c.1920) and the cab roof sports only one whistle.The angle of photography shows a particular Robinson feature off nicely: on many of his engines a gentle 'S'-shaped curve accommodated a slight change in platform (footplate) width just ahead of the leading coupled wheels. On the Atlantics and 8C 4-6-0 this increased from 8ft.3ins. to 8ft.9½ins. Conversely, the main frames-of 1¼ins. steel plate- were bent inwards behind the leading coupled wheel tyres to give increased side clearance for the rear bogie wheels. The bend was followed by a gentle inclination inwards to give similar clearance for the front bogie wheels and was reinforced front and back by motion plates, outside for the slide bars and inside for the valve spindle guides.Though the first Simple G.C.Atlantic was superheated in 1912, 262 was not so treated until 1925. Apart from the fitting of piston valves no other major changes were wrought on the class throughout their long life which spanned two World Wars and saw them into the British Railways era.

Collection of G.H.Platt

An immediate success, the Atlantics were put to work on the best trains, the Manchester to Marylebone expresssses. Gorton and Neasden sheds shared the allocations, with Leicester coming on stream with a number from 1906 onwards. Notable through workings for the class in their early days were cross-country trains as far as Bristol and even to Plymouth. In 1909 a complicated working took an Atlantic from Oxford to Sheffield, across to York and back again the following day. By Grouping, two sheds shared the allocation of Atlantics - Leicester and Woodford with 16 and 11 engines respecively.

In LNER days the Atlantics remained on their home territory but by the mid-1930s they were showing their age and were displaced from top-link duties by B17 4-6-0s. Still a useful and sturdy locomotive, the Atlantics found work on the lines of the former G.N and G.E. sections, from Lincoln to New Holland and Cleethorpes becom-

ing well-established rosters for the class. Cambridge too became a home for a former Leicester engine which worked into King's Cross on duties which included the well-known Cambridge Buffet Car Express. A contingent of Atlantics was still found at Leicester, however, where light duties such as stopping and night trains as far north as Newcastle were the order of the day.

Post-war days saw the Atlantics entering into decline. Two engines had slipped from the scene during the War and Lincolnshire was to be the final home for the remainder of the class with concentrations at Immingham, Lincoln and Boston. Pick up goods and local passenger duties were the only work available for what were then locomotives of almost fifty years of age. In December 1950 G.C.R. no. 260 then British Railways no. 62918, was withdrawn. Thus ended one of the most significant chapters of the Robinson locomotive history.

And so to the engines themselves. Though the 8C 4-6-0

SUMMARY OF CLASS 8B 4 - 4 - 2 (LNER C4)

NUMBER	BUILDER	DATE BUILT	WITHDRAWN
192,194	Beyer Peacock & Co.	December 1903	Both November 1950
263 - 267	Beyer Peacock & Co.	July 1904	Oct 1943-Jun 1949
1083 - 1094	North British Loco.Co.	October & November 1905	Nov 1939-Nov 1950
260/261/262,358/360-363	Gorton	February to August 1906	Feb 1948-Dec 1950

Notes:

a) Last Gorton batch intended to be 10 engines but Nos.364 & 365 were constructed as Compounds instead.

b) Superheating commenced in March 1912 with No.361. Others were superheated in due course and most (but not all) received cylinders and piston valves of the 8K pattern, in a few cases concurrently. The details are as follows:-

NUMBER	SUPERHEATED	P.V.CYLINDERS
192	September 1920	November 1927
194	October 1925	October 1932
260	February 1935	Not fitted
261	January 1927	February 1937
262	April 1925	April 1925
263	June 1926	Not fitted
264	July 1921	November 1931
265	September 1920	April 1927
266	May 1921	Not fitted
267	September 1920	April 1927
358	May 1920	February 1932
360	October 1920	February 1931
361	March 1912	March 1912
362	March 1928	January 1942
363	February 1921	September 1933

NUMBER	SUPERHEATED	P.V.CYLINDERS
1083	January 1921	October 1932
1084	August 1929	Not fitted
1085	January 1925	January 1925
1086	August 1914	December 1925
1087	September 1920	November 1930
1088	December 1926	Not fitted
1089	June 1920	Not fitted
1090	March 1914	September 1922*
1091	April 1925	April 1925
1092	March 1921	July 1925
1093	November 1927	June 1937
1094	January 1936	Not fitted

* Dealt with separately under Class 8J (3-cylinder rebuild).

No.264 stands alongside platform 5 at Manchester Central fully coaled-up, blower on and ready to go. The engine is, of course, immaculately groomed with all brass and steelwork polished, not forgetting the 4 pillars of the Ramsbottom safety valves, the chimney-polished right to the top-and the 2 whistles. The livery is the darker 'Brunswick' green with black and white lining adopted with the construction of the first Atlantics and 8C 4-6-0's in 1903; a brief description of this livery was recounted in the story of the 11A 4-4-0 - with the Atlantics the claret shade was applied to the cylinder clothing as well as to the footplate edging. Splasher tops were painted green lined white as seen here, reflected in the shine on the boiler clothing. Initially, and perhaps surprisingly, it was intended to have the first two Atlantics painted black. Happily, this did not come to pass, although in the economies of the post 1928 period, the LNER did apply a simple black livery to the entire class.264 and her train are probably bound for Marylebone; 264 will leave Manchester Central over the Castlefield Viaduct past a myriad of canal wharves and cotton warehouses. Leaving the CLC Liverpool line at the curiously-named Throstle Nest East Junction she will bark her way through the murk of Throstle Nest Tunnel and out over the Cheshire Lines to Chorlton. Veering south-east, away from the rival Midland route via Derby, through Alexandra Park and Fallowfield her green and crimson form will arrive at Guide Bridge. From this first stop, on the Pennine fringe, the train will head east up a 1-in-201 gradient through the dark and sulphurous hell of the infamous Woodhead Tunnel.To Sheffield Victoria and on to Annesley, end of the old MS&L and start of Watkin's dream, south through England's heartland and the still open countryside north of London, this beautiful machine will arrive in the capital.

Collection of G.H.Platt

A splendid action picture of no.358 roaring away from Godley Junction (3 miles east of Guide Bridge) with an up express. The mixed proportions of the 11-coach train indicate some form of excursion working; the first 3 vehicles are G.N.R.6-wheelers. At any rate, the locomotive is certainly going places with the enormous heap of coal on the tender!

Collection of G.H.Platt

built at the same time was a handsome (and capable) machine, somehow the lines of the Atlantic were just that bit more finely balanced, that small additional degree of rarification - a design that looked 'just right'

Following the introduction of the first two locomotives Beyer, Peacock built a further batch of five engines - delivered in July 1904. The years 1905 and 1906 saw delivery of twelve and eight engines respectively, the 1905 batch being built by The North British Loco. Co. and having boilers pressed initially to 200lbs p.s.i. in contrast to the 180lbs used in the other series. The last engines were built by the G.C. themselves at Gorton in 1906.

The tenders with coal rails were of the 3250 gallon pattern coupled to the first two engines - 192 and 194. these were built with water pick up gear from new, operated by what looked very much like a ship's wheel. Unique to Robinson, this carried six spokes with a projecting handle attached at the wheel rim. On the tenders for these first two Atlantics, the wheel was given steam-powered assistance. A cylinder of 5ins diameter and 9ins stroke was fitted behind the wheel on the left hand side of the tender. Steam was admitted to the cylinder by pulling over a small handle. When the piston had completed the first 4ins of its stroke it uncovered an exhaust passage thus relieving the pressure in the cylinder and pushing the operating arm back to its original position.

Records show the remainder of the 8B series as having been coupled to 4000 gallon tenders, with the characteristic sheet steel coal plate, from new. Some photographs show later engines with coal-railed tenders indicating changes at a heavy repair or tenders taken aside for repairs and an earlier tender exchanged.

The 'small batch, detail difference' theme was evident with production of the Atlantics as elsewhere. Apart from the Compounds which will be described separately, there existed differences in firebox depth, boiler pressure and number of boiler tubes. Later modifications saw the Atlantics (no. 365 which we will deal with separately) in May 1911 using the Schmidt system over which Robinson had enthused in 1909. Superheating of the Simples was begun in March 1912 using Robinson's own pattern superheater - a field in which he had made rapid and competent progress. A 24-element pattern was used initially with variations to 18 elements, 22 elements becoming the standard arrangement later on.

The first Atlantics quickly proved themselves and with the recurrent motive power shortgages on the G.C. more were soon ordered. Beyer, Peacock were chosen again to build a batch of five engines - delivered in the July of 1904. Differences occured in this batch with the fitting of a deeper firebox - the original two engines shared an identical firebox arrangement with the two 8C 4-6-0s restricted in depth because of the rear coupled axle of the latter.

A vintage Great Central scene at Leicester. No.1094, one of 12 Atlantics built by the North British Loco.Co. in 1905, gets away smartly with the 2.15 p.m.Manchester to Marylebone express. The train was due to arrive in the capital at 6.43. The coaching stock is in the short-lived G.C.livery of dark brown with cream upper panels, replaced from around 1910 onwards by an all-over varnished teak.

G.M.Shoults

Class 8B Type 4-4-2. No of Engines ... 27.

Maker	Year Built	No of Engines	Maker	Year Built	No of Engines	Maker	Year Built	No of Engines
Beyer Peacock	1903	2	G. C. R.	1906	8			
"	1904	5						
North British	1905	12						

Figures in red refer to Superheated Engines.
" red & green " Engines 361 & 1090 only.   Total Superheated ... 15

CYLINDERS.
Diameter .... 21" 19"
Stroke .... 26"
Centres .... 6' 8"

BOILER.
Class .... No 6 Standard
Working Pressure .... 180 ...Lbs. per ☐"
Barrel Dia. Outs. Max. .... 5' 0"
Barrel Length .... 15' 0"
Barrel Thickness of Plates .... 5/8"

TUBES.
Large No. ... 22 ... Dia. Outs. ... 5¼"
Small No. 226 110 Dia. Outs. 2" 2"
Length between Tubeplates ... 15' 4⅞"

SUPERHEATER.
Kind of Header .... Front Cover
Elements { Dia. Outs. .... 1⅜"
    { Dia. Ins. .... 1.⅛"
    { Number 22

IF FITTED WITH
Draft Retarder ....
Circulating Valve .... Yes
Header Discharge Valve .... Yes
Pressure Release Valves ....
Combined Pressure Release } .... Yes
    and Piston Valves }

FIREBOX SHELL.
Length Outs. at Bottom .... 8' 6"
Width " " " .... 4' 0½"
" " " Top .... 5' 2¾"
Thickness of Plates—
    Back 21/32. Casing. ⅝". Throat ¾"

COPPER FIREBOX.
Length of Grate .... 7' 9½"
Width " " .... 3' 4½"
Depth to Top of Ring, Front .... 6' 5½"
    " " " Back .... 5' 3"

Width of Ring.
Back and Front .... 3" Sides .... 3"
Thickness of Plates—
    Back 9/16". Casing 9/16". Tube { ⅞"
               { 9/16"

HEATING SURFACE.
Firebox Outside .... 154 154 .Sq. ft.
Large Tubes .... 464 "
Small Tubes .... 985 1818 "
Superheater Inside .... 242 ...... "
        Total 1745 1972 "

GRATE AREA. .... 26 ...Sq. ft.

WHEELS. Diameter, See Diagram.
Tyres Thickness .... 3"

JOURNALS.   Dia.   Length.
Leading Bogie or Truck .... 6"   9"
Leading Coupled .... 8"   9"
Driving .... 9"   9"
Intermediate ....
Trailing Coupled (outs) 6½"   11"
Trailing Bogie or Truck (ins) 7"   5⅞"
Tractive Power at { Lbs. 17,800 21,300
85% Boiler Pressure { Tons 7.95 9.5
Adhesion Coefficient. Lbs. per Ton .. 590 576
Height. Rail to Top of Chimney .. 13' 3"
  "   " Centre of Boiler .. 8' 6"

VALVES. Kind Balanced Slide Pist.

CYLINDER LUBRICATOR } Mechanical or Intensifore
                Kind Sight Feed
If Fitted with Steam Sanding Apparatus .. Yes
  "   " Train Warming " .. Yes

BRAKE. .... Steam & Auto Ejector

TENDER. Capacity. Water, Gallons 4.000
     "   Coal, Tons 6

WHEELS. Diameter .... 4' 4"

JOURNALS. Dia. .. 6" Length .... 11"

In the years following 1906, Leicester shed became something of a natural habitat for G.C.Atlantics. Leicester was a change-over point for expresses to and from the north and engine crews from there became noteworthy for the fine performances they put up with these celebrated locomotives. When Mr.G.M.Shoults called at Leicester shed on Sunday, June 4th.1911, Atlantic no.192 was 'at home', together with 9J 0-6-0 no.1038. Tantalising glimpses of other Great Central engines, tank and tender types alike, are also visible.

G.M.Shoults

Dwarfing the Sacre' Class 12AM tank behind it, no.196 rests at Neasden, tender well filled with coal and ready for work again. The engine is in the earlier condition-the four safety valves retain their open form and have yet to be cased-in. The splendid condition of the engine reflects the immense pride and effort the company put into maintaining its loco fleet. Though a product of cheap and plentiful labour, this manifest smartness was deemed an essential part of the image that the company presented to its travelling public who were, after all, their paymasters.

Collection of W.A.Brown

Class 8c Type 4-6-0. N° of Engines 2.

Maker	Year Built	N° of Engines	Maker	Year Built	N° of Engines	Maker	Year Built	N° of Engines
Beyer Peacock	1903	1						
" "	1904	1						

Particulars in red refer to Engine 195.

CYLINDERS.
Diameter .... 21" 19"
Stroke .... 26"
Centres .... 6' 8"

BOILER.
Class .... 8C & 8F
Working Pressure .... 180 Lbs. per □"
Barrel Dia. Outs. Max. .... 5' 0"
Barrel Length .... 15' 0"
Barrel Thickness of Plates .... 5/8"

TUBES.
Large No. ...... − Dia. Outs. −
Small No. 226 Dia. Outs. 2"
Length between Tubeplates .... 15' 4 7/8"

SUPERHEATER.
Kind of Header .... −
Elements { Dia. Outs. .... −
{ Dia. Ins. .... −
{ Number .... −

IF FITTED WITH
Draft Retarder .... −
Circulating Valve .... −
Header Discharge Valve .... −
Pressure Release Valves .... −
Combined Pressure Release } .... −
and Piston Valves }

FIREBOX SHELL.
Length Outs. at Bottom .... 8' 6"
Width " " " .... 4' 0 1/2"
" " " Top .... 5' 2 3/4"
Thickness of Plates—
Back 21/32" Casing 5/8" Throat 3/4"

COPPER FIREBOX.
Length of Grate .... 7' 9 15/32"
Width " " .... 3' 4 1/8"
Depth to Top of Ring, Front .... 5' 5 1/2"
" " " Back .... 4' 5 1/2"

Width of Ring.
Back and Front 3" Sides 3"
Thickness of Plates—
Back 9/16" Casing 9/16" Tube { 7/8"
{ 9/16"

HEATING SURFACE.
Firebox Outside .... 133 Sq. ft.
Large Tubes .... − "
Small Tubes .... 1818 "
Superheater Inside .... − "
Total .... 1951 "

GRATE AREA. .... 26 Sq. ft.

WHEELS. Diameter. See Diagram.
Tyres Thickness .... 3"

JOURNALS. Dia. Length.
Leading Bogie or Truck .... 6" 9"
Leading Coupled .... 8" 12"
Driving .... 8" 9"
Intermediate ....
Trailing Coupled .... 8" 12"
Trailing Bogie or Truck ....

Tractive Power at { Lbs. 17,800 21,300
85% Boiler Pressure { Tons 7.95 9.5
Adhesion Coefficient. Lbs. per Ton. 349 382
Height. Rail to Top of Chimney 13' 3"
" " Centre of Boiler 8' 6"

VALVES. Kind Balanced Slide

CYLINDER LUBRICATOR. Kind Sight Feed
If Fitted with Steam Sanding Apparatus Yes.
" " Train Warming " Yes.

BRAKE. .... Steam & Auto Ejector

TENDER. Capacity. Water, Gallons 4000
" " Coal, Tons 6

WHEELS. Diameter .... 4' 4"

JOURNALS. Dia. 6" Length. 11"

86

Class 8C 4-6-0

Eclipsed by the more numerous and certainly more celebrated Atlantics, the Class 8C 4-6-0 was still a capable and impressive machine. Some comparisons with later 4-6-0 types serve to prove the size of this particular design. Outline dimensions of the 8C were thus: length over buffer planks 36'-3½", width over platform (footplate) 8'-9½", height (rail to chimney) 13'-3", weight (in working order) 72 tons, 13 cwt. Comparisons with modern 4-6-0s put the dimensions of the 8C into perspective. Figures in the same order put the LMS Royal Scot at 38'-2½", 8'-3", 12'-5½", weight 83 tons. GWR Castle at 38'-3", 8'-8", 13'-3¾", weight 79 tons 17 cwt. When comparing weight however, it should be remembered that the 8C was a 2-cylinder machine whereas the 'Scot' had 3 cylinders and the 'Castle' 4.

The first 8C, no.195, was given a superheated boiler in 1912 and received 21"bore cylinders with piston valves of the type carried by the 8K 2-8-0's. only to revert back to a saturated version in 1920. 195 and 196 differed slightly in cylinder diameter; no.196 had cylinders of 19" compared to the 19½" bore of the earlier engine.

Cylinder diameters were changed again when super-heater boilers were fitted. This part of the 8C story now begins to spill into LNER days as no.196 did not receive her superheater until 1927. By then the class had become re-classified 'B1' and were subject to various visual changes, not least in the area of boiler mountings. Chimneys and sundry detail changes will be covered in a later work dealing specifically with G.C.engines in the LNER era.

Gorton and Neasden shared the two engines when built, after which they wandered in a state of 'no fixed abode.' Sheffield played host to the pair around the time of the First War after which no.195 went to Neasden. In 1923, Immingham became the engines' home base followed by Neasden again and then Woodford from where they worked trains between Banbury and Sheffield. This was followed by a spell on fish trains between Banbury, Doncaster and Grimsby. Colwick, Leicester, Neasden and finally, Annesley were all stabling points for one or other of the pair between 1940 and their withdrawal at the end of 1947.

SUMMARY OF CLASS 8C 4 - 6 - 0 (LNER B1)

NUMBER	BUILDER	DATE BUILT	WITHDRAWN
195	Beyer Peacock & Co.	December 1903	December 1947
196	Beyer Peacock & Co.	January 1904	Decembner 1947

No.196, the second engine of the pair is caught here at Neepsend shed. Compared with the Atlantic, the third pair of coupled wheels gives an added dimension, albeit perhaps illusory, of size and power.

Collection of G.H.Platt

Sir William in person: All the glory of the Edwardian railway locomotive seems to ooze from no.365 *Sir William Pollitt* in this particularly splendid shot taken on Neasden shed in what must have been the early days of the engine's career.

Collection of G.H.Platt

Compound Atlantics
Classes 8D & 8E

Like many locomotive engineers, Webb on the LNWR and Gresley on the LNER, Robinson looked to compound expansion in a bid to improve efficiency in the motive power field. He appears to have been impressed by W.M.Smith's system developed for the N.E.R. Smith's son incidentally, J.W.Smith, was appointed Works Manager at Gorton in 1906 having been Chief Locomotive Draughtsman under S.W.Johnson on the Midland Railway at Derby.

A 3-cylinder arrangement for the Compound Atlantics was adopted; a high-pressure inside cylinder of 19″ bore exhausting into 2 outside cylinders of 21″ bore. Only 4 Compounds were built and all were constructed in the G.C's own shops at Gorton between the end of 1905 and 1906. The second pair were originally intended as simple engines but emerged instead as Compounds. Differences in frame design ensued and it was this alteration that brought about the different class designations-8D and 8E-for the first and second pairs respectively.

Along the right-hand side of the smokebox was set the reinforcing valve-a feature of the Smith compound system. This enabled live steam at 50 p.s.i. to be admitted briefly to the low-pressure (outside) cylinders to aid starting. The system also had the advantage of enabling the engine to be worked in a semi-compound fashion when the locomotive was pressed hard, on a rising gradient for example. A rod passing through the r.h. boiler handrail controlled this particular feature, visible in the photographs along with the valve itself.

Boiler mountings, identical with those of their Simple sisters exhibited one subtlety: on the Compound series the finely flowing chimney (1′10¼″tall) was set 3″ further along the smokebox towards the front of the engine. This was to accommodate the extra pipework inherent in the smokebox of the Compound which would have resulted in the blast pipe being set further forward.

The reversing rod was extended via an extension through the front of the leading splasher to operate the

Compound Atlantic no.259 *King Edward VII* **looks about 'ready for the road' alongside Manchester London Road 'A' platform. This may well have been a cross-country working, for a North-Eastern bow-ended corridor coach can just be seen behind the tender. Steam roars from the safety valves and an upward plume from the engine's blower with a 'pop' from the whistle all add to the atmosphere. The cloth cap worn by the driver appears to have been** *de rigeur* **for G.C.drivers of the period in contrast to the uniform peaked caps sported elsewhere. A human footnote to this picture is portrayed by the three young lads, one of whom is actually on the engine getting some 'hands on' experience. How typical it all seems of the fascination of railways that captivated us all at a tender age.**

Collection of G.H.Platt

lifting arms of the valve gear for the inside cylinder. Cleaners and fitters working inside the frames of a Compound Atlantic must have had something of an adventure. Apart from the pear-shaped crank webs of the leading coupled axle, no less than six eccentrics with their attendant rods would have been encountered. The slide valves for the outside cylinders were driven by eccentrics on the rear coupled axle. Eccentric rods-on 8'11½" centres- were hooped over the crank axle with the 2 expansion links of the Stephenson valve gear suspended ahead of it. The high-pressure cylinder was set well forward to drive the leading axle. Steam was fed via piston valves situated underneath the cylinder and inclined upwards. What an incredible sight all this machinery must have presented when the engine was running!

In 1919 no.259 was fitted with a Galloway-Hill furnace. This was a device whereby steam was blown into a modified ashpan creating a vacuum into which air was drawn; the idea being a controlled increase in the air supply to the fire according to the working conditions of the locomotive. The furnace was retained when the engine was superheated in 1921 but was removed in early LNER days.

No.365 *Sir William Pollitt* was the first of any of the Atlantics to be superheated- in May 1911 using the Schmidt system which required some sundry external alterations. Reference to the second picture in our series

shows the Wakefield lubricator seen above the l.h.outside cylinder along with the oil pipe to the steam chest. The projecting box above the front bufferbeam covered the tail rod for the inside cylinder. Set in the centre of the smokebox was the damper for the superheater. This took the form of a louvre-type arrangement which cut off the hot gases passing through the boiler flues. It was controlled from a steam-operated cylinder which worked automatically when the blower was used. The device could also be hand-operated from the cab, the rod extending through the boiler handrail.

Later modifications to the Compounds included fitting of a boiler carrying Robinson's own design of superheater with 24 elements, substituted by the 22-element pattern later on. The Wakefield mechanical lubricators were replaced also- with his 'Intensifore'system of lubrication with sight feeds in the locomotive cab.

The Compounds spent the greater part of their G.C.lives allocated to Gorton shed where they were regarded as the pride of the G.C.'s fleet. Naturally enough, they would have been deployed on the company's expresses to and from Manchester over the Woodhead route. In the period 1920-23 the four engines were transferred to Leicester where one of them, no.259 *King Edward VII* became the personal engine of Fred Lancashire to whom we referred biographically in the section on the 11B 4-4-0s.

SUMMARY OF CLASS 8D/E 4 - 4 -2 (LNER C5)

NUMBER	BUILDER	DATE BUILT	NAME	WITHDRAWN
258	Gorton	December 1905	*The Rt.Hon.Viscount Cross G.C.B. G.C.S.I.*	December 1946
259	Gorton	February 1906	*King Edward VII*	April 1947
364	Gorton	December 1906	*Lady Faringdon**	December 1947
365	Gorton	December 1906	*Sir William Pollitt*	August 1947

* *Lady Henderson until 1917*

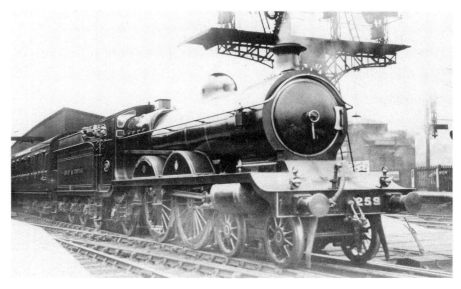

No.259 *King Edward VII* **stands at Guide Bridge at the head of an up express for Marylebone in 1922. The four Compounds appear to have been regarded as something rather special. Perhaps this was due to the names they carried or maybe alluded to the fact that the quartet were mechanically different. Had an original intention been put into practice no.259 would not have been named after the reigning monarch at all. Initially, it had been the company's idea to name the first two Simple engines , nos. 192 and 194,** *King Edward VII* **and** *Queen Alexandra* **respectively. However, the idea was abandoned a few weeks before the two pioneers emerged.**

Collection of G.H.Platt

In April 1910 no.258 *The Rt.Hon. Viscount Cross K.C.B.G.C.S.I.* storms under Powdrills Bridge Whetstone with the 10.59 a.m. Leicester-West of England express. The train was due into Plymouth at 6.30 p.m. Records state that the Compounds did not work through to Plymouth, although there is evidence of their having worked as far as Bristol in the 1906-10 period.

G.M.Shoults

Classes 8D & E Type 4.4.2 № of Engines 4

8D Class.			8E Class						
G. C. R.	1905	1	G. C. R.	1906	2				
"	1906	1							

CYLINDERS. (*Three*)
Diameter .... (1) 19" (2) 21"
Stroke .... 21"
Centres ...... 6'-8" between outs.

BOILER.
Class ...... № 6 Standard
Working Pressure ...... 180 Lbs. per □"
Barrel Dia. Outs. Max. ...... 5'.0"
Barrel Length ...... 15'.0"
Barrel Thickness of Plates ...... 5/8"

TUBES.
Large No. ... 22 ... Dia. Outs. ... 5¼"
Small No. 226.110 Dia. Outs. 2 ... 2"
Length between Tubeplates ...... 15'.4⅜"

SUPERHEATER.
Kind of Header ...... Front Cover
Elements { Dia. Outs. ...... 1⅜"
{ Dia. Ins. ...... 1 1/16"
{ Number 22

IF FITTED WITH
Draft Retarder ......
Circulating Valve ...... Yes
Header Discharge Valve ...... Yes
Pressure Release Valves ......
Combined Pressure Release }
and Piston Valves }

FIREBOX SHELL.
Length Outs. at Bottom ...... 8'.6"
Width "   "   " ...... 4'.0½"
  "   "   " Top ...... 5'.2¾"
Thickness of Plates—
Back 21/32. Casing 5/8. Throat ¾.

COPPER FIREBOX.
Length of Grate ...... 7'.9 15/32"
Width "   " ...... 3'.4⅛"
Depth to Top of Ring, Front 6'.5½"
  "   "   " Back ...... 5'.3"
Width of Ring.
Back and Front ...... 3" Sides ...... 3"
Thickness of Plates—
Back 9/16. Casing 9/16. Tube { 7/8"
{ 9/16"

HEATING SURFACE.
Firebox Outside ...... 154 154 Sq. ft.
Large Tubes ...... 404 – "
Small Tubes ...... 885 1818 "
Superheater Inside ...... 242 – "
Total 1745 1972 "

GRATE AREA. ...... 26 Sq. ft.

WHEELS. Diameter. See Diagram.
Tyres Thickness ...... 3"
JOURNALS. Dia. Length.
Leading Bogie or Truck ...... 6" 9"
Leading Coupled ......
Driving ...... HP 8" 9"
Intermediate ...... LP 8" 9"
Trailing Coupled ...... Outs 6½" 11"
Trailing Bogie or Truck Ins. 7" 5⅝"

Tractive Power at { Lbs. 13350
85% Boiler Pressure { Tons 5.97
2/3 BP Power in HP Cylinder
¼ "   " LP
Adhesion Coefficient. Lbs. per Ton. 361
Height. Rail to Top of Chimney ... 13'.3"
  "   " Centre of Boiler ...... 8'.6"
VALVES. Kind { HP Piston (Inside Admission)
{ LP Unbalanced Slide
CYLINDER LUBRICATOR. Kind Mechanical or
Intensifier. Sight Feed Yes
If Fitted with Steam Sanding Apparatus ... Yes
  "   " Train Warming " ...... Yes
BRAKE. ...... Steam & Auto Ejector
TENDER. Capacity. Water, Gallons 4000
  "   Coal, Tons 6
WHEELS. Diameter ...... 4'.4"
JOURNALS. Dia. ... 6" Length ... 11"

No.1096, the second of the 8F's completed in June 1906 at a cost of £4260. Inflation is regarded in the U.K. as a phenomenom of our time but statistics available show the terrific inflationary effect of World War I on prices. In the post-1918 era Robinson 4-6-0s were costing around £15000-£17000 each, a massive increase from these palmy Edwardian days. Though the engines in question were bigger and were built with superheaters, the comparison is interesting nevertheless. I would date this picture as being taken somewhat earlier than that of *Immingham*. Differences emerge, and I am tempted to think that this is a green-liveried engine. The safety valves have not yet been cased in, piston tail-rods are still carried and only the centre splasher panel carries the company coat of arms. Given that the black no.1097 was repainted from green it is reasonable to suppose that the re-painting of the splasher panels was done at the same time. 1096 stands behind the cab roof- a feature not seen on any other G.C. 4-6-0s at this time. 1096 stands alongside platform 2 at Guide Bridge with an up express. This station was something of a focal point for the Great Central in Manchester in a similar way that Marple and later Chinley was for the Midland. Trains to and from Sheffield, the East Coast ports, Humberside all called here. Prior to 1922, slip coaches from Hull-Liverpool trains, by-passing Manchester on the Godley to Glazebrook line, were brought in here en route to Manchester London Road. Guide Bridge was also served jointly by the L.NWR who had their own goods facilities here and a direct line to Stockport via Denton Junction. The LNW were also involved jointly with the G.C. in the Oldham, Ashton and Guide Bridge (O.A & G.B.) line which provided connections east and west of Guide Bridge with the important Lancashire mill towns of Ashton and Oldham. Guide Bridge also saw G.C. traffic arriving from Manchester Central and Liverpool over the Cheshire Lines Committee. The line from Central joined the G.C. main line at Fairfield Junction about one mile due west of the station, tracks between these points having been quadrupled, such was the intensity of traffic, in 1906/07.

Collection of G.H.Platt

'Immingham' Class 8F 4-6-0

If any name sums up the thrusting enterprise and ambition of the Great Central Railway, that name, surely, is 'Immingham.' Anxious to develop further the deep-water port and dock facilities of Grimsby, the G.C.were forced to seek cheaper land along the Humber Estuary.The site chosen was some five miles upstream, at Immingham. Work began on the 1000-acre dock and port complex in July 1906. When, after almost exactly six years work, its royal opening took place, Sam Fay-the company's redoubtable General Manager-was knighted by King George V on the spot.

It was at this place that, on July 12th 1906, Lady Henderson, wife of Sir Alexander, the G.C. Chairman, cut the first sod in what has been described as the jewel in the company's crown. The train carrying the Chairman, his wife and other worthies was hauled to Immingham by one of Robinson's brand new 4-6-0s, the third Class 8F no.1097 named *Immingham* especially for this most prestigious occasion.

Essentially, the 8F was not really a new class at all. Robinson took the already successful 8C 4-6-0 design, 2 of which had already been built for comparison with his Atlantics and reduced the coupled wheel diameter by 2″ to 6′7″. As will be seen, this was to become a familiar

Robinson tactic: the fine tuning of one design by altering the coupled wheel size for a specific purpose. Not that this was a practice confined to the Great Central; S.W.Johnson on the Midland had done an exactly similar thing with his slim boilered 4-4-0's built from 1876 onwards.

Whereas the 8C was purely an express passenger design, the later 8F was intended for express goods and fish traffic, something of a Great Central speciality for which the company was noted. With a coupled wheel diameter of almost express proportions, the 'Immingham' engines were something of a Mixed Traffic design; indeed, our pictures show them at work on express trains. Ten 8Fs were built, all by Beyer,Peacock & Co.and delivered in the short space of just 28 days from early June to the beginning of July 1906.

Newly-built, the engines were divided between Neasden, Gorton and Grimsby. Though intended for express goods and fish traffic, the class were equally at home on express passenger trains, as our pictures will show. In First War days half the class were moved to Mexborough and worked troop train specials as far as Banbury. In early 1921, Mexborough and Woodford had four engines apiece with two stationed at Gorton.

Eight cove-roof coaches have been supplemented by five 6-wheelers to give this Manchester-Cleethorpes train a look of very mixed proportions. Godley Junction, dividing point with the C.L.C's line to Glazebrook, is the setting as 11A 4-4-0 no.681 and *Immingham* **4-6-0 no. 1102 storm past c.1922.**

Collection of G.H.Platt

By Grouping, a shift in movement had occured and all ten locomotives were based on the northern half of the G.C. system, in the centre of operations, so to speak, at Sheffield.

All 10 of the class were superheated between 1926 and 1928 and 6 were fitted with 21″ cylinders and piston valves of the very successful type developed for the 8K 2-8-0 freight engine. The LNER found work for the class on former G.E. and G.N. territory, the West Riding district of Yorkshire being a notable area of operation. The engines at this time wore the attractive lined passenger green of the company lined, as in their early Great Central days, black and white. Prior to the Second War, members of the class were based at March and Lincoln, working the Harwich Boat trains from between there and York.

Soldiering on through the War, the 8Fs (as LNER B4) were concentrated at Copley Hill (near Wakefield), Lincoln and Ardsley working goods, local trains and excursions. Four engines survived to become the property of British Railways. Appropriately enough, *Immingham* was the last to go, withdrawn in November 1950.

SUMMARY OF CLASS 8F 4 - 6 - 0 (LNER B4)

NUMBER	BUILDER	DATE BUILT	WITHDRAWN
1095 - 1104	Beyer Peacock & Co.	June and July 1906	Feb 1944*- Nov 1950

Notes:
a) Only one engine named No. 1097 Immingham.
b) Several engines were fitted with 21″ bore cylinders and, piston valves of the pattern fitted to the 8K 2-8-0.
Dates of fitting and engines concerned were:-
1095   October 1927
1098   August 1934
1100   May 1932
1102   June 1927
1103   May 1927
1104   March 1927

* No.1095 first withdrawn in July 1939 but put back into traffic in October of that year.

No.1096 showing her sinistral side whilst standing east of Guide Bridge station. The lattice- post signals which appear in the background, pneumatically-operated and replicas of those used on the LSWR, were unique to this part of the G.C. They were installed parallel with the Ardwick-Hyde Junction widening, completed in 1907. Aside from the rolled-up tarpaulin, the condition of the engine appears to be the same as in our previous picture. Though the smokebox door ring and brass beading are a little lacklustre, the cylinder lagging bands and overall lining show well enough.

Collection of G.H.Platt

No.1102 'square-on' outside Manchester London Road. Through the haze, the outlines of St.Andrew's church in the Ancoats district of the city stand ghost-like just a hundred yards or so away from the railway boundary. St.Andrew's stood almost on top of the Midland's extensive goods depot in Ancoats, an indication of the intense competition that existed amongst the individual companies for goods traffic. The sight of one of the Great Central goods warehouses at Ducie Street, alongside London Road, to the left of our picture, reinforces this; it would have been to here that 1102 and her sisters would have worked from time to time.

Collection of G.H.Platt

Class 5ᴬ Type o.6.o. Nº of Engines ... 5.

Maker	Year Built	Nº of Engines	Maker	Year Built	Nº of Engines	Maker	Year Built	Nº of Engines
G.C.R.	1906	4						
-"-	1914	1						

CYLINDERS.
Diameter .... 13"
Stroke .... 26"
Centres .... 6' 6¾"

BOILER.
Class 5
Working Pressure ...... 150 Lbs. per ☐"
Barrel Dia. Outs. Max. .... 3'-6¹⁵⁄₁₆"
Barrel Length .... 9'-3"
Barrel Thickness of Plates ...... ¹⁵⁄₃₂"

TUBES.
Large No. ...... - Dia. Outs. ...... -
Small No. 124 Dia. Outs. 1¾"
Length between Tube plates .... 9'-7 ⁹⁄₁₆"

SUPERHEATER.
Kind of Header .... -
Elements { Dia. Outs. .... -
            Dia. Ins. .... -
            Number .... - }

IF FITTED WITH
Draft Retarder .... -
Circulating Valve .... -
Header Discharge Valve .... -
Pressure Release Valves .... -
Combined Pressure Release } .... -
  and Piston Valves }

FIREBOX SHELL.
Length Outs. at Bottom ...... 4'-6"
Width   "   "   " .... 3'-7⅞"
  "   "   " Top .... 3'-7⅞"
Thickness of Plates—
  Back ½" Casing ¹⁵⁄₃₂" Throat ⁹⁄₁₆"

COPPER FIREBOX.
Length of Grate .... 3'-9¹³⁄₁₆"
Width   "   " .... 3'-0"
Depth to Top of Ring, Front 4'-5⅞"
  "   "   " Back 4'-0⅝"

Width of Ring.
Back and Front 3" Sides 3"
Thickness of Plates—
  Back ⁹⁄₁₆" Casing ¹⁵⁄₃₂" Tube { ¾" ⁹⁄₁₆" }

HEATING SURFACE.
Firebox Outside .... 60 Sq. ft.
Large Tubes .... "
Small Tubes .... 530 "
Superheater Inside ...... - "
              Total 590 "

GRATE AREA. 11 Sq. ft.

WHEELS. Diameter. See Diagram.
Tyres Thickness .... 3"
JOURNALS.   Dia.   Length.
Leading Bogie or Truck ......
Leading Coupled .... 6" 7"
Driving .... 6" 7"
Intermediate ....
Trailing Coupled .... 6" 7"
Trailing Bogie or Truck ......
Tractive Power at { Lbs. 10218
85% Boiler Pressure { Tons ...... 4·5
Adhesion Coefficient. Lbs. per Ton 280
Height. Rail to Top of Chimney .... 11'-0"
  "   " Centre of Boiler .... 6'-0"

VALVES. Kind *Unbalanced Slide*
CYLINDER LUBRICATOR. Kind *Roscoe*
If Fitted with Steam Sanding Apparatus ...... No
  " " Train Warming ...... No
BRAKE. *Steam & Auto Ejector*
TANK
Capacity. Water, Gallons 950
  " " Coal, Tons 1½
WHEELS. Diameter ...... -
JOURNALS. Dia .... - Length .... -

Outside Gorton Works no.321 has been stripped of its motion and, judging by the very worn condition of its paintwork, is awaiting a visit to the works for a heavy repair. As with the Class 5s a warning bell is mounted on the engine, this time on top of the firebox. Apparently this was transferred around the time of the Grouping to the right-hand side of the engine where the bell could be sounded automatically from the motion. Notice, again, the wooden 'sandwich' pattern of buffer plank, and drip-feed lubricators sited above the front sandboxes. The first two engines built, G.C.nos. 60 and 61 were fitted with condensing apparatus owing to their location as station pilots at Liverpool's Central Station and their subsequent deployment in the tunnelled dock areas. Essentially a dock tank design, the seven Class 5As found their way into fairly specific areas: Liverpool's Huskisson Dock, Grimsby and Immingham all being listed as work stations for these locomotives. Though the stovepipe chimney of the Pollitt era was discarded by Robinson, it is interesting to compare the outline shape as similar save for the graceful cap-another one of those little touches of Robinson's artistry. Running back from the smokebox is the vaccuum ejector pipe, though the locomotives themselves did not carry a vacuum brake and were steam-braked only. 3-link couplings appear to have sufficed for the whole of the engines' career.

Collection of G.H.Platt

Though the phrase: 'camera-shy' is a trifle nonsensical in respect of a railway locomotive, the term 'camera-friendly' is hardly applicable to the Class 5A tank engines! In consequence we have to move into the LNER era in search of further pictures. Still retaining its Robinson chimney is the former G.C.R.no.157 now seen in late LNER days working at Birkenhead Docks on April 12th 1947. Oval-head buffers have been fitted although the left hand one seems to have gone somewhat awry! Twin handles appear on the smokebox door, replacing the familiar Great Central spoked wheel and handle. In contrast to the other six engines no.157 used lever reverse in lieu of the wheel and screw fitted to the rest.

Class 5A 0-6-0 Tank

Robinson produced this neat little design in 1906. Though shunting engines for dockside work are hardly likely to tax any designer of locomotives, Robinson was able to take the tidy and workmanlike Pollitt Class 5 saddle tank and suitably modify it.

The result formed the Class 5A shunting tank, six of which were built at Gorton in 1906 with one further engine appearing 8 years later, in 1914. Robinson retained the essential working parts of the Pollitt engine i.e: mainframes, cylinders, wheels, motion and boiler with saddletank removed. In its place appeared side tanks, increasing the water capacity by over 50%, from 600 to 950 gallons. With typical style, the rather stark and upright Pollitt cab was replaced by a somewhat flatter affair with a characteristic front curve.

Numbering of the 5As was somewhat random, unusually for the G.C.who were quite orderly in this respect compared to, say, the LNWR who operated a beautifully higgledy-piggledy system!The numbers were: 60, 61, 89, 157, 321 & 538-all built in 1906. 277-one engine only-built in 1914. All were constructed at Gorton Works.Withdrawal took place in the wake of the Diesel shunter invasion-from 1953 onwards. The other 5 1906 engines disappeared between January 1955 and April 1956. the last to go was the 1914 locomotive, no.277- (then (British Railways no. 68210) dispatched in February 1957.

SUMMARY OF CLASS 5A 0 - 6 - 0 TANK ENGINES (LNER J63)

NUMBER	BUILDER	DATE BUILT	WITHDRAWN
60/61,89,157,321,538	Gorton	August to November 1906	Oct 1953-Apr 1956
277	Gorton	June 1914	February 1957

Class ... 8F Type 4.6.0 Nº of Engines ... 10.

Maker	Year Built	Nº of Engines	Maker	Year Built	Nº of Engines	Maker	Year Built	Nº of Engines
Beyer Peacock	1906	10						

CYLINDERS.
Diameter ... 19"
Stroke ... 26"
Centres ... 6' 8"

BOILER.
Class ... 8C & 8F
Working Pressure ... 180 Lbs. per □"
Barrel Dia. Outs. Max. ... 5' 0"
Barrel Length ... 15' 0"
Barrel Thickness of Plates ... 5/8"

TUBES.
Large No. ... — Dia. Outs. —
Small No. ... 226 Dia. Outs. ... 2"
Length between Tubeplates ... 15' 4 3/8"

SUPERHEATER.
Kind of Header ... —
Elements { Dia. Outs. ... —
Dia. Ins. ... —
Number ... —

IF FITTED WITH
Draft Retarder ... —
Circulating Valve ... —
Header Discharge Valve ... —
Pressure Release Valves ... —
Combined Pressure Release } —
and Piston Valves }

FIREBOX SHELL.
Length Outs. at Bottom ... 8' 6"
Width " " ... 4' 0½"
" " Top ... 5' 2¾"
Thickness of Plates—
Back 21/32" Casing 5/8" Throat ¾"

COPPER FIREBOX.
Length of Grate ... 7' 9 15/32"
Width " " ... 3' 4 1/8"
Depth to Top of Ring, Front ... 5' 5½"
" " " Back ... 4' 5½"

Width of Ring.
Back and Front ... 3" Sides ... 3"
Thickness of Plates—
Back 9/16" Casing 9/16" Tube { 7/8" / 9/16"

HEATING SURFACE.
Firebox Outside ... 133 Sq. ft.
Large Tubes ... — "
Small Tubes ... 1818 "
Superheater Inside ... — "
Total ... 1951 "

GRATE AREA. ... 26 Sq. ft.

WHEELS. Diameter. See Diagram.
Tyres Thickness ... 3½"

JOURNALS. Dia. Length.
Leading Bogie or Truck ... 6" 9"
Leading Coupled ... 8" 9"
Driving ... 8" 9"
Intermediate ...
Trailing Coupled ... 8" 12"
Trailing Bogie or Truck ...
Tractive Power at { Lbs. ... 19,180
85% Boiler Pressure { Tons ... 8.11
Adhesion Coefficient. Lbs. per Ton ... 367
Height. Rail to Top of Chimney ... 13' 3½"
" " Centre of Boiler ... 8' 6½"

VALVES. Kind Balanced Slide
CYLINDER LUBRICATOR. Kind Sight Feed
If Fitted with Steam Sanding Apparatus ... Yes
" " Train Warming " ... Yes
BRAKE. Steam + Auto Ejector
TENDER. Capacity. Water, Gallons ... 4000
" Coal, Tons ... 6
WHEELS. Diameter ... 4' 4"
JOURNALS. Dia ... 6" Length ... 11"

No.1110 tops up its boiler outside Manchester London Road whilst pausing between duties, the fireman pausing in his work to do a spot of reading. Livery for the class appears to have been fairly uniform: the company crest appearing in the the centre splasher surrounded by a single line and polished brass beading. All-over, the main colour was black relieved by red and white lining. Cylinder covers and tail rods being of the usual polished steel.Earlier pictures such as this one depict the engines carrying 20-ton screw jacks for re-railing purposes. Supplied by Messrs.Tangye of Manchester, the jacks weighed 135 lbs. each which must have made manoeuvring them into position something of a feat.1110 was one of six of the class to be withdrawn in 1947. As LNER 1474 she was taken out of service in October of that year.

Collection of W.A.Brown

1108, the fourth engine of the 8G class on a stopping passenger train at the west end of Guide Bridge station. The overbridge in the background carries Guide Lane over the railway and leads into the town of Ashton-under-Lyne. Dated around 1920, this was very much the era of the tram and the gas light as the scene depicts. Condition of the engine is far from pristine although the brass-beading on the splashers is still clean and the decorated panels remain intact. By coincidence, both locos illustrated have suffered bent handrails alongside the smokebox-modellers please note!

Collection of G.H.Platt

Class 8G 4-6-0

Beyer, Peacock & Co. worked in a close harmony with the Great Central and, despite some petty friction between them, produced many fine well-engineered locomotives. The two companies were very close neighbours, the G.C.'s locomotive, carriage and wagon works lying on the north side of their Manchester to Sheffield line with Beyer, Peacock's Gorton Foundry immediately opposite, on the south side. This close liaison was apparent in 1923 when the Great Central's redoubtable Sir Sam Fay became Beyer, Peacock's Chairman. He was joined, a year later, by Robinson himself who became a director of the company following his departure from Gorton. Undoubtably Beyer, Peacock's close proximity to the G.C. Works nucleus had been of immense benefit to the company over the years, giving them an almost 'in-house' operation in engineering expertise and experience.

Though renowned as builders of locomotives, Beyer, Peacock were also large producers of machine tools and a report in the company archives laments the relatively few machine tools bought from them by the MS&L and the G.C. It has been suggested that the friction between them was due to their being close neighbours and drawing their respective workforces from the same area.

Within two months of the completion of the last 'Immingham' 4-6-0 (Class 8F) Beyer, Peacock began construction of what was essentially a smaller wheeled version of this express goods design. Designated Class 8G (the G.C. classification could be quite logical if studied) the coupled wheel diameter was set at 5'-4" underlining the suitability of this new locomotive for goods work also.

As mentioned elsewhere, loco policy under Robinson was to build, in the main, small batches of engines, modifying details from batch to batch in an endeavour to either improve performance or to match the varied design to a specific traffic need.

The 8G used the same boiler barrel as the 'Immingham' and 8C 4-6-0s and also the Atlantics. It was coupled, however, to a shorter firebox -7'-9" as opposed to 8'-6". Aesthestically the 8G was a pleasing design. The coupled wheel size, allied to the disposition of the two outside cylinders, led to the footplate being dropped to provide for the appearance of three splashers. Some observers have remarked on this as being a mere cosmetic exercise. One could hardly have expected Robinson to have done otherwise.

Though not quite as stately as their bigger-wheeled

Maximum effort seems to be indicated in this shot of 8G no.1108 as she labours up the 1 in 117 bank near Crowden prior to 'hitting the hole', that is to say entering the Woodhead Tunnel. Sheeted open wagons, vans and cattle wagons give a thoroughly mixed air to 1108's train. The 5ft.4ins. coupled wheels would have given these engines a good turn of speed on such trains commensurate with the limitations of loose couplings. Notice the loops on either side of the line here, well-polished rails indicating a high degree of use on what was a very heavily-trafficked line.

G.M.Shoults

10 8Gs were built in all, 6 being delivered in September 1906 and a further 4 in the October of that year. No.1110, the sixth locomotive to be delivered, is seen on Gorton shed in post-First War days; 4 of the class are shown as being based here in the 1921 allocation list. Gorton engines would have found themselves working out of the Great Central Ducie Street depot alongside the London Road passenger station. The cylinders of 1110 are minus the tail rods fitted to the engines when built. The 2 cylinders, with slide valves mounted beween them, are shown on the maker's drawing with a bore of 19 ¼ins. This rather odd size seems to have been changed by Grouping-19 ins.being recorded before 1923. The engine is paired with a 3250 gallon coal-railed tender. These were not standard issue for the class in G.C.days, 4000 gallon types with solid coal guards being supplied from new. By the look of the enormous pile of coal in her tender those coal rails are going to be needed! The decidedly mixed appearance of this fuel suggests some fire-cleaning will be required before many miles have been covered.

Collection of G.H.Platt

Class 8G *Type* 4.6.0 *Nº of Engines* 10.

Maker	Year Built	Nº of Engines						
Beyer Peacock	1906	10						

CYLINDERS.
Diameter.................................19"
Stroke ....26"
Centres ....6'-8"

BOILER.
Class 8G
Working Pressure ....180. Lbs. per □"
Barrel Dia. Outs. Max..............5'-0"
Barrel Length ....15'-0"
Barrel Thickness of Plates ....⅝"

TUBES.
Large No............ — Dia. Outs. —
Small No......226 Dia. Outs. 2"
Length between Tubeplates ..15'-4⅜"

SUPERHEATER.
Kind of Header .... —
Elements { Dia. Outs. .... —
Dia. Ins. .... —
Number .... —

IF FITTED WITH
Draft Retarder .... —
Circulating Valve .... —
Header Discharge Valve .... —
Pressure Release Valves .... —
Combined Pressure Release } .... —
and Piston Valves }

FIREBOX SHELL.
Length Outs. at Bottom ....7'-9"
Width ,, ,, ,, ...4'-0½"
,, ,, ,, Top ....5'-2¾"
Thickness of Plates—
Back 21/32" Casing ⅝" Throat ¾"

COPPER FIREBOX.
Length of Grate ....7'-0 15/32"
Width ,, ,, ...3'-4⅛"
Depth to Top of Ring, Front ...5'-10"
,, ,, ,, Back ....4'-11"

Width of Ring.
Back and Front ....3" Sides ....3"
Thickness of Plates—
Back 9/16" Casing 9/16" Tube { ⅞"
{ 9/16"

HEATING SURFACE.
Firebox Outside ....133....Sq. ft.
Large Tubes .... — ,,
Small Tubes ....1818 ,,
Superheater Inside.............. — ,,
Total 1951 ,,

GRATE AREA. ....23·5 . Sq. ft.

WHEELS. Diameter. See Diagram.
Tyres Thickness ....3½"
JOURNALS. Dia. Length.
Leading Bogie or Truck ....6" 9"
Leading Coupled ....8" 9"
Driving ....8" 9"
Intermediate..............
Trailing Coupled ....8" 12"
Trailing Bogie or Truck ......
Tractive Power at { Lbs. 22,400
85% Boiler Pressure { Tons 10
Adhesion Coefficient. Lbs. per Ton....428
Height. Rail to Top of Chimney .....13'-0½"
,, ,, Centre of Boiler .....8'-3½"
VALVES. Kind....Balanced Slide
CYLINDER LUBRICATOR. Kind Sight Feed
If Fitted with Steam Sanding Apparatus ....Yes
,, ,, Train Warming ,, ...Yes
BRAKE. Steam & Auto Ejector
TENDER. Capacity. Water, Gallons 4000
,, Coal, Tons 6
WHEELS. Diameter.................4'-4"
JOURNALS. Dia.........6" Length....11"

sisters, these machines which incidentally were painted in the standard black goods livery, still had all the usual Robinson refinements. That splendid chimney which, as J.N. Maskelyne noted, had not a straight line on it, measured 2'-1¼" from base to lip. In our pictures we observe that No.1108 carries brass-cased safety valves, though the Beyer Peacock drawing shows four 4" valves uncased as on No.1110. These are indicated as blowing off at 200 p.s.i. although all other applications of the boiler show a 180lb setting. Unlike 1110 this engine is coupled to the conventional 4000 gallon tender, with the 'ships wheel' for the water pick up gear behind the driver.

Built as saturated engines, the 8G 4-6-0s were given superheated boilers from 1924 onwards. These were of 4'-9" diameter (one engine had already carried a smaller size boiler from 1910 to 1919) as fitted to the Class 8A 0-8-0. The new boilers were raised to clear the rear coupled axle and this high pitched appearance completely altered their original looks. Just one engine, the former no.1109 was fitted with 21 in. piston valve cylinders (of the 8K pattern) in November 1924 at the same time as it received its new boiler. Thus the story of the 8G in the original Robinson guise ended, more or less, with the disappearance of the Great Central itself.

The small wheeled 4-6-0s were allocated when built to Gorton and Lincoln sheds where they were deployed on fast goods trains. The Manchester engines worked fitted freights to Marylebone and the East Coast ports, those at Lincoln saw regular service over the Pennines on similar duties to Manchester.

Post-Grouping days saw the Lincoln detachment sent en-bloc to Gorton with some engines going to Trafford Park in the later part of the decade. These engines worked express freight traffic from the former Great Northern goods depot in Manchester, travelling over the Woodhead route to destinations southwards.

In both pre and post-Grouping days the 8G class found useful work on both stopping and, to a lesser extent, on express passenger trains. In the 1930s a role was also found for these locomotives in working excursion traffic; forays over the MSJ&A line and C.L.C. lines to Aintree Racecourse are recorded. By the outbreak of the Second War the ten members of the 8G class (LNER B9) were mostly employed on secondary duties. Stockport's Heaton Mersey (a former G.C. and Midland shed) played host to the engines in the War period, one duty being the working of through coaches to Liverpool from Godley Junction of the down Mail Train from London. In immediate post-War days no. 6109 (ex 1109) was working local passenger and freight trains over the Fairfield to Chorlton Junction line. From this point until their demise in 1949, the class were working over what had become something of a happy hunting ground for elderly Great Central locomotives, the Cheshire Lines. Withdrawal took place from June 1947 onwards; final extinction coming in May 1949 with the departure of no 61475 (G.C. 1111) already withdrawn just before the War and returned to traffic in September 1939.

SUMMARY OF CLASS 8G 4-6-0 (LNER B9)

NUMBER	BUILDER	DATE BUILT	WITHDRAWN
1105 - 1114	Beyer Peacock & Co.	September and October 1906	Jun 1947-May 1949

Notes:
1) No.1111 (as LNER 6111) was first withdrawn in July 1939 but was put back into traffic the following September.
2) No.1109 was fitted with 21" cylinders and 10" piston valves of the 8K pattern in November 1924.

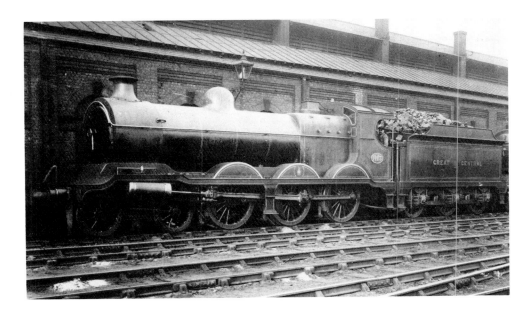

No.1113 of October 1906 showing the final condition of the 8G class in their Great Central days: cased safety valves, no tail rod covers to cylinders, single whistle and short pattern ash ejector to l.h. of smokebox. Photograph taken on Lincoln shed on 15th March 1924.
A.W.Craughton

No.1171, one of the four Wath Bankers built by Beyer,Peacock & Co. in December 1907/January 1908. Nicknamed locally as 'Daisies', an affinity to the Class 8A 0-8-0s will be detected; the Wath engines had been based on this design using similar coupled wheels (4ft.8ins.) and wheelbase spacing. Likewise, axles, axleboxes, coupling and connecting rods were all freely interchangeable with the parent design. Standardisation was obviously in Robinson's mind at the drawing board stage; the boiler was the same as that carried by the Atlantics, 8C and 8F classes fitted with Belpaire firebox of course. Three independent sets of Stephenson's Link Motion drove the valves, of the balanced slide pattern. To make life easier for the driver, steam-operated reversing gear was fitted. This must have been a bonus on the footplate as endless backward and forward running would have been daily practice.

Collection of G.H.Platt

SUMMARY OF CLASS 8H 0 - 8 - 4 TANKS (LNER S1)

NUMBER	BUILDER	DATE BUILT	WITHDRAWN
1170	Beyer Peacock & Co.	December 1907	January 1956
1171	Beyer Peacock & Co.	December 1907	January 1957
1172	Beyer Peacock & Co.	January 1908	January 1956
1173	Beyer Peacock & Co. January 1908	March 1954	

1) No.1171 was fitted with a trailing booster from January 1932 until January 1943
2) All four engines were superheated by the LNER on the dates given:-
*   1170   November 1951*
*   1171   January 1932*
*   1172   July 1940*
*   1173   December 1941*
3) The LNER built a pair (Nos.2798 and 2799) in 1932, both being booster fitted and superheated from new. The boosters were removed in December and June 1943 respectively. Further coverage of these locos will be given in a subsequent volume.

Class 8H. Type 0.8.4 Nᵒ of Engines ... 4.

"Beyer Peacock ₁ 6"	1907	2						
" " -	1908	2						

CYLINDERS. (Three)		FIREBOX SHELL.		WHEELS. Diameter. See Diagram.	
Diameter	18"	Length Outs. at Bottom	8' 6"	Tyres Thickness	3½"
Stroke	26	Width	4' 0½"	JOURNALS.	Dia. Length.
Centres	6' 8"	" " " Top	5' 2⅞"	Leading Bogie or Truck	
BOILER.		Thickness of Plates—		Leading Coupled	8" 9"
Class	Nᵒ 6 Standard	Back ²¹/₃₂ Casing ⅝" Throat ⁹/₁₆"		Driving	8" 9"
Working Pressure	180 Lbs. per ☐"	COPPER FIREBOX.		Intermediate	8" 9"
Barrel Dia. Outs. Max.	5' 0"	Length of Grate	7' 9¹⁵/₃₂"	Trailing Coupled	8" 12"
Barrel Length	15' 0"	Width "	3' 4⅝"	Trailing Bogie or Truck	7" 11"
Barrel Thickness of Plates	⅝"	Depth to Top of Ring, Front	6' 3½"	Tractive Power at { Lbs.	40524
TUBES.		" " " Back	5' 3"	85% Boiler Pressure { Tons	18
Large No. Dia. Outs.		Width of Ring.		Adhesion Coefficient. Lbs. per Ton.	550
Small No. 179. Dia. Outs. 2¼"		Back and Front 3" Sides	3"	Height. Rail to Top of Chimney	13' 3⁷/₁₆"
Length between Tubeplates 15' 4⅞"		Thickness of Plates—		" " Centre of Boiler	8' 6½"
SUPERHEATER.		Back ⁹/₁₆" Casing ⁹/₁₆" Tube { ⅞"		VALVES. (3) Kind Balanced Slide	
Kind of Header		{ ⁹/₁₆"		CYLINDER LUBRICATOR. Kind Sight Feed	
Elements { Dia. Outs.		HEATING SURFACE.		If Fitted with Steam Sanding Apparatus	No.
{ Dia. Ins.		Firebox Outside	154 Sq. ft.	" " Train Warning	No.
{ Number		Large Tubes		BRAKE. Steam & Auto Ejector	
IF FITTED WITH		Small Tubes	1818 "	Capacity. Water, Gallons	3000
Draft Retarder		Superheater Inside	"	" " Coal, Tons	5
Circulating Valve		Total	1972 "	WHEELS. Diameter	
Header Discharge Valve				JOURNALS. Dia. Length	
Pressure Release Valves					
Combined Pressure Release } and Piston Valves }		GRATE AREA.	26 Sq. ft.		

'Wath Banker'
Class 8H 0-8-4 Tank

The first decade of the 20th century was a busy one for the Great Central. The great works at Immingham, widening of the lines between Ardwick and Hyde near Manchester and also between Neasden and Northolt, pneumatic signalling installations on the route out of Manchester London Road - all fired by the determination and foresight of Sam Fay, one of the most dynamic General Managers ever to head a British railway company.

On top of this there was another particularly apposite and ambitious project: the construction of a wagon sorting yard at Wath-on-Dearne, situated in South Yorkshire in the heart of one of the world's richest coalfields. Some idea of the volume moved in those days can be given by looking at what was referred to as 'the great coalfield'. Lying in South Yorkshire, Nottinghamshire and Derbyshire and including part of Lincolnshire - it was estimated to hold some 49 **billion** tons of coal in the first years of this century. Much of this field was in G.C.territory, the company moving around 23 million tons of coal and coke per annum in the years up to the outbreak of the First War.

The new yard at Wath was laid out on the 'hump' system - a principle used extensively in later British freight yards. Wagons were propelled up to the 'hump' on a maximum gradient of 1 in 146 and locomotives in the yard were required to push trains of 80 loaded wagons (about 1200 tons). Once over the top, the wagons were broken from the train and ran by gravity down into the various sorting sidings which were laid out 'gridiron' fashion in a fan of parallel lines.

Robinson developed a locomotive able to produce a high tractive effort at a moderate speed; a principal requirement was a regular, even turning moment and to this end a 3-cylinder design was adopted with cranks set at 120 deg. to each other - features that were to become a *sine qua non* for H.N.Gresley when he began locomotive production on the Great Northern in 1912, though he would not have approved of the divided drive used in the 8H design.

'Not to be moved' warns the plate fitted to the front of no.1171 standing on shed displaying her right-hand flank. The 8H was something of a brute in appearance, displaying little of the elegance of so many of Robinson's other designs. That much said, the steam locomotive was essentially a functional device and Robinson was primarily an engineer and secondly an artist.Built for a specific need, the 8H tanks inevitably spent the greater part of their existence in the Wath concentration yard and were based at Mexborough. Some minor migrations were recorded however: no.1171 was dispatched to former N.E.R.territory in early 1928 but returned in a very short space of time, work in that area never being recorded. 1170 was moved to Whitemoor in April 1930 for trials in the new marshalling yard there, spending three weeks away before returning. Nos.1172 and 1173 were sent to March in July 1932 where they were to remain until ousted by Diesel shunters in 1949. Following this they were dispersed to Frodingham where they were deployed on movements of steel from the yards there. Unsuited for this work, the two were moved back to Mexborough. 1173 (then British Railways no.69903) was tried out at Immingham on dock shunting duties, a use for which it was not suited. It was Doncaster Works that provided the last work for these sturdy and robust-looking engines. Moving engines in and out of the 'Plant' was not the most glamorous work; but then, the 8H was not that kind of engine. Final forays shunting in the Frodingham steelworks yards was the lot that befell the erstwhile no. 1171 (B.R.69901) and the LNER-built no.69905. Both were withdrawn in January 1957 and were cut up at Darlington.It is worth recording that the LNER pair (then of Class S1) lasted only more or less as long as the Great Central engines. 69905 has been mentioned, 69904 built in May 1932 was withdrawn in January 1956.

Collection of W.A.Brown

A.F. Bound's pneumatically-operated signals with their characteristic lattice posts form a frame for this photograph of no.1090, at the head of an up express at Guide Bridge, the arrangement of the Walschaerts valve gear can be clearly identified. This engine was most definitely a curiosity in the line of Atlantics–notice the raised platform in front of the splashers designed to cover the tops of the expansion links, arranged in line across the locomotive at this point. The long radius rod-offset away from the connecting rod–precluded the use of a footstep beween the splashers; in lieu of this, a footstep was provided ahead of the cylinders which gave the front of the engine an altogether different appearance.

Collection of G.H.Platt

Class 8J 4-4-2
3-Cylinder Rebuild

An interesting variant of the Simple Atlantics was the rebuilding of No.1090, carried out at the end of 1908. 1090 had originally been built by the North British Locomotive Company in 1905 as a conventional 2-cylinder engine. In the manner of the Compounds, 3 cylinders were used in the rebuild, but simple expansion was preferred, using cylinders of 16″ bore x 26″ stroke. The drive was divided; the 2 outside cylinders driving the rear coupled wheels - as with the rest of the engines - and the inside cylinder driving onto the front coupled axle.

Unusually for that period of locomotive development and certainly for the G.C.R., Walschaerts valve gear was used, a set of motion being provided for each of the three cylinders. The expansion links for the gear were all driven from the rear coupled axle. An advantage of the Walschaerts gear, aside from the provision of constant lead, was the need for only one eccentric rod and slotted link per set of motion. Steam was fed to all three cylinders using balanced slide valves situated on top of the cylinders.

1090 was superheated in March 1914, an 18-element superheater being fitted. The engine was converted back to two cylinders in September 1922 and fitted with the conventional Stephenson valve gear. Clearly, the outside Walschaerts motion could not have been retained. The move back to Stephenson gear was done in the interests of standardisation, as in this second rebuilding, cylinders were sized at 21″ bore and were fed via piston valves 10″ in diameter - the same arrangement used in the very successful 8K 2-8-0.

SUMMARY OF CLASS 8J 4 - 4 - 2 (LNER C4)

G.C.R.number 1090.(1 engine only)
Originally built by North British Locomotive Co. in November 1905.Rebuilt to 3 cylinder Simple in December 1908.
Superheated in March 1914.
Rebuilt again, back to 2 cylinders, in September 1922 with cylinders and piston valves of the 8K pattern.
Withdrawn in November 1939 as LNER no.6090.

1090 in 1913 heading up the Chorlton Junction to Fairfield line in South Manchester just near to Alexandra Park Station. The train is the 3.22 p.m. Manchester Central to Cleethorpes express; the three ex-MS&L 6-wheelers forming the front part of the passenger accommodation must have given an exhilarating ride! Perhaps surprisingly, 1090 was the first of the Atlantics to be withdrawn-in November 1939. The four Compounds were gone before 1948 and, although the majority of the Simple engines survived Nationalisation, the early B.R.years saw them gradually picked off. The obsequies carried out at Dukinfield Carriage Works in those last years are perhaps best not featured here. Rather better to pass from these particularly magnificent engines with the memory of Sir William Pollitt-beautifully picked out with polished brass, burnished steel and shining green paintwork. Sadly, the Great Central Atlantic-the 'Jersey Lily' of music hall fame, has gone for ever.

G.M.Shoults

The 9N quickly established a sound reputation for itself, as such a big, solid and well-thought out design would do. A further batch of six was outshopped from Gorton in 1912, the Locomotive Committee resolving on the 6th October 1911 that....the programme of loco building for the year 1912 shall be as under:- All engines to be fitted with Mr. Robinson's new superheater, 18 at least 8K Class eight wheels coupled leading pony truck, superheating tender engines. Six wheels coupled bogie tender passenger and goods engines (Immingham Class). Six 9N Class six wheels coupled superheater passenger tank engines. Total 30. Five more 9Ns appeared from Gorton during the First War, in 1917. This batch was numbered 371-4 and (alone) 5411. As was inevitable with a class built over a long period, design detail differed. We journey to Guide Bridge again to look at no.371, the first of the wartime engines. Under the cab can be seen the bracket supporting the 'Reliostop' mechanism. This was an early and ingenious attempt at automatic train control. Pioneered by A.F. Bound, the GC Signalling Superintendent and W. Rowland, Robinson's chief locomotive draughtsman, the system consisted of a rubber disc - visible at the base of the arm - which was set to engage a series of ramps in front of distant and stop signals. At a distant signal showing danger, a siren would sound in the cab and a partial brake application would be made. Although the driver could cancel this, it was reinforced by another brake application should the corresponding stop signal be at danger. The driver was unable to cancel this latter part of the sequence thereby, it was hoped, rendering the system foolproof. 'Reliostop' was fitted to 20 engines only and, though it worked well, development was halted at the Grouping. The only obvious drawback was the mechanical nature of its operation which could have left the operating mechanism prone to wear and damage, a feature eschewed by the G.W.R system which was adopted, with modifications, as the B.R. standard. 'Reliostop' was never used in the Manchester area (which shows no.371 as being off her home territory) and was confined to the Marylebone outer suburban lines which these engines had been built to serve. All of the 9Ns built in Great Central days had been allocated to Neasden and the probability is that the engine is running-in from Gorton prior to returning home. Behind 371's bunker is one of the celebrated 'Barnum' coaches. Undoubtedly the child of American practice, these unconventional vehicles had a maximum body width of 9ft.0ins. and measured 60ft.0ins. in length over headstocks.

Collection C.H.Platt

Class 9N 4-6-2 Tank

The second series of Robinson 4-4-2 tanks, the 9L Class - 12 in number - had been delivered in 1907. On July 9th 1909 Robinson pointed out to the Locomotive Committee the existing shortage of tank engines for suburban traffic and stated he would consult the General Manager - Sam Fay - on the subject.

The matter was raised at a meeting of the Great Central Board at London Road, Manchester on August 5th, 1910.

An extract from the minutes of that meeting read as follows:

Subject 26. Programme of locomotive building for next year.

Chairman: *Then looking well ahead and not as in the past leaving things to the last moment with regard to our locomotive building. We want you to approve a programme for 1911. Mr. Fay has been looking very carefully into what we shall require and he has come to the conclusion we want a more powerful tank engine for working our London local traffic and Mr. Robinson agrees that our trains are increasing in weight.*

Mr. Fay: *We want them accelerated, and to start more quickly.....cannot keep ace with the Metropolitan Company......it is an unusual type of engine for Southern service.*

Chairman: *These are on Renewal Account not capital. 30 new engines on Renewal Account next year. Suggest 10 should be of this class. 20 of the biggest eight-wheeled coupled to be rather larger engines than our largest engine today - with superheaters.*

Mr. Beazley: *What will it cost?*

Chairman: *I haven't that; Mr. Robinson gives me figures but all his arrangements are to enable him to build cheaply; you two gentlemen were there yesterday and we are going this afternoon.*

Mr. Viccars: *As usual he wants a little more expenditure and some of it ought to be done. I suppose there would not be superheaters in the tanks?*

Chairman: *Oh yes there will be. It would not be unreasonable if we liked to charge some of the cost to Capital as these eight-wheels coupled are equivalent to two or three of the old type of engine*

The Committee resolved:

After a careful and long discussion, and hearing Mr. Robinson's explanations, it was decided, on the recommendation of the General Manager and Chief Mechanical Engineer, that the programme of locomotive building for the year 1911, on renewal account, be as under:

10 six-wheels coupled tank passenger engines, and 20 eight-wheels coupled goods engines, fitted with superheaters.

In the final analysis, the 10 six-coupled tanks appeared, as the first of the 9Ns. The 20 eight-wheeled goods engines projected for 1911 suffered a shortfall of eight; 9 Class 8K 2-8-0s appearing with the addition of 3 8A 0-8-0s, the last of the class to appear.

9N, no.168, seen at Neasden in the early years of its life. Robinson adopted the Schmidt superheater (as used on the 9J 0-6-0) for the first eight of the ten engines built in 1911. Incidentally, it was the appearance of these first engines that caused some enginemen to dub them 'Coronation Tanks'-George V having been crowned in that year.Imaginatively, the 9Ns were turned out in the superb dark green livery with claret frames above the footplate. This darker colour was relieved with a vermillion line to contrast with the black and white lining applied to the green paintwork elsewhere. Notice here the wheels are lined white, the touch of an artist to complement the main green colour.

Collection of G.H.Platt

Suburban traffic out of Marylebone had been growing steadily. The late Victorian and Edwardian decades had seen the beginnings of the development and expansion of the north-west London suburbs, famed as 'Metro-Land' and later immortalised in the poetry and writings of Sir John Betjeman. Of significance too was the opening in 1906 of the GW & GC Joint Line from Northolt Junction to Ashendon Junction via High Wycombe and Princes Risborough. This cut-off line opened up new territory for the Great Central and provided a more gently-graded route to Aylesbury and the north.

The engine that emerged to cope with this new traffic was the 9N 4-6-2 tank. An almost complete departure from previous essays in this field was made; only the coupled wheel diameter - at 5 ft.7 inches remained the same as in previous series. The most striking feature was the wheel arrangement, the 4-6-2 layout having only appeared on 3 designs at that time: the Worsdell class W and Raven class Y tanks of the N.E.R. in 1907 and 1910 respectively and Churchward's infamous 'Great Bear' on the G.W.R. in 1908

Robinson took advantage of developments with his first 4-4-0s, using the superheated boiler produced for the rebuilt 11B (which became 11D). Thus, a milestone in Great Central locomotive history was reached: the 9N becoming the first design to be sueprheated throughout from new. Piston valves - generously sized at 10 inches

ments was to follow over the next few years; initially on the 9Ns he used the Schmidt system, the first eight of the class - built between March and June 1911 - being so fitted. For the last two built in that year he used his own variation of the apparatus, an 18-element pattern the same as the Schmidt engines.

The second series of Robinson 4-4-2 tanks, the 9L Class-12 in number-had been delivered in 1907. On July 9th 1909 Robinson pointed out to the Locomotive Committee the existing shortage of tank engines for suburban traffic and stated he would consult the General Manager-Sam Fay-on the subject.

The matter was raised at a meeting of the Great Central Board at London Road, Manchester on August 5th.1910.

An extract from the minutes of that meeting read as follows:

*Subject 26. Programme of locomotive building for next year.*Chairman: *Then looking well ahead and not as in the past leaving things to the last moment with regard to our locomotive building. We want you to approve a programme for 1911. Mr.Fay has been looking very carefully into what we shall require and he has come to the conclusion we want a more powerful tank engine for working our London local traffic and Mr.Robinson agrees that our trains are increasing in weight.*

Mr.Fay: *We want them accelerated, and to start more quickly..cannot keep pace with the Metropolitan Com-*

SUMMARY OF CLASS 9N 4 - 6 - 2 TANK (LNER A5)

NUMBER	BUILDER	DATE BUILT	WITHDRAWN
23/24,165-170,447/448	Gorton	March to August 1911	Dec 1942-Nov 1960

This summary covers the 21 engines built to Class 9N in the G.C.era. Engines built for the LNER at Gorton and by Hawthorn, Leslie & Co. will be dealt with in more detail in a subsequent volume.

were provided, admitting steam to 20 x 26 inch cylinders.

The onset of superheating posed problems for locomotive designers in two main respects: one was to provide an adequate lubrication system as the much drier steam at a much higher temperature lacked the almost self-lubricating properties of saturated steam. The Wakefield mechanical lubricator was used on the first of the class and can be seen on in our photograph of No. 168, built in 1911. Eventaully, all the class were fitted with Robinson's own 'Intensifore' system.

The other problem was to find a satisfactory means of keeping the superheater elements cool when steam was shut off. An early Robinson device to obviate this was the steam-operated flue damper which can be seen on the left-hand side of No. 168's smokebox in our first photograph. This fitting was carried by all ten of the class built in 1911. Later batches of 9Ns carried the early pattern of draught retarder whereby steam was blown through the superheater flues from small nozzles when the blower was used.

At this point, Robinson was developing his own ideas in the field of superheating. A positive rash of develop-

pany; ...it is an unusual type of engine for Southern service.

Chairman: *These are on Renewal Account not Capital. 30 new engines on Renewal Account next year.Suggest 10 should be of this class. 20 of the biggest eight-wheeled coupled to be rather larger engines than our largest engines today-with superheaters.*

No.5045 built at Gorton in 1923, one of ten 9Ns completed that year by the LNER.

H.A.White, courtesy of W.A.Brown

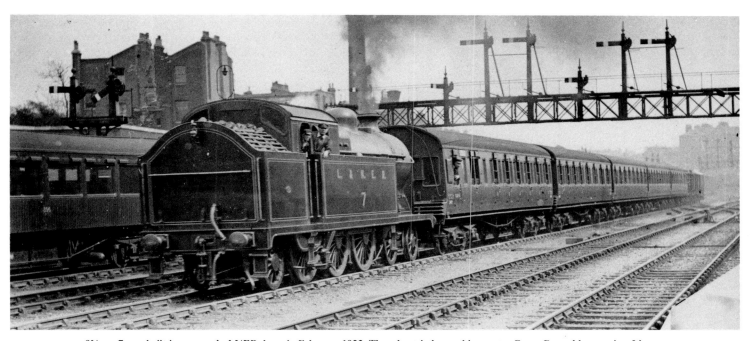

9N no. 7 was built in very early LNER days, in February 1923. Though, strictly speaking, not a Great Central locomotive, I have included this picture for several reasons. Seen thundering out of Marylebone early in its career, the engine is very much on home ground and doing exactly the sort of work the class was conceived for-London suburban traffic. The picture shows splendidly the rear aspect of the class and illustrates the development applied to all the post-Grouping engines and ultimately to the class as a whole, the fitting of side-window cabs. Notice the coaches have Robinson's anti-collision fenders, bulky steel corrugations above the headstocks. Yet another of his innovations, these were designed to prevent telescoping in a collision. Thankfully, this contingency was never tested in practice. No.7 became LNER 5007 in 1924 and no.9822 in the company's 1946 re-numbering. She was withdrawn by British Railways as no.69822 in November 1958.

Collection of G.H.Platt

Class __9N__ Type __4-6-2__ N° of Engines ... __22.__

Maker	Year Built	n° of Engines	Maker	Year Built	n° of Engines	Maker	Year Built	n° of Engines
G. C. R.	1911	10	L. N. E.	1923				
"	1912	6						
"	1917	5						

CYLINDERS.
Diameter ... 20"
Stroke ... 26"
Centres ... 2'0"

BOILER.
Class ... No 4 Standard
Working Pressure ... 180 Lbs. per □"
Barrel Dia. Outs. Max ... 5'0"
Barrel Length ... 11'6"
Barrel Thickness of Plates ... 5/8

TUBES.
Large No. ... 22 Dia. Outs. ... 5¼"
Small No. ... 134 Dia. Outs. ... 1⅞"
Length between Tubeplates ... 11'10⅞"

SUPERHEATER.
Kind of Header ... Front Cover
Elements { Dia. Outs. ... 1⅜"
Dia. Ins. ... 1 1/16"
Number ... 22

IF FITTED WITH
Draft Retarder ...
Circulating Valve ... Yes
Header Discharge Valve ... Yes
Pressure Release Valves ...
Combined Pressure Release } ... Yes
and Piston Valves }

FIREBOX SHELL.
Length Outs. at Bottom ... 7'0"
Width ,, ,, ... 4'0½"
,, ,, ,, Top ... 5'2¾"
Thickness of Plates
Back 7/32 Casing 5/8 Throat ¾"

COPPER FIREBOX.
Length of Grate ... 6'4 15/32"
Width ,, ,, ... 3'4⅛"
Depth to Top of Ring, Front ... 6'7¼"
,, ,, ,, Back ... 5'10½"

Width of Ring.
Back and Front ... 3" Sides ... 3"
Thickness of Plates—
Back 9/16" Casing 9/16" Tube { 7/8"
9/16"

HEATING SURFACE.
Firebox Outside ... 136 Sq. ft.
Large Tubes ... 359 ,,
Small Tubes ... 780 ,,
Superheater Inside ... 178 ,,
Total ... 1453 ,,

GRATE AREA. ... 21 Sq. ft.

WHEELS. Diameter. See Diagram.
Tyres Thickness ... 3"
JOURNALS. Dia. Length.
Leading Bogie or Truck ... 6" 9"
Leading Coupled ...
Driving ... 8" 9"
Intermediate ... 8" 12"
Trailing Coupled ... 8" 12"
Trailing Bogie or Truck ... 8" 14"
Tractive Power at { Lbs. ... 23435
85% Boiler Pressure { Tons ... 10.6
Adhesion Coefficient. Lbs. per Ton ... 440
Height. Rail to Top of Chimney ... 13'3"
,, ,, Centre of Boiler ... 8'10"
VALVES. Kind ... Piston (Ins. admission)
CYLINDER LUBRICATOR. Kind ... Intensifore
If Fitted with Steam Sanding Apparatus ... No
,, ,, Train Warning ,, ... Yes
BRAKE. ... Steam & Auto Ejector & Reliostop
TANK. Capacity. Water, Gallons ... 2280
,, Coal, Tons ... 4¾"
WHEELS. Diameter ...
JOURNALS. Dia. ... Length ...

Mr. Beazley: *What will it cost?* Chairman: *I haven't that; Mr. Robinson gives me figures but all his arrangements are to enable him to build cheaply; you two gentlemen were there yesterday and we are going this afternoon.* Mr. Viccars: *As usual he wants a little more expenditure and some of it ought to be done. I suppose there would not be superheaters in the tanks.*

Chairman: *Oh yes there will be. It would not be unreasonable if we liked to charge some of the cost to Capital as these eight-wheels coupled are equivalent to two or three of the old type of engine.*

The Committee resolved:

After a careful and long discussion, and hearing Mr. Robinson's explanations, it was decided, on the recommendation of the General Manager and Chief Mechanical Engineer, that the programme of locomotive building for the year 1911, on renewal account, be as under:

10 six-wheels coupled tank passenger engines, and 20 eight-wheels coupled goods engines, fitted with superheaters.

In the final analysis, the 10 six-coupled tanks appeared, as the first of the 9Ns. The 20 eight-wheeled goods engines projected for 1911 suffered a shortfall of eight; 9 Class 8K 2-8-0s appearing with the addition of 3 8A 0-8-0s, the last of the class to appear.

Suburban traffic out of Marylebone had been growing steadily. The late Victorian and Edwardian decades had seen the beginnings of the development and expansion of the north-west London suburbs, famed as 'Metro-Land' and later immortalised in the poetry and writings of Sir John Betjeman. Of significance too was the opening in 1906 of the GW & GC Joint Line from Northolt Junction to Ashendon Junction via High Wycombe and Princes Risborough. This cut-off line opened up new territory for the Great Central and provided a more gently-graded route to Aylesbury and the north.

The engine that emerged to cope with this new traffic was the 9N 4-6-2 tank. An almost complete departure from previous essays in this field was made; only the coupled wheel diameter-at 5'-7" remained the same as in prevous series. The most striking feature was the wheel arrangement, the 4-6-2 layout having only appeared on 3 designs at that time: the Worsdell class W and Raven class Y tanks of the North Eastern in 1907 and 1910 respectively and Churchward's infamous *Great Bear* on the Great Western in 1908.

Robinson took advantage of developments with his first 4-4-0s, using the superheated boiler produced for the rebuilt 11B (which became 11D). Thus, a milestone in Great Central locomotive history was reached: the 9N becoming the first design to be superheated throughout from new. Piston valves-generously sized at 10" were provided, admitting steam to 20" X 26" cylinders.

The onset of superheating posed problems for locomotive designers in two main respects: one was to provide an adequate lubrication system as the much drier steam at a much higher temperature lacked the almost self-lubricating properties of saturated steam. The Wakefield mechanical lubricator was used on the

first of the class and can be seen on in our photograph of no. 168, built in 1911. Eventually, all the class were fitted with Robinson's own 'Intensifore' system.

The other problem was to find a satisfactory means of keeping the superheater elements cool when steam was shut off. An early Robinson device to obviate this was the steam-operated flue damper which can be seen on the left-hand side of no. 168's smokebox in our first photograph. This fitting was carried by all ten of the class built in 1911. Later batches of 9Ns carried the early pattern of draught retarder whereby steam was blown through the superheater flues from small nozzles when the blower was used.

At this point, Robinson was developing his own ideas in the field of superheating. A positive rash of developments was to follow over the next few years; initially on the 9Ns he used the Schmidt system, the first eight of the class-built between March and June 1911- being so fitted. For the last two built in that year he used his own variation of the apparatus, an 18-element pattern the same as the Schmidt engines.

The massive bulk of the design, weighing in at 85 tons, 18 cwt in working order, will be observed at a glance. Length over buffers was 42'11⅞" and height from rail level to chimney top measured 13'3" (a 'Duchess' Pacific was a mere 13'2⅝"!!) Robinson fitted top feeds to the later series of 9Ns, devices rare on British locomotives of that period-certainly outside of Swindon, in whose practices Robinson had been schooled of course. Though top feeds were carried by many of the 9Ns, the device was eventually removed. Sticking 'clack' valves are reported as having been the main source of trouble, though a contemporary observer noted fracturing of pipes and valves due to their having been attacked in a rather brusque fashion by enginemen wielding coal hammers! 'Pop' safety valves were later fitted in lieu of the cased Ramsbottom pattern of the pre-War engines. Maximum use of platform width was made to accommodate water tanks which held 2280 gallons. The class were built with water pick-up gear which lasted until early B.R. days when it was removed. Subtly, Robinson curved in the platform to avoid any unnecessary appearance of bulk, one of his skilfull touches that so helped to balance his designs and make them look 'right.'

A contemporary account of the of the class, after its introduction, taken from 'The Railway Engineer' of June, 1911 gives some useful technical details and is of interest in its own right: *We illustrate herewith the new 4-6-2 Tank Engines which have recently been built at the Great Central Railway's locomotive works at Gorton to the designs of Mr. J.G. Robinson, M.Inst.C.E., the chief mechanical engineer, and which have been specially designed, at the desire of Mr. Sam Fay, the general manager, with rapid accelerating powers to cope with the growing traffic of the suburban lines out of Marylebone into North Middlesex and Buckinghamshire, and which is one of the most beautiful residential districts round London.*

The engines will also be used for the trains from London to Leicester and Nottingham over the two joint lines via

Aylesbury and High Wycombe and for some of the excursions. Ten of them have been built.

The wheel arrangement is new in this country, and gives great tractive power and an easy running engine.

In spite of the long wheel-base of 32'-9" the engine will readily pass through a 5-chain curve, as the bogie has been allowed the somewhat unusual range of 6½", the frames being cut away to allow it to run below them. The radial axle has a cross travel of 3½" and is controlled by springs as shown in the drawing.

The cab, which is built up to the limits of the loading gauge, is very roomy and provides an excellent outlook in both directions in spite of the large size of the boiler and its height (8' 10") above the rails.

The boiler and most of the other important parts of the engine being interchangeable with other standard modern classes of Gt. Central engines the cost of maintenance will be considerably reduced.

The boiler is fitted with a superheater having 18 elements.

Cast steel is largely used, the bogie centres, superheater header, steam pipes, frame stays, horn-blocks, spring hangers, wheel centres and rear pony truck frame being all of this material.

The motion is entirely of mild steel except some of the pins, which are of wrought-iron case-hardened.

The axles are of steel, the crank axle having elliptical checks surrounded with wrought-iron hoops.

The boiler tubes are of steel.

the boiler works at 160 lbs.per sq.in., and is fitted with four 4 in.safety valves.

Hitherto Gt.Central R.engines have worked at a pressure of 180lbs.per sq.in., but Mr.Robinson's experience during the past 18 months with a goods engine fitted with a superheater has led hime to the conclusion that a big saving in firebox repairs can be effected by using a lower pressure in conjunction with highly superheated steam.

The superheater tube ends open into a damper box, the doors of which are automatically opened by a small cylinder which is supplied with steam from the main steam pipe. this ensures that the superheating pipes shall not be overheated when steam is not passing through them.

The smokebox is of ample capacity, and is fitted with louvre plates on the door to throw down cinders, and with a spray pipe at each end through which steam can be blown to lift the accumulated ashes into the influence of the blast, by which they are ejected as required.

The boiler is fed by one 9 m/m and one 10 m/m combination injectors.

The cylinders, which are 20" by 26" stroke, have inside admission piston valves 10" diam. on top worked by secondary Stephenson link motion.

The piston rods are carried forward into dummy glands on the front covers.

Valves, pistons and piston rod dummy glands are connected up to a Wakefield 8-way mechanical lubricator driven from the left-hand crosshead.

The coupled wheels are 5ft.7ins. diam., a size which, though being large enough to permit of high speeds, is not too big to allow of a high starting effort, and consequent combination without necessitating abnormal stresses in the crank axle, horn-blocks, etc.

Water tanks have a capacity of 2,280 gallons, and are fitted with a pick-up to work in either direction.

The engines have steam brakes to the coupled wheels, worked in combination with the Vacuum Brake Co.'s latest combination ejector for the automatic train brake, and is fitted with the necessary fittings for train warming........ .

High, wide and certainly handsome, the Robinson 4-6-2 tank was a successful and well-liked design. Their success can surely be measured by their perpetuation in post-1923 days, a further 10 were built at Gorton in the first half of that year. Doubtless these would have been ordered in any event by the Great Central and no attempt was made to bring them from the generous G.C.loading gauge to LNER standards. In the years 1925-26, Hawthorn,Leslie & Co. of Newcastle-on -Tyne built a further 13 engines-now classified A5. Some modifications were made to the original design; externally these hinged around alterations to boiler mountings, cab roof and width of tanks and bunker to bring them within the designated LNER standard loading gauge. Mechanically, longer-travel valves were used with the size of the piston valve reduced from 10" diameter to 8". Though this sounds strange, the reasons probably hinged around standardisation as the same cylinder design was adopted for the LNER standard 0-6-0 goods designs of Class J38 and J 39 introduced at the same time. These 1925 engines were required for work on the ex-North Eastern section and it must seem a compliment to Robinson that his design was chosen by Gresley as opposed to that of either Worsdell or Raven. This second LNER batch would have been distinguished at the time by their side-window cabs which eventually became standard for the whole class, although one engine no.450, had been dealt with in this manner in 1921.

Largely unmodified over the years, the 9Ns soldiered on well into the B.R.era. Well-remembered is the sight of them, albeit somewhat grimy and in prosaic black livery, slogging their way up the bank of the Fairfield Loop Line from Chorlton Junction to Guide Bridge with Liverpool to Harwich and Hull Boat Trains in the 1950s. There was something very special about the sight of these giant tank engines even if it was a product of youthful admiration.

Perhaps surprisingly, it was engines from the Great Central batches that survived the longest. One engine, G.C.no.447, was withdrawn in 1942 having suffered severely cracked frames. Withdrawal in B.R.days began in 1957 and was completed by the end of 1960.

278's frontal aspects show off the Robinson chimney, a corroded rim suggesting a later G.C. period. The very unusually-shaped buffer beam consists of a wooden plank faced with steel. Looking like an afterthought, the buffer casings resemble those fitted to coaching stock.
Collection of G.H.Platt

Class 4 Type 0.6.0. N⁰ of Engines ... 2.

Makers	Year Built	N⁰ of Engines	Makers	Year Built	N⁰ of Engines	Makers	Year Built	N⁰ of Engines
Manning Wardle	1876	1	Engine 407ᴮ					
Hudswell Clarke	1909	1	" 278					

Contractors Engines. Particulars below refer to Engines 407ᴮ ▬▬ For other 4 Class, see Page

CYLINDERS.
Diameter .... 14"
Stroke .... 20"
Centres .... 2'-4"

BOILER.
Class 4
Working Pressure .... 130 .. Lbs. per □"
Barrel Dia. Outs. Max. ... 3'-6"
Barrel Length .... 9'-1⅜
Barrel Thickness of Plates .... ½"

TUBES.
Large No. ... — .. Dia. Outs. ... —
Small No. ... 124 .. Dia. Outs. ... 1¾"
Length between Tubeplates ..... 9'-6"

SUPERHEATER.
Kind of Header ....
Elements { Dia. Outs. ....
{ Dia. Ins. ....
{ Number ....

IF FITTED WITH
Draft Retarder ....
Circulating Valve ....
Header Discharge Valve ....
Pressure Release Valves ....
Combined Pressure Release } ....
and Piston Valves }

FIREBOX SHELL.
Length Outs. at Bottom ...... 3'-11"
Width ,, ,, ,, ... 3'-6"
,, ,, ,, Top .... 4'-0¾"
Thickness of Plates—
Back ½" ...Casing ½" Throat ⅝"

COPPER FIREBOX.
Length of Grate .... 3'-3¾"
Width ,, ... 2'-11"
Depth to Top of Ring, Front 4'-4¼"
,, ,, ,, Back 4'-4¼"

Width of Ring.
Back and Front 2½" .. Sides 2½"
Thickness of Plates--
Back 9/16" ..Casing ½" .. Tube { ¾"
{ 9/16"

HEATING SURFACE.
Firebox Outside .... 52 .. Sq. ft.
Large Tubes .... ,,
Small Tubes .... 540 .. ,,
Superheater Inside.............. — ,,
Total 592 ,,

GRATE AREA. .... 9½ .. Sq. ft.

WHEELS. Diameter. See Diagram.
Tyres Thickness .... 3'
JOURNALS. Dia. Length.
Leading Bogie or Truck ....
Leading Coupled .... 5½" 6¾"
Driving .... 5½" 6¾"
Intermediate ....
Trailing Coupled .... 5½" 6¾"
Trailing Bogie or Truck ....
Tractive Power at { Lbs. 9,626
85% Boiler Pressure { Tons .... 4·3
Adhesion Coefficient. Lbs. per Ton 364
Height. Rail to Top of Chimney ... 11'-8½"
,, ,, Centre of Boiler ...... 6'-0"

VALVES. Kind.... Unbalanced Slide

CYLINDER LUBRICATOR. Kind ....
If Fitted with Steam Sanding Apparatus ...... no
,, ,, Train Warming ,, ... no

BRAKE. .... Hand
~~TENDER~~ Tank. Capacity. Water, Gallons 1300
,, Coal, Tons ... 1 Ton 5cwts.

WHEELS. Diameter............
JOURNALS. Dia. .... — Length..... —

Class 4
0-6-0 Saddle Tank

In June 1911 the G.C.R. took into its locomotive stock an 0-6-0 saddletank, one Humber, an engine built by Hudswell, Clarke & Co. in 1909 for the Grimsby and Immingham Light Railway. Humber was grouped under the umbrella of 'Class 4', a rather loose classification which encompassed a mixed bag of 4 and 6-coupled former contractors' shunters in the Grimsby and Immingham areas. Nine of these had been withdrawn between 1903 and 1907; of the survivors, three were 0-6-0s of the saddletank variety and two were 0-4-0s. The latter lasted into LNER days to become Class Y2.

Humber became G.C.R. No. 278 in December 1911.

Reference to the Class 18T saddletanks will recall that No. 18 of that class was withdrawn in December 1910. The number 278 was carried in the interim by one of the two 0-4-0 saddletanks referred to.

Coupled wheels of just 3'-1½" were fitted to no.278; notice the slender coupling rods, the bearings are of the split pattern with gib and cotter adjustment-a hangover from earlier MS&L practice.

278 survived Grouping to become, along with the former no.407B, one of only two members of Class J61. A unique little engine, she was withdrawn, as LNER no.5278, in April 1931.

The dimunitive, yet attractive, no.278 spent its life on dock shunting duties around the ports of Grimsby and Immingham. Strictly functional in appearance, 278 had none of the comparative suavity that graced each of the other two Great Central dock shunting classes-5 and 5A.In this picture 278 pauses along the dockside at Grimsby in what appear to be the most dilapidated surroundings. A remnant of G.C. livery remains, some lining being just visible on the bunker and cab sides, even the running number is only feintly discernible.

Collection of G.H.Platt

The powerful, workmanlike and yet majestic form of the Robinson 8K 2-8-0 revealed in a somewhat begrimed no.379 standing at Stalybridge around the time of World War I. An immediate resemblance to the earlier 8A 0-8-0 is detected, but whereas the previous freight engine had a rather unbalanced look at the front end this imbalance had been avoided with the 2-8-0. 379 was one of 11 8Ks built at Gorton in 1913; the top feed is in front of the dome, a feature not present in the first engines, but appearing on nos. 385-399 turned out from Gorton in 1913-1914 . The fitting was applied retrospectively to the earlier locomotives but not, be it noted to the R.O.D. series. The Belpaire firebox, a now well-established Great Central standard, shows a 'waisted' form below the bottom of the boiler barrel. Earlier designs such as the first 4-6-0s and Atlantics had exhibited a straight side to the firebox which was actually a cosmetic appendage. With the arrival of the 8K this 'waisted' effect became visible; in the case of *Sir Sam Fay* and its successors the waisting was incorporated skilfully into the design by careful blending into the splasher panel. In later years, under LNER auspices, many of the Robinson 2-8-0s were rebuilt with round-topped fireboxes of Doncaster origin with associated alterations to cab, superheater, boiler mountings and other details. This wholesale rebuilding activity, to provide a wide variety of sub-classes was rivalled in complexity only by the Great Eastern *Claud Hamilton* 4-4-0 rebuilds. Such details will be described in a subsequent volume.

Collection of G.H.Platt

Class 8K 2-8-0

A former LNER engine driver was asked 'Which type of heavy goods engine was the best one you drove in your career?' Unequivocally came the reply: 'The Robinson 04 of the Great Central.' As an ex-Great Northern man the driver might well have favoured the Gresley 01 or 02 or even the Ivatt 'Long Tom' - GNR K1 0-8-0 (LNER Q1 and Q2).

That driver was Bill Johnson who began his career on the Great Northern at Manchester's Trafford Park shed in 1912. Driver Johnson spent the greater part of his career driving freight trains over the GC's Woodhead route in LNER days when, of course, the Robinson 2-8-0 was the staple motive power of such traffic. Then classed as 04 these engines remained unchallenged as prime movers of freight over Woodhead until the line was electrified under the Manchester-Sheffield-Wath scheme in 1954.

In Bill Johnson's opinion the Robinson engines were excellent steamers and even during the weary years of World War II when maintenance was limited he recalled the 2-8-0s giving him little or no trouble. Using the colloqualism of 'Tinies' (a name also given to the 8A 0-8-0) he records no instance of ever slipping to a halt in the satanic confines of Woodhead Tunnel. It was the passage through this tunnel that gave rise to truly horrendous conditions for footplate men. Johnson recalls occasions when smoke was such a problem that if an engine was in 'poor nick' it was not uncommon for the driver and his mate to tie a handkerchief round their faces, open the regulator wide, get down on the cab floor and hope for the best!

Robinson's 8K 2-8-0 had its origins in his 8A 0-8-0 introduced as far back as 1902 and built up to 1911 to number 89 engines. The need for a bigger goods engine arose out of the anticipated rise in coal and mineral traffic that would ensue when the GC's colossal Immingham Dock complex opened in July 1912.

It was the opening of the port facilities at Immingham and the ensuing rise in traffic that brought about the need for a heavy goods engine of the size of the 8K. Reference is made elsewhere in this book to the vastness of this Humber port and at this point in the locomotive history mention of Immingham's capacity will give some idea of the loco power required to operate the traffic from there.

A wide variety of cargo could be dealt with at Immingham. Described by contemporary sources as 'the finest coal port in the North of England' eight hydraulic hoists could each load 700 tons of coal per hour. Storage and other sidings were provided capable of holding 150,000 to 170,000 tons of coal. Empty wagon capacity for about 5,500 coal wagons was also provided. Figures for the rapid loading of coal were impressive. The Great Central boasted 2,800 tns of coal shipped aboard the S.S. Zuid Holland in 7½ hours. During the year 1913, over 2¼ million tons of coal were shipped from the port.

Coal shipment was however only part of Immingham's story. Elaborate arrangements had been put in hand for dealing with pig iron, iron ore, wood pulp, timber, pit props and other cargo. A grain elevator of 15,000 tons capacity was available, whilst the import of wool from Australia was to flourish at Immingham also - the port being ideally located for the West Riding of Yorkshire. A dockside warehouse with a capacity of 40,000 bales was established, 21,000 bales being landed in 1914. At the time of Immingham's opening, iron and steel production in the neigbouring Frodingham district was expanding. To feed this the GC were able to cope with a record discharge of 4,427 tons of iron ore in 43 hours from the S.S. Porjus.

With the opening of Immingham as a backdrop, a water area of upwards of 45 acres and 170 miles of running lines and sidings, the company had found the right tool for the job in Robinson's 8K 2-8-0. Lamentably though, it was the agonies of war that were to provide for the multiplication of the engine on a grand scale that could never have been foreseen by its designer.

Taking the 8A as a successful foundation, Robinson enlarged the boiler, shared with the Class 8 'Fish Engines' of 1902. The diameter was increased from 4ft 3ins to 5ft 0ins. Boilers in steam days were usually rolled up from steel plate into a series of rings. that for the 8K 2-8-0 was made from plate in three telescoping rings; the largest, in front of the firebox, being 5ft in diameter. The length of the barrel remained at 15ft whilst the firebox was increased in length from 7ft 9ins outside to 8ft 6ins in the new design. Working pressure was 180lbs p.s.i. though the boiler had been designed to operate at 200lbs., pitch above rail level was 8'-6½". Under the Great Central classification the boiler was designated 'No. 6 Standard'.

The new goods engine thus had a boiler of outline dimensions similar to that provided for the Atlantics. Considerable differences existed internally however, notably in the number of firetubes and in the provision of superheating - applied new with the 2-8-0s and fitted only retrospectively to the Atlantics.

A Robinson 18-element superheater, an early type applied the first 9N tanks, was fitted to no. 966 when built in September 1911. Thereafter, Robinson used the Schmidt apparatus on a further nine engines before reverting to his own type for future construction. Schmidt fitted engines were later turned over to Robinson's apparatus also. Progressing from the original 18-element superheater, a move was made to the 24-element variety, as used on the first Atlantic, in engines built up to 1914. A further switch was made, when in 1916 the 22-element apparatus was standardised for the whole class (as per the 1923 engine diagram); the 18-element system becoming obsolete and some engines being converted from 24 to 22 elements. Pressure of armanents work at Gorton in the First World War caused three 8Ks to become saturated engines for a period i.e. nos. 1208/1240 and 1252 were fitted with non-superheater boilers in early 1917 and did not receive superheaters again until 1920 (nos. 1208 and 1240) and 1919 (no. 1252).

Coupled wheels of 4'-8" diameter, the same as those used on the 8A 0-8-0 were used. Cylinders for the 2-8-0 were sized at 21ins bore 2ins wider than in the 8A design and used the almost universal stroke of 26ins. 10inch piston valves were provided, driven from the third coupled axle by the ubiquitous Stephenson valve gear. Motion both inside and outside were common to the 8A class also. The highly successful cylinder configuration was later implanted into Atlantics, 8A 0-8-0s. 8G and 8N 4-6-0s.

In its construction overall, the 8K was almost wholly straightforward. The design was simple, made no use of unconventional features and, above all, was solid and very well engineered. Mainframes, machined from 1¼" steel plate were massively braced at the front end by the cylinders, inclined with the valves at an angle of 1 in 24. Side play for the front coupled axle was made available by bending the mainframes inwards immediately ahead of the second coupled wheel. The cylinders, with valve chests integral, were cast in two separate halves, one for each side of the engine. A rectangular space was cut in the main frames through which the valve chests were inserted. The casting was then bolted around the hole in the frames, the two abutting faces of the steam chests - along the centre line of the locomotive were then being bolted together. This solid mass also acted as a support for the smokebox tubeplate. Adding support and guid-

ing this was the pony truck pivoted from the leading driving axle with 6ins side play and sprung via lateral laminated and two underslung coil springs.

Tenders fitted to all but three of the 8K class were of the standard Robinson 4000 gallon variety with water scoop. Some of the class ran with earlier pattern tenders equipped with coal rails. The rails were later plated over, though some dealt with in LNER days had the plating fitting to the inside of the rails, leaving these still visible. Coal capacity was a nominal 6 tons, but the tenders fitted to the ROD engines (which had no water scoop) had a recorded coal capacity of 7 tons. Nos. 377/380 and 382 were coupled to 3250 gallon tenders for a period in late GC days, but all had been re-equipped with bigger tenders by 1925.

Construction of the new goods engines began at Gorton in September 1911, thirty locomotives being delivered by the end of 1912. On October 4th 1912 Robinson spoke to the Locomotive Carriage & Wagon Committee on the subject of engine renewals for 1913. Referring to the 8K design, he proceeded ...*With regard to the eight wheels coupled mineral engines of Gorton build, 28 have been turned out to the present and we are going on with 12; and as the Committee will be aware, 70 of the same type were ordered from the North British Locomotive Co. and Messrs Kitson & Co. all of which, according to contract, should be delivered by the end of the present year. When these orders are completed, including those under construction at Gorton, the company will have a total of 197 eight wheels coupled mineral engines. It is therefore a matter for consideration whether in the 1914*

A view at Guide Bridge of 8K no.1234 fitted with a Caille-Potonie feed-water heater. This curious-looking apparatus was fitted to the engine in June 1921 and the engine is seen running with this attached at Guide Bridge. The heater, one of many such contrivances invented to improve the very low thermal efficiency of the steam locomotive, took exhaust steam from the blastpipe in the manner of an injector. Passing through the base of the smokebox, in the arrangement observed here, the exhaust steam passed through a grease separator and was then fed along a large diameter pipe lying above the splashers to a box-type heater directly under the cab. The pre-heated water was then pumped into the boiler via the locomotive's top feed. The apparatus did not find continued favour and was removed at the end of 1923.

Collection of G.H.Platt

8K no.8 stands in the siding roads adjacent to Ashton Moss South Junction. At this location the Great Central owned capacious sorting sidings related to the movement of trans-Pennine freight where the 2-8-0s would have been a very familiar sight. The Junction was formed with the Oldham, Ashton & Guide Bridge joint line from Guide Bridge to Oldham. This affair, managed by the G.C. and LNWR connected with the L&Y's Ashton Branch by means of a sharp curve from Ashton Moss South round to Ashton Moss North on the L&Y line itself.No.8 was a product of the wartime production of the R.O.D.series of 2-8-0s. Gorton Works, fully occupied with armaments production, built only three of these engines; six were to have been constructed but the Locomotive Committee agreed on April 11th 1919 to cancel the remaining three and to take those already built into the company's account. Like many of her classmates, no.8 was rebuilt with a round-topped boiler of the Doncaster pattern from Class 02. Becoming part of Class 04/5 in 1932 and then 04/8 (with a modified tube layout) in 1955. She was withdrawn as British Railways no.63628 in September 1965.

Collection of G.H.Platt

programme a further lot of engines of this type should be constructed...

At this juncture it is worthwhile including the details of arrangements entered into by the Great Central and the North British Loco Company regarding the order for 50 8K engines considered in February 1912. The GC negotiated a hire-purchase agreement for payment of the locomotives, priced at £4,500 each. Recorded in the Locomotive, Carriage & Wagon Committee mnutes as 'deferred payment principle', the North British Company agreed to charge the GC interest at 3⅝% without guarantee for the payment of half-yearly instalments. (North British, thou shouldst be living at this hour!) Four engines were to be delivered by August 15th 1912 and 12 per month thereafter until the contract was completed.The payment was to be spread over 10 equal half-yearly instalments commencing January lst. 1913. Accrued interest was due half-yearly. The North British stated they would have to put tenders out to sub-contractors such was the quantity of material required. Ever-canny, the Great Central requested a list of such firms for approval by the General Manager and the contract was let subject to such approval forthcoming.

Robinson went on to say that the company's coal traffic was continually on the increase and that the Superintendent of the Line could find use for many more eight-wheeled goods engines than were available. Significantly, Robinson also complained of congestion in block sections on busy parts of the railway, delays occuring due to the low speeds around 15/20 mph,

maintained by the heavy freight engines. A suggestion is made by him that a higher powered six-wheeled goods engine could easily be built using standard components and highly superheated steam. This proposal which would have produced a super-powered 9J ('Pom-Pom') suggests an improvement of 30% in power over existing designs. In the event, of course, such an engine was never built, the First War intervening. What did happen was the production of a large-boilered 2-8-0, class 8M delivered towards the end of the War, in January 1918. Discussion of this engine will be entered into in a subsequent volume.

Mention of the First War brings into play the role of the Robinson 2-8-0 on a much broader front (literally) than the designer could ever have anticipated. It was the great conflict of 1914/1918 that threw up the need for a heavy goods locomotive to work behind the lines on the Continent. Mention is made elsewhere of the supply of 8A and 9J locomotives to sustain the War effort in France and a good many other companies similarly loaned engines to assist abroad in these dire times.

Partly because of political problems in France and Belgium and the fact that something like about 600 locomotives were already on loan from British railway companies, including the GC, it was not until 1916 that a decision was made by the British Ministry of Munitions to select the Robinson 8K 2-8-0 as the standard locomotive for the Railway Operating Department.

This department of the British Army's Royal Engineers had been formed in the First War and had begun

Class ... 8K.   Type ... 2.8.0   Nº of Engines ... 129.

G.C.R.	1911	9	North British	1912	48	G.C.R.	1914	15
"	1912	21	" "	1913	2	"	1919	3
Kitson	1912	20	G.C.R.	1913	11			

CYLINDERS.
Diameter .... 21"
Stroke .... 26"
Centres .... 6'.8"

BOILER.
Class ... Nº 6 Standard
Working Pressure ...... 180 Lbs. per □"
Barrel Dia. Outs. Max. ...... 5'.0"
Barrel Length ...... 15'.0"
Barrel Thickness of Plates ...... 5/8"

TUBES.
Large No. 22 ... Dia. Outs. 5¼"
Small No. 110 ... Dia. Outs. 2"
Length between Tubeplates ... 15' 4⅜"

SUPERHEATER.
Kind of Header ... Front Cover
Elements { Dia. Outs. 1⅜"
       Dia. Ins. 1 1/16"
       Number 22

IF FITTED WITH
Draft Retarder ....
Circulating Valve ...... Yes
Header Discharge Valve ...... Yes
Pressure Release Valves ....
Combined Pressure Release } Yes
   and Piston Valves

FIREBOX SHELL.
Length Outs. at Bottom ...... 8'.4"
Width   "   " ...... 4'.0½"
   "   "   Top ...... 5'.2¾"
Thickness of Plates—
   Back 21/32" Casing 5/8" Throat 9/4"

COPPER FIREBOX.
Length of Grate ...... 7'.9 5/8"
Width   " ...... 3'.4⅛"
Depth to Top of Ring, Front ... 6'.5½"
   "   "   Back ... 5'.3"

Width of Ring.
Back and Front ...... 3"   Sides ... 3"
Thickness of Plates—
   Back 9/16" Casing 9/16" Tube { 7/8"
                 9/16"

HEATING SURFACE.
Firebox Outside ...... 154 Sq. ft.
Large Tubes ...... 464 "
Small Tubes ...... 885 "
Superheater Inside ...... 242 "
       Total   1745 "

GRATE AREA. ...... 26 Sq. ft.

WHEELS. Diameter. See Diagram.
Tyres   Thickness ...... 3½"

JOURNALS.   Dia.   Length.
Leading Bogie or Truck ...... 6"   9"
Leading Coupled ...... 8"   9"
Driving ...... 8½"   9"
Intermediate ...... 8"   9"
Trailing Coupled ...... 8"   12"
Trailing Bogie or Truck ......

Tractive Power at { Lbs. 30813
85% Boiler Pressure { Tons 13.75
Adhesion Coefficient. Lbs. per Ton ... 465
Height. Rail to Top of Chimney ... 13' 3½"
   "   Centre of Boiler ... 8'.6½"

VALVES. Kind Piston (Ins. Admission)

CYLINDER LUBRICATOR. Kind Mechanical
If Fitted with Steam Sanding Apparatus ... No
   "   Train Warming   " ... Yes

BRAKE. Steam & Auto Ejector

TENDER. Capacity. Water, Gallons 4000
   "   Coal, Tons 6

WHEELS. Diameter ...... 4'.4"

JOURNALS. Dia. ... 6" Length ...... 11"

Pictures of R.O.D. 2-8-0s will be presented in the next volume in this series. As a taster, here is a view of one such engine to give the reader a view of this historic locomotive for comparative purposes. R.O.D. no.2124 had been built by the North British Loco.Co. at their Queen's Park Works Glasgow in 1919, part of a batch of 50 and one of the penultimate batch to be built. The principal differences in the R.O.D.version were: steel instead of copper plate for the inner fireboxes which, incidentally, saved nearly 1 ton in weight. This move, obviously made on grounds of cost, never found undue favour in the U.K., many of the surplus engines purchased after the war had their steel fireboxes replaced by the conventional copper plate. No water pickup was fitted to the ROD engines and other detail differences were Ross 'Pop' safety valves, small rectangular numberplates, and ribbed taper- shank buffers. To suit Continental practice, side chains were fitted either side of the draw hook and screw jacks were furnished, carried on each side of the smokebox. Operationally and visually, the most singular change was the provision of the Westinghouse donkey pump for the air brakes, carried prominently on the right-hand side of the smokebox. The first batch of engines carried both Westinghouse and steam brakes. Those ordered in between February and August 1918 had only Westinghouse equipment as previously described.In sparkling condition, no.2124 stands outside Strawberry Hill sheds on the LSWR. Revealing her N.B.parentage, a diamond-shaped works plate is carried on the splasher. She presents a fine sight standing in front of a sister engine and amongst the strange bedfellows of the southern company. Sadly, this locomotive saw little in the way of an active life. It did not work overseas, and was loaned to the LSWR in November 1919. From July 1920 until May 1925 2124 was stored at Stratton, near Swindon, one of many 'dumping' sites around the country where the war-surplus engines were laid up. Purchased by the GWR in June 1925, the engine was withdrawn by that company at the end of 1929.

Collection of G.H.Platt

operations in France and Belgium in 1916. The acronym ROD was to become firmly established in railway parlance in later years and in similar vein, present day enthusiasts can refer to the Riddles 2-8-0s and 2-10-0s built for the Ministry of Supply that saw service from World War II into the latter days of BR steam.

Though the Robinson 2-8-0 had been thoroughly well established before the First War began, it had two powerful backers from its home stable, one was Sir Sam Fay, currently deployed as Director of War Transport, the other was Mr. G.S. Lynde who was serving as chief of the ROD's workshops which were situated at Audruicq in North East France between Calais and St. Homer. Lynde was a former Gorton apprentice who later became CME of the New Zealand Government Railways.

SUMMARY OF CLASS 8K 2 - 8 - 0 (LNER O4)

NUMBER	BUILDER	DATE BUILT	WITHDRAWN
26/69/93,102/133/155, 331-335,400/402/408,966	Gorton	September 1911 to May 1912	Aug 1959-Oct 1965
346 - 355	Gorton	June to September 1912	Apr 1959-Dec 1962
1183 - 1202	Kitson & Co.	July to October 1912	Jul 1959-Jul 1965
1203 - 1252	North British Loco Co.	August 1912 to January 1913	Feb 1959-Oct 1965
375 - 384	Gorton	April to September 1913	Jul 1962-Jun 1965
271,385-399	Gorton	December 1913 to June 1914	Mar 1959-Nov 1965
1/5/8	Gorton	January to March 1919	See notes

Notes:
1) Nos.1/5 and 8 were built as part of an ROD order.
2) Withdrawal dates shown relate to engines remaining in British Railways stock. A total of 25 8Ks and 67 of the ROD engines were sold to the War Department in December 1943 for service in the Middle east, Iran and Russia. The erstwhile G.C.R. nos.1202 and 1335 were lost at sea en route. All were taken out of LNER stock and none returned to the U.K.
3) Nos.5/69,1215 and 1222 (along with one of the ROD series) were requisitioned for service in Egypt in 1952. Like their earlier counterparts, they too remained abroad.
4) Nos.1 and 8 were withdrawn as BR nos.63626 and 63628 in June 1961 and September 1965 respectively.

The crew of 8K 2-8-0 no.1206 gaze intently at the photographer as their engine stands on the Down no.1 Loop outside Guide Bridge close to Ashton Junction at the head of a coal working. This locomotive was built by the North British Loco.Co. in August 1912 and was the fourth of a series of 50 built by them up to the beginning of 1913. Prominent on the side of the smokebox is the superheater header discharge valve. This was a Robinson-inspired device which, linked to the regulator, caused steam from the superheater header to be directed to the base of the blastpipe when the former was closed. The device was removed from the class in LNER days and replaced by Gresley's somewhat simpler arrangement of a snifting valve behind the chimney to give the superheater elements protection from overheating when steam was shut off.

Collection of G.H.Platt

Construction of the ROD series began quickly and a total of 233 engines had been ordered by the end of June 1917. The first one, ROD no. 1801 one of an initial batch of 141 locomotives from the North British Loco Co. was handed over in September 1917 for immediate service in France. Perhaps surprisingly, the Great Central only built three of the ROD 2-8-0s and these were never regarded as deliveries to the Government being taken into the company's stock and numbered 1, 5 and 8. The biggest supplier by far was the North British Locomotive Co.with 369. Robert Stephenson & Co. with 82, Nasmyth Wilson & Co. (like Beyer, Peacock a Manchester based concern) built 32 engines and Kitsons of Leeds built 32. Locomotives were still being turned out after the Armistice up to 1920 in fact, to sustain an industry geared up to wartime production and otherwise starved of materials and work.

Largely because of the very widespread dispersal of the Robinson ROD engines after the war, not only to British companies but to overseas ones as well, this locomotive has probably seen service in more countries than almost any other. These peregrinations extended into the Second War as well, Robinson's famous desgn finding its way into the USSR, via Iran. Disposal of the engines took place from 1919 onwards and it was not until 1927 that the final few were cleared. It should be recorded that this tardiness had nothing to do with the engines as such but only that the Government of the day, who were the owners, were asking the exhorbitant price of up to £12,000 per engine secondhand in 1921; this is

notwithstanding the building price of about £6,000 - £8,000 for each engine when new! At this juncture it is perhaps relevent to quote that the Kitson and North British 2-8-0s of 1912 cost the GC £4,550 and £4,512 each respectively.

Some ROD 2-8-0s were loaned to British railway companies, including the Great Central after the First War and were duly returned. The actual sale and disposal is complicated and goes beyond the scope of this work, the minutes of this being faithfully recorded elsewhere*.

Principally the ROD engines were bought by the LNWR, GWR and only naturally, the GCR themselves who purchased three currently under construction in their own works. Minor purchasers included the L&Y LSWR and SECR. Apart from the GC engines only those owned by the Great Western lasted into the latter days of BR to 1958. In deference to the Robinson desgn it has to be said that not all railways had widespread use for such a heavy goods engine and that the Great Central's generous loading gauge was, doubtless, an inhibiting factor in the locomotives usefulness.

The Robinson 8K became the standard heavy goods workhorse of the Great Central. The raison d'etre of the class was, as described, the construction of the new port facilities at Immingham and the necesary movement in

(*Heavy Goods Engines of the War Department. Vol l. ROD. 2-8-0 - J.W.P. Rowledge. Springmead Railway Books 1977)

The obverse side of no.1234 at the same time as the previous view. Careful scrutiny of the original photograph reveals the box of the Caille-Potonie apparatus under the opposite side of the cab. The fitting visible beneath the right hand cabside is a twin vertical pump working in conjunction with the feed-water heater to supply the heated water to the top feed; an inspection door has been fitted beneath the numberplate. No.1234 had been built by the North British Loco. Co. in November 1912. An otherwise straightforward specimen, she became LNER Class 04 no.6234 as late as 1927. Later re-numbered 3581, the engine lasted until February 1959 when it was withdrawn by British Railways as no.63581.

Collection of G.H.Platt

No.69 was the third 8K to be built, emerging from Gorton in December 1911. Continuing largely unmodified as LNER 04/1 no.5069, she was re-numbered 3580 in 1947. In 1952, along with four others of the class, she was 'called up' for military duties in the Middle East. The engine was shipped to Adabiya in Egypt and named *Whitehall* on arrival there. Following the British withdrawal in Egypt in the wake of the Suez crisis, the five 2-8-0s were handed over to The Egyptian State Railways. It is thought they lasted in service until 1961.

Collection of G.H.Platt

and out of freght, especially coal and minerals. In consequence it was to the northern and midland sections of the system that the 8Ks were sent initially. During the First War, three engines were despatched to Neasden for working coal trains to London with some movement of these to Woodford by around 1920. At the end of 1922 Mexborough shed had the largest contingent of the class with 58 locomotives allocated, Annesley and Gorton had 24 each, Staveley (north east of Chesterfield) had 9, Neepsend (Sheffield) had 8. Immingham shed was allotted 6 8Ks and, finally, Keadby (west of Scunthorpe) had just 2.

After Grouping, augmented by War-surplus ROD engines, the class began to penetrate the further reaches of the LNER system. For example, Doncaster formerly a GN shed, received an allocation taking on board workings into ex-GC territory and travelling via Lincoln to March.

Beginning in 1929 Gresley began a programme of rebuilding of what were then Class 04 with round-topped fireboxes of his own design and carried by the former GN 02 2-8-0s. Further developments arose towards the end of the Second War when Thompson's proposed ideas for a standard LNER heavy goods engine were put into practice. These brought about further variations of the 8K/04 locomotive. Bearing in mind these many permutations, the story of the Great

Central 2-8-0 though not complete here, must be left to another volume, in which details and illustrations of the various rebuilds will be covered along with their allocations and work.

With the appended summary the description of the Robinson 8K 2-8-0 comes to an end, at least as far as its progress in Great Central days goes. Undoubtedly one of the 'greats' of the steam age. Robinson is known to have regarded this design as one of his finest, if not the finest. Highly regarded, widely-travelled, incredily useful and utterly reliable. Other designs have, it is true fulfilled some of those criteria, some others 'got about' in their time. Partisanship aside, the 8K was a damn good engine and who better to have said that than an engine driver.

PRESERVATION: Great Central no. 102, the first Gorton engine of 1912 was selected for preservation when she was withdrawn in June 1963. Then based at Frodingham as British Railways no. 63601, the engne had various homes before finally coming to rest at the Dinting Railway Centre at Glossop, where she is currently displayed. Her final place of exhibition is yet to be decided, as the Dinting centre is likely to close before the end of 1989.

No.423, *Sir Sam Fay* himself seen on shed at Neasden early on in the engine's life. The use of 2 inside cylinders on a G.C. 4-6-0 was a new idea and suggestions have been made that Robinson had been influenced by Mc.Intosh's 'Cardean' on the Caledonian Railway in 1906 which used a similar wheel arrangement. The presence of a Wakefield mechanical lubricator on the immaculately-groomed engine will be noted. A necessary appendage on a superheated engine, these lubricators gave way after a few years to Robinson's own 'Intensifore' pattern.

Collection of G.H.Platt

Sir Sam Fay
Class 1 4-6-0

The history of the steam locomotive is a catalogue of success and failure. Likewise, those who have studied and written about its many engineers and designers have been shrewd in their analysis of the triumphs and disasters of these giants of the drawing board. Inevitably, as in any endeavour initiated and controlled by human design, the products of that design will mirror the frailties of their makers.

More than enough of a meal has been made of J.G. Robinson's engines that were not up to the mark of their contemporaries. Again and again, writers have remarked on this engineer's work in the most general, and usually disparaging, of terms. Much the same fate befell F.W. Webb of LNWR whose Compounds, though doubtless a mixed bag, are taken - very mistakenly - as being the benchmark of the man's whole life and work.

Thus, we come to the 'Sir Sams'. The bestowal of the name of the General Manager on the first engine of the class - built in 1912 - gave the engines an unofficial title. Signalmen on the G.C. section of the LNER knew them as 'Big Sammies' though their official G.C. designation was Class 1, far too prosaic for railwaymen and enthusiasts who much prefer names to numbers!

The 'Sir Sams' were massive machines with fine, flowing lines. A complete break had been made with previous design concepts; here was a brand new thing

with Robinson giving full reign to his ideas. All the stops seemed to have been pulled out to produce what was surely intended to be this engineer's magnum opus and the flagship of the Great Central's express passenger fleet.

Superheating was built into the design from new and, in consequence, the combined blower and draught retarder was fitted to the engines when built, it can be seen in the photographs as a projection from the top of the smokebox - a small flange coupled to a pipe. Almost certainly, Robinson would have fitted his improved version of this device for which he filed a patent in June 1912. This ingenious apparatus consisted of a small steam jet to each element of the superheater connected to the blower pipe. This served to neutralise the draught through the flues containing the superheater elements when the blower was in action, thus preventing any chance of overheating the elements when steam was shut off. The improved version incorporated a valve which enabled the steam supply to be more precisely set than in the earlier design (patented in 1911) which had no such adjustment.

Notwithstanding Robinson's ability in this field it is perhaps surprising to find that the layout and design of the superheater in this prestigious class left something to be desired, two modifications to the design of the tubes

The big 4-6-0 was put into the front rank of Great Central express working when built, between Manchester and London. Here the pioneer of the class waits to depart from Manchester's London Road station with the 3.40 pm to Marylebone when new. The locomotive is in spanking condition, the driver-no doubt very proud of his charge-has engaged full forward gear ready for a brisk departure. A typical journey time in 1912/13 from London Road to Marylebone was around five hours, the 3.40 timed at just one minute inside this schedule.

Collection of G.H.Platt

and flues of the apparatus being made before the Grouping.

But, sadly, the Sir Sam Fay design was not the success it should have been. Such a splendid appearance, such an apparition of engineering magnificence as was rolled out of Gorton Works in the closing days of 1912 belied a rather poor locomotive. The shortcomings that emerged in the 'Sir Sams' were surprising in the light of Robinson's prowess at that time.

Sir Sam's cylinders had been set at 21½" diameter, certainly the largest Robinson had used up until then and, indeed, one of the largest employed on any British railway at that period. Such innovation, unfortunately, meant restricted room between the frames for adequate coupled wheel bearings. These received a thrashing from the massive cylinders, a process reflected in overheating. This defect was partially mitigated when the cylinders of three of the class were lined up to 20 inches in later G.C. and LNER days.

The immediate impression given, even from a casual glimpse of Sir Sam Fay was the majesty and power that this class of engine exuded. The deep main-frames under the smokebox supported the two massive inside cylinders with their respective piston valves set on top and driven by rocking shafts. It was in the design of the valves themselves, together with their associated steam passages, that the chief weaknesses of the class lay. Such a massive boiler should have been able to supply all the steam required, even by such large-sized cylinders. However, the narrow firebox dictated by the Belpaire design was also fairly shallow - a deficiency that should

have been recognised by then from experience with the 8B and 8C designs of Atlantic and 4-6-0 some eight years earlier. A considerable problem lay in the length of the firetubes - inherent with such a long barrel. This length - at 17 ft.3 inch was out of proportion to the size of the firebox. In the later years of steam locomotive development, designers increased their barrel length - while keeping tube length short - by the provision of a combustion chamber. This device, essentially a 'neck' at the front of the firebox, did wonders for steam-raising. The accompanying smaller-wheeled replica, shows something of the ashpan layout which was also to prove troublesome; lacking ventilation at the back made it prone to blockage after a short period of running. Sadly, the dictum that: .....*a boiler's ability to raise steam is limited by its capacity to boil water.....* seldom seemed truer.

That much aside, the 'Sir Sams' were certainly not Robinson's best design. As to why the class was built in the first place, the answer is uncertain. Maybe publicity was the reason and it has been suggested that the class was built at the behest of Fay, although the study of G.C. history reveals engineers engaged in a more or less constant struggle against their management for more motive power resources. Authority would hardly have been given for a prestige locomotive as such, even if it did carry the name of the General Manager and was to be exhibited abroad. The company had no need of such a huge engine; events were to prove that a somewhat smaller machine could handle all their needs for the immediate future.

No. 424 *City of Lincoln* **in 'as built' condition stands outside Manchester Central in what looks like pre-First War condition. The Great Central gained access into this station by virtue of its membership of the Cheshire LInes Committee, a Triumvirate which it shared with the Great Northern and Midland companies.** *City of Lincoln* **is standing in front of the water tower which fronted on to a turntable. Though the G.C.shared locomotive facilities with the other two Cheshire Lines companies at nearby Trafford Park there is no record of the Class 1s being stationed there. Gorton shed, the eventual home of all the class, was a good way off from Central Station. Thus, rudimentary stabling facilities were provided here; fire and smokebox cleaning appear to be in evidence and the fireman on top of the tender is paying attention to a rather large heap of coal.**

Collection of G.H.Platt

Class 1. Type 4.6.0   N° of Engines ... 6.

Maker	Year Built	N° of Engines	Maker	Year Built	N° of Engines	Maker	Year Built	N° of Engines
G C R	1912	1						
"	1913	5						

Particulars in red refer to 28 element headers. Particulars in green refer to engines with 20" cylinders.

CYLINDERS.
Diameter .... 20" 21½"
Stroke .... 26"
Centres .... 2' 0½"

BOILER.
Class .... N° 7 Standard
Working Pressure .... 180 Lbs. per □"
Barrel Dia. Outs. Max. .... 5' 6"
Barrel Length .... 17' 3"
Barrel Thickness of Plates .... ⅝"

TUBES.
Large No. .... 24 28 Dia. Outs. 5¼"
Small No. .... 139 116 Dia. Outs. 2¼"
Length between Tubeplates .... 17' 7⅞"

SUPERHEATER.
Kind of Header .... Front Cover
Elements { Dia. Outs. .... 1⅜"
Dia. Ins. .... 1¼"
Number 28 24

IF FITTED WITH
Draft Retarder ....
Circulating Valve .... Yes
Header Discharge Valve .... Yes
Pressure Release Valves ....
Combined Pressure Release and Piston Valves } .... Yes

FIREBOX SHELL.
Length Outs. at Bottom .... 9' 6"
Width " " " .... 4' 0½"
" " " Top .... 5' 8¾"
Thickness of Plates—
Back ⁿ/₃₂ Casing ⅝" Throat ¾"

COPPER FIREBOX.
Length of Grate .... 7' 9⅛"
Width " " .... 3' 4½"
Depth to Top of Ring, Front .... 6' 6⅛"
" " " " Back .... 5' 0⅝"

Width of Ring.
Back and Front .... 3" Sides .... 3"
Thickness of Plates— .... ⅞"
Back ⁹/₁₆ Casing ⁹/₁₆ Tube ⁹/₁₆"

HEATING SURFACE.
Firebox Outside .... 163 163 Sq. ft.
Large Tubes .... 672 579 "
Small Tubes .... 1303 1442 "
Superheater Inside .... 343 294 "
Total .... 2477 "

GRATE AREA. .... 26 Sq. ft.

WHEELS. Diameter. See Diagram.
Tyres Thickness .... 3"
JOURNALS.   Dia.   Length.
Leading Bogie or Break .... 6" 9"
Leading Coupled ....
Driving .... 9" 9"
Intermediate .... 8" 12"
Trailing Coupled .... 8" 12"
Trailing Bogie or Truck ....
Tractive Power at { Lbs. ... 22750 19300
85% Boiler Pressure { Tons ... 10.15 8.6
Adhesion Coefficient. Lbs. per Ton ... 396 336
Height. Rail to Top of Chimney ... 13' 3¾"
" " Centre of Boiler ... 8' 11"

VALVES. Kind .... Piston (Ins. admission)
CYLINDER LUBRICATOR. Kind .... Intensifore
If Fitted with Steam Sanding Apparatus .... No
" " Train Warming .... Yes
BRAKE. .... Steam & Auto Ejector
TENDER. Capacity. Water, Gallons ... 4000
" Coal, Tons ... 6
WHEELS. Diameter .... 4' 4"
JOURNALS. Dia. ... 6" Length ... 11"

Sir Sam Fay en route from Gorton to Manchester Central early in 1913. The locomotive is standing at the down home signal outside Alexandra Park station ('Wilbraham Road' in later years) on the Chorlton Junction to Fairfield line. This spot has a touch of nostalgia for the writer, connected with the engine in question. Wilbraham Road station was closed in 1958 when stopping passenger services on the line ceased. The buildings were of particular interest to me as I was keen to model the station in 4mm scale (which I did.) Vandalism was then an up and coming sport amongst the teenage population of Manchester and, on one of my trips there, I was rebuked by a local resident. After explaining the purpose of my visit we began a serious conversation about railways and about this stretch of railway in particular. 'I remember this line when Sir Sam Fay was the engine of the day' remarked the resident. Progress after that was unimpeded and my model was finished without hindrance! Carrying an Indicating Shelter, the locomotive is obviously going to be put through its paces. The use of Indicating Shelters on Great Central engines would appear to be rare, unlike on the Great Western where they seem to have been commonplace. A touch of the latter company's practice can be seen at the top of the chimney; this is copper-capped, a unique feature for a G.C.loco. *Sir Sam Fay* was to have been exhibited at an engineering exhibiton in Ghent, Belgium and the company obviously wanted their pride and joy to look its very best. The exhibition of locomotives abroad was an established practice in those days; the Midland, LNWR and Great Eastern companies all having sent engines at one time or another for showing on the Continent. As it happened, 'Sir Sam' never set foot out of the country, but a model was sent, as well as a mock-up of a boiler front showing one of Robinson's patent superheaters.

Collection of G.H.Platt

Whatever the reasons for producing the Class 1 4-6-0, the design in the form of an express engine was not repeated, although the Glenalmond class 4-6-0 of 1913 was something of a replica and mirrored the faults of the parent class to a large extent. For passenger working Robinson turned back to the 4-4-0 type; therein lay his strength.

Standard 4000-gallon tenders with nominal 6-ton coal capacity were fitted to the locos from new. These all carried water pick-up gear operated by the now familiar 'ship's wheel' situated on top of the bulkhead on the driver's side of the tender. These tenders remained with the class throughout their lives and no swapping or interchanging of tenders, as with other G.C. classes, appears to have taken place.

Following the appearance of Sir Sam Fay at the end of 1912, four more engines appeared in the first three months of 1913. These were followed by a fifth locomotive in the December of that year. Such a long time gap between the fourth and fifth engines seems strange, the design flaws in the type being surely obvious in the

interim. As stated already though, the Great Central seemed to be continuously short of motive power throughout its history and maybe Robinson felt a commitment to fulfill the original order on these grounds alone.

Photographs will show the engines working on Manchester-Marylebone expresses when new. Their shortcomings caused them to be displaced from these services fairly quickly, the immediately successful Directors taking their place. Hereafter, three engines were sent to Immingham; the eastern half of the G.C. system becoming something in the nature of home ground for the class. First War duties saw the engines working on overnight fast goods trains between Manchester and Marylebone. Second division working had now become the norm, Manchester becoming the home base for the engines for most of the 1920s, trips between here and Sheffield forming the greater part of the workload for the Sam Fays at this time. In 1927 through working between Manchester and March on the Harwich Boat train was instituted with Sir Sams taking charge; No.424

SUMMARY OF CLASS 1 4 - 6 - 0 (LNER B2)

NUMBER	BUILDER	DATE BUILT	NAME	WITHDRAWN
423	Gorton	December 1912	*Sir Sam Fay*	April 1947
424	Gorton	January 1913	*City of Lincoln*	November 1945
425	Gorton	February 1913	*City of Manchester*	July 1947
426	Gorton	March 1913	*City of Chester*	December 1944
427	Gorton	March 1913	*City of London*	November 1947
428	Gorton	December 1913	*City of Liverpool*	April 1947

Note: Only nos.423 and 428 carried names from new. No.427 (as LNER 5427) had its name removed in september 1937. The title was then carried by one of the streamlined B17s, no.2870.

At the same spot outside Manchester Central, a nameless no.428 rests between duties.

Author's Collection

A 'Sir Sam' in the later years of the G.C:Watched by a lady with a parasol, No.427 *City of London* passes under St.Werburgh's Road bridge on the outskirts of Manchester and takes G.C.metals at Chorlton Junction with the 3.22 p.m.Manchester Central to Cleethorpes train in August 1920. By this time the class had long been relegated to secondary services, working chiefly between Manchester and Sheffield. The 6-coach train is composed of clerestory stock then finished in the varnished teak favoured by the company. *City of London* appears to be painted green, although when new (along with nos.424 & 426) she was turned out in the Great Central goods livery of black lined red and white. The date of repainting is not known but the picture provides a clue that all had been given the green livery by 1923. This engine was the one to lose its name when in 1937 the title was passed on to the LNER streamlined B17 4-6-0 no.2870.

G.M.Shoults

City of Lincoln being noted as one such engine.

Cross country trips between Manchester, Sheffield, Hull and Cleethorpes were typical duties for the class in the 1930s. At the outbreak of the Second War, allocations were split between Lincoln and Immingham. Some notably heavy wartime passenger train workings were recorded by members of the class during these years, haulage of 15 and 16 coach trains being recorded.

Immingham was the final shed to which the Sir Sams were assigned. No. 426 (LNER 1475 - Class B2) was the first of the class to be withdrawn, in December 1944. The remaining five had gone by the end of 1947.

Names of cities served by the company were chosen for application to the remaining members of the class in due course - only the first and last engines actually appeared carrying names when built. Lincoln, Manchester, Chester, London and Liverpool were the selected titles. The omission of Sheffield seems odd but the remainder were, perhaps, fair enough, although Chester and Liverpool were only reached by joint or absorbed concerns.

Few observers could have failed to be impressed by the majestic appearance of Sir Sam Fay. Though beauty itself will always be a subjective matter, surely this locomotive must rank as one of the finest-looking 4-6-0s ever to take to the rails. The front end reminds us strongly of the 9N 4-6-2 tank introduced in 1911. Rearwards, the outline of the cab - always roomy and commodious on a Robinson engine - bore familiar outlines. Here though, it was combined in an upward sweep of the running plate over the coupled wheels. This feature was to be retained for future designs and gave something of a 'family' look to Great Central engines of the period.

The neat brass-cased safety valves completed the ensemble on top of the boiler. These would give way to the more functional-looking Ross 'Pop' variety in the 1921-22 period. Altered over the years, it was perhaps the removal of their original boiler mountings that did so much to change the original lines of many Great Central locomotives.

Earl Kitchener of Khartoum No. 279-another oil-burner and the penultimate member of the class, turned out from Gorton in December 1914. *Earl Kitchener* is seen at Guide Bridge at the head of, unusually, an express passenger working. The date is c.May-October 1921 (Q.V.) Worthy of mention are the massive bosses of the coupling rods and the small cross painted on the top of the smokebox door. The latter, together with a variation the form of a star, seem to be Gorton hallmarks of the period. The black livery is in the usual fine fettle with all lining visible and a good degree of sheen apparent.

Collection of G.H.Platt

'Glenalmond'
Class 1A 4-6-0

Before the last Class 1 4-6-0 had appeared, Robinson-true to form-produced a smaller-wheeled version of his erstwhile magnum opus, a 4-6-0 with coupled wheels of 5'-4" diameter.

The Great Central no.4, *Glenalmond*, appeared at the end of June1913, just over 7 months after *Sir Sam Fay* had steamed out of Gorton Works for the first time. Thirteen months then elapsed before the second of the class appeared. In the meantime, the rest of the 'Sir Sams' took the rails with the mixed results already described.

No.439 *Sutton Nelthorpe*-the second 'Glenalmond', delivered in July 1914, began a sequence of 10 locomotives built over the period to January 1915-now well into the start of the First War.

Such an overlap between the introduction of two classes that were almost mechanically identical is worthy of consideration. If Robinson had known of the deficiencies in the original design why was an engine that was almost a replica constructed? Perhaps the answer lay in the duties for which the respective classes were assigned to. Whereas *Sir Sam Fay* had been designed for express work, the *Glenalmond* was intended for fast goods and mixed traffic work. On the whole, the lower wheel speeds involved in slower running would have meant less strain on the coupled wheel axleboxes. Correspondingly, piston speed would also have been lower and consequently less hindered by the awkward layout of the steam passages. As with the Class 1s, the drive was taken to the front coupled axle-the journals of which measured only 9" long by 9" in diameter. Thus, at a slower pace, the foibles of the pioneer design would have been somewhat less manifest.

In the manner of the Class 1, alterations were made to both the cylinder and boiler layout of the 'Glenalmonds' none of which bore much fruit.

Oil-burning was a short-term measure introduced by various British railway companies in times of fuel crises. A coal strike in 1921 had forced the Great Central to adopt oil-firing for several locomotives, including three 'Glenalmonds'-nos.279/443/and 445, equipped with Robinson's favoured 'Unolco' system in May and June of that year. The coal space in the tender was occupied wholly by the enormous oil tank which, as with other classes, came to within the very limits of the loading gauge. In this tender-first view at Guide Bridge, no.443 displays her cab fittings to advantage and a tarpaulin is rolled up on top of the back of the cab. The superheater header discharge valve can be seen on the smokebox side and the 'Wakefield' lubricator, carried from new, has given way to Robinson's 'Intensifore' system. In 1927, no.443 had her cylinders lined up to 20" in a bid to improve performance, although the full 21" bore was re-instated in 1935. As with the Class 1s, alterations were made to the boiler layout: the number of tubes being reduced progressively from 157 tubes of 2¼" diameter on the class as built, to 139, then 116 tubes in the final version. 443 became LNER no.1354 in the 1946 scheme of things. She fared a little better than some of her colleagues, managing to serve under the new re'gime in 1948. She was withdrawn in the March of that year.

W.A.Brown collection

Earl Kitchener of Khartoum in its original condition, a view affording an interesting contrast to previous pictures. The locomotive is in coal-burning condition, carries cased Ramsbottom-pattern safety valves and 'Wakefield' mechanical lubricator. A superheater header discharge valve appears on the smokebox side and Robinson's patent blower and steam circulating device (improved draught retarder) is also fitted. These oft-mentioned devices, though novel and effective,were, possibly, a little too sophisticated. They were replaced after Grouping by Gresley's pattern of snifting valve, situated behind the chimney. *Earl Kitchener* was another survivor of the LNER, passing into the British Railways era. As no.1358 as part of Class B8, she was withdrawn in August 1948, outlived by only two others of the class. None received B.R. numbers.

W.A.Brown collection

Like the 'Sir Sam Fay' design the 'Glenalmond' was superheated from new. Robinson's own superheater was used, differing from the Schmidt system in having the ends of the tubes expanded directly into the headers. At first (as with the Class 1) a 24-element superheater was tried. The diameter of the pipes forming these was then reduced from 1 ⅜″ to 1 ¹/₁₆″. In the third (and final) version the number of elements was increased from 24 to 28 but with the smaller size elements being retained.

The Drawing Office copy of the G.C.diagram book records the engines as being fitted with both Robinson's steam circulating valve and header discharge valve. Incidentally, the former device was originally patended under the name of 'steam jet draught retarder.' This invention was supplanted a year later in 1912 when a patent was filed for an improved version. This was described as an 'improved steam draught retarder.' Both devices worked in conjunction with the blower-a small supply of steam being directed along the superheater flue pipes to prevent their overheating. The second (improved) version carried a valve that could be pre-set to accurately control the flow of steam; the idea being

that at any given setting of the blower, the jets of steam issuing along the flues would be just sufficient to neutralize the draught.

'Glenalmond' was the name of Sir Alexander Henderson's (the G.C's Chairman) Scottish country home. A distinguished name indeed and one that could have set something of a precedent; however, only three of the remaining ten locomotives received names. Appropriately enough for the wartime years of their production, two of these were named in honour of heroes of the conflict.

The parent engine was based at Gorton when newly-built with Neasden and Immingham also receiving 'Glenalmonds' and forming, in effect, three points of a triangle around which the engines moved fast goods, fish and passenger trains. In early LNER days four of the class migrated to March for work on fitted goods services, whilst later in the 1920s, express goods trains from Colwick (east of Nottingham)and Annesley kept the engines busy.

In the decade prior to the Second War, coal trains to and from Annesley and Woodford were worked by

'Glenalmonds', whilst excursion workings over a wide area from the Nottingham district saw the class deployed on the passenger side.

More westerly points were reached by the remainder of the engines after the War. Turns over the Woodhead route were recorded by the survivors of the class and the C.L.C., once again, hosted the last remnants of a Great Central passenger locomotive.

In the event, the projected 'Glenalmonds' were not built, the class becoming complete with no. 280 - finished in the January of 1915. Construction of the so-called 'Heavy Tanks' had began in 1914 and a further 18 were built over the period 1915 to 1917. No further 'Directors' were constructed until the 'Improved' or 11E series emerged over the years 1919/22. The 10 London Surburban Tanks (9N) were restricted to a series of five built in 1917, further examples not appearing until after the Great Central's demise, in 1923.

As will be seen, further exhortations by Robinson for extra motive power resources in this crucial operiod were to prove less than fruitful. Express pasenger design was halted until the appearance of the majestic 9P or 'Valour' 4-6-0 of 1917, wartime activity at Gorton being restricted to the engines described, repairs and, of course, a heavy involvement in munitions work.

Somehow the appearance of the last of the 'Glenalmonds' marked something of a boundary between the old and new orders. The palmy days of Edwardian England when the railways were in the heyday of their supremacy, had been left behind. The growth of industry to which the railways had contributed so much, had given man the means for mechanised destruction and conflct on a scale never seen before. It was more than the flower of the Nation's youth that perished in the mud of Flanders and Northern France in those dark years, it was a way of life that was never to return.

The sight of the last of the 'Glenalmonds' plodding their way through the fields of Cheshire in the early days of British Railways is a sad one. No. 446, *Earl Roberts of Kandahar* was the last survivor, withdrawn in April 1949. Then grubby and down at heel, the 'Glenalmonds' represented part of what one man expressed as his best intentions. Sturdy and hard-working beasts they were; better, they might have been.

No.443 has backed down Ducie Street goods yard alongside Manchester London Road station. Great Central goods operations from here were impressive; the company boasting a full range of facilities including a massive grain warehouse, part of which can be seen in the background. With this broad view, part of no.443's train is visible:four vans behind the tender and three sheeted wagons with a brake van can be made out further down the yard. In the distant background, the outlines of the LNWR's goods warehouse, underlining the separate facilities existing here, will be noticed. Sadly, one of the failings of railway photographers over the years has been their reluctance to photograph anything of any significance of goods operations. This is understandable as, obviously, the prestige express engines tended to steal most of the limelight. Enthusiasts of today take their photography for granted; film and cameras are cheap nowadays compared with the era we are studying. Then, each subject was photographed on an expensive glass plate, equipment was far from compact and photography was something of a rich man's hobby. Blending into the background of the grain warehouse is an oil tank atop no.443's tender. 3 'Glenalmonds' were converted to oil-firing using Robinson's 'Unolco' (United Oil & Coal Corporation Ltd.) in May and June of 1921 to combat coal strikes which, of course, posed a dire threat. We can date the photograph fairly accurately as it is known that the oil-burning apparatus was removed from no.443 (and no.279) in the October of the same year. Steam issuing from the safety valves serves to point out the Ross 'Pop' type of valve in lieu of the traditional Ramsbottom brass-cased variety with which the engines had been built. Incidentally, these famous valves fitted to so many British designs over the years were manufactured by R.L.Ross & Co.Ltd. at their Premier Works in Stockport, Cheshire. The fitting above the vacuum ejector pipe on the right-hand side of the smokebox is an ash ejector-a device controlled by the driver whereby live steam could be admitted to the base of the smokebox when the engine was working and the residual ash blown up into the exhaust and out through the chimney. This device was later modified to obviate the abrasive action that the steam blown ash caused against the smokebox tubeplate. Modifications were recognised by the appearance of a longer pipe alongside the smokebox. Robinson's ingenuity anticipated the move towards the 'self-cleaning' smokeboxes that appeared in the latter days of steam. Ash ejectors seemed to have remained with the 'Glenalmonds' at least until the time of the Second War.

Collection of G.H.Platt

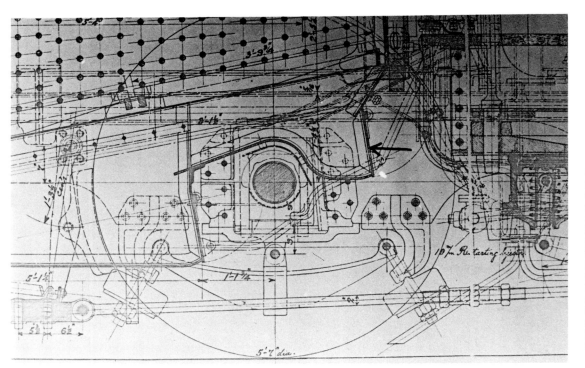

Reference to sections of the 'Glenalmond' drawing shows the three unfortunate areas of weakness reflected in this and the parent design-the *Sir Sam Fay*-Class 1. Shown here is: FIREBOX AND ASHPAN: Close proximity of rear coupled axle to firebox restricts depth of latter. In particular, ashpan layout at rear is awkward, with limited capacity at back. This would give rise to the choking effect of ash on supply of air frequently reported with these engines. Note, however, that dampers have been provided for both sections of the ashpan.

Class ... 1ᴬ Type 4·6·0 Nº of Engines ... 11.

G C R	1913	1						
"	1914	9						
"	1915	1						

CYLINDERS.
Diameter .... 21½"
Stroke .... 26"
Centres .... 2'0½"

BOILER.
Class ... Nº 7 Standard
Working Pressure ...180...Lbs. per ☐"
Barrel Dia. Outs. Max .... 5'6"
Barrel Length .... 17'3"
Barrel Thickness of Plates ...... ⅝"

TUBES.
Large No. ...24... Dia. Outs. 5¼"
Small No. ...139... Dia. Outs. 2¼"
Length between Tubeplates ...17'7⅞"

SUPERHEATER.
Kind of Header ... Front Cover
Elements { Dia. Outs. ...... 1⅜"
Dia. Ins. ...... 1¹⁄₁₆"
Number 24

IF FITTED WITH
Draft Retarder ....
Circulating Valve .... Yes
Header Discharge Valve ...... Yes
Pressure Release Valves ......
Combined Pressure Release } Yes
and Piston Valves }

FIREBOX SHELL.
Length Outs. at Bottom ...... 8'6"
Width „ „ „ ...... 4'0½"
„ „ „ Top ...... 5'8¾"
Thickness of Plates—
Back ...²⁴⁄₃₂.. Casing ⅝" Throat ¾"

COPPER FIREBOX.
Length of Grate .... 7'9¹⁵⁄₁₆"
Width „ „ .... 3'4⅛"
Depth to Top of Ring, Front 6'6⅛"
„ „ „ Back 5'0⅞"

Width of Ring.
Back and Front 3" Sides 3"
Thickness of Plates—
Back ⁹⁄₁₆ Casing ⁹⁄₁₆ Tube { ⅞"
⁹⁄₁₆"

HEATING SURFACE.
Firebox Outside ...... 163 ...Sq. ft.
Large Tubes ...... 578 „
Small Tubes ...... 1442 „
Superheater Inside ...... 294 „
Total ...... 2477 „

GRATE AREA. ...... 26 ...Sq. ft.

WHEELS. Diameter. See Diagram.
Tyres Thickness .... 3"
JOURNALS. Dia. Length.
Leading Bogie or Truck ...... 6" 9"
Leading Coupled ....
Driving .... 9" 9"
Intermediate .... 8" 12"
Trailing Coupled .... 8" 12"
Trailing Bogie or Truck ......

Tractive Power at { Lbs. 27,400
85% Boiler Pressure { Tons 12.25
Adhesion Coefficient. Lbs. per Ton ...494
Height. Rail to Top of Chimney ...13'1¼"
„ „ Centre of Boiler ...8'8⅞"
VALVES. Kind ... Piston (Ins. adm)
CYLINDER LUBRICATOR. Kind ...Intensifore
If Fitted with Steam Sanding Apparatus ...Yes
„ „ Train Warming „ ...Yes
BRAKE. ... Steam & Auto Ejector
TENDER. Capacity. Water, Gallons ...4000
„ „ Coal, Tons 6
WHEELS. Diameter .... 4'4"
JOURNALS. Dia. ...6" Length ...... 11"

No.441 at Neasden shed on September 17th 1921. Ross 'Pop' valves have now replaced the cased Ramsbottom variety carried from new. A small detail often missed in descriptions of these engines is the anti-vacuum valve sited on the mainframes roughly on the smokebox centreline. Designed to prevent smokebox ash from being sucked down into the cylinders when running with steam shut off, it was a feature fitted to all the class except no.4.

W.A.Brown collection.

SUMMARY OF CLASS 1A 4-6-0 (LNER B8)

NUMBER	BUILDER	DATE BUILT	NAME	WITHDRAWN
4	Gorton	June 1913	*Glenalmond*	November 1947
439	Gorton	July 1914	*Sutton Nelthorpe*	August 1947
440 - 445	Gorton	August to November 1914		May 1947-Mar 1949
446	Gorton	November 1914	*Earl Roberts of Kandahar*	April 1949
279	Gorton	December 1914	*Earl Kitchener of Khartoum*	August 1948
280	Gorton	January 1915	--	March 1947

Earl Kitchener of Khartoum **on the Gorton shed turntable during its brief oil-burning career. The engine reverted to coal-firing in October 1921.**

Railway Revivals Collection

EXPRESS WORKING ON THE
MS&L - MANCHESTER - KINGS CROSS

A BRIEF HISTORICAL OUTLINE

The Manchester, Sheffield & Lincolnshire Railway, in partnership with the Great Northern Railway had begun through services from Kings Cross to Manchester on August 1st 1857 - the year of the celebrated Manchester Exhibition. The aim was for the Great Northern to capture some of the traffic from the hostile London & North Western and to break the latter's monopoly in the process. Such activity on the part of the upstart MS&L angered the LNWR with the resultant arrest of passengers who had arrived at Manchester's London Road station from Kings Cross via Sheffield.

For several years there were some five trains in each direction between Kings Cross and Manchester. Initially the journey time was set at 5 hours 20 minutes including stops at Penistone, Sheffield, Retford, Grantham, Peterborough and Hitchin. Later, the fastest train did the journey in around 4¾ hours a similar travelling time to that provided by the Midland and the LNWR.

In 1883, at the behest of Sir Edward Watkin the MS&L Chairman, the Manchester-Kings Cross trains were further accelerated. The journey time was reduced to 4½ hours, stops being made only at Sheffield and Grantham. Hitherto, a stop had been made at Retford, where engines were changed. A year later, in 1884, the 2.00 pm trains in each direction between the two cities were further speeded up - the journey time now being reduced to 4¼ hours. This acceleration produced speeds that were reputed then to be the fastest in the world; the down train reached Grantham in just under two hours, averaging out at 53½ mph. On the up journey, the 54 mph average between Grantham and Kings Cross was certainly the fastest in the country at that time. Most of these services carried through carriages for Bradford which travelled via Penistone and Huddersfield over the L&Y system.

This joint service was certainly enterprising and led to the introduction of special rolling stock; joint expenditure between the two companies resulting in the production of lavishly equipped dining and sleeping cars. Both the MS&L and the GN had invested in the Victoria Hotel which adjoined the similarly-named station in Sheffield, the MS&L buying out the GN's share in 1883.

The abolition of the Retford stop had led to an alteration in the arrangements for locomotive working between the two companies. Prior to 1883, Retford had been the point where engines were changed, the GN providing motive power between here and Kings Cross, the MS&L correspondingly being responsible for running between here and Manchester London Road via Sheffield. With an engine change at Grantham, distances became a little more equitable; the GN's 105½ miles to Kings Cross equating roughly with the MS&L's 97¼ miles to Manchester. Geographically though, the MS&L crews got the rough end of things, their journey

in the up direction included a 3 mile slog at 1 in 201 through the notorious Woodhead Tunnel whose sulphureous single bores were reckoned on occasions to bring engine crews to near asphyxiation. Returning to Manchester was no sinecure either; the eastern portal of the Woodhead Tunnel just beyond Dunford Bridge was almost 1,000 feet above sea level reached by gradients varying from 1 in 120 to 1 in 132 over the 18½ miles from Sheffield Victoria.

For the MS&L's part the motive power used on these Manchester trains had run the full gamut of Class 14, his various 2-4-0 types - the Fairbairn Class 25 of 1859, the fascinating 12A followed by the similar looking Class 6B 4-4-0 of 1877, all had plied the tortuous Woodhead route. Like Sacre before him, Thomas Parker had developed a 2-4-0 type before producing a 4-4-0 design - the 6'-9" Class 2 of 1887. Hereafter 4-4-0s with 7'-0" wheels were given preference with the Kings Cross expresses and then the GC's own London Extension trains uppermost in the designers' minds.

On March 15th 1899, the Great Northern began its own service from Manchester Central to Kings Cross. It was no concidence that the Great Central's own regular service over its newly opened London Extension had begun that same day. Not that this was quite the end of the joint services; through coaches were coupled to the 3.40 pm express from Manchester London Road, detached at Sheffield and worked by a Neepsend engine as far as Grantham. Manchester, then the centre of Britain's cotton industry and a city with a vast amount of heavy manufacturing capacity, particularly in the engineering trades, was a lucrative proposition. The GN went as far as building special 4-coach trains for its independent Manchester services which it brought into use in August 1906. These trains, designated 'Special Through Dining Car Expresses' covered the down journey in 4 hours with one stop at Sheffield Victoria. But even in these palmy days four contenders were, perhaps, just that one too many.

In 1910 the GN service had shrunk to two trains per day each way with a best time of 4 hours 3 minutes in the down direction. Other tmings of 5 hours 12 minutes and 5 hours 30 minutes in the up direction suggest that the company had given up the ghost as far as competition for the Manchester passenger traffic was concerned. Subsequently the day services were replaced by one overnight express in each direction. These reached Manchester via Godley Junction, Woodley Stockport, Tiviot Dale and then over the Manchester South District Line to Central Station.

At the beginning of 1917 these overnight trains ceased to carry passengers, becoming instead parcel trains. By 1920 these trains too had disappeared, not that this was the end of the GN's involvement in Manchester, far from it. At great expense the company had opened its

Deansgate goods warehouse in July 1898. By way of its membership of the CLC and by means of running powers, the GN had access to a considerable variety of routes. Even today, 66 years after its demise, the legend: 'Great Northern Railway Company's Goods Warehouse' stands out proudly above the building, still largely intact and approaching the centenary of its construction.

The Manchester-Kings Cross trains had laid the foundation stone for top-link MS&L motive power.

Fired by Watkin's determination and ruthlessness the company had acquired its own route to London, something which would have been viewed with incredulity in the early years of the alliance with the GN.

A study of the development of MS&L motive power is something for another work but, hopefully, the beginning of GC services to London and the development of the locomotives that hauled them can now be viewed as a part of an evolutionary process rather than a sudden birth.

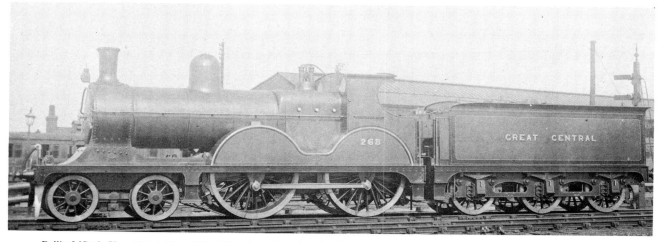

Pollitt MS&L Class 11A 4-4-0 no.268 at Grantham, the point of engine change-over on the Manchester-Kings Cross expresses. The loco is in 'as built' condition and as such forms a useful introduction to the Pollitt 11A Class (Q.V.)Green in one shade or another had been the dominant colour for MS&L engines from earliest times and was perpetuated by the new company. A dark, 'Brunswick' green had been used by Sacre' and continued by Thomas Parker. Around 1893, a change to a lighter shade of green took place as exhibited by no.268. The main frames above the footplate, footplate edging, footsteps and tender frames were all painted a chocolate shade lined in yellow. On our example, the contrast between the green and chocolate areas can be readily discerned. The yellow lining shows nicely too, as does the polished brass beading of the coupled wheel splashers. Wheel centres were the same shade of green as the main engine colour, with the boiler and firebox lagging bands coloured chocolate lined yellow on each side. Wheel tyres, guard irons and coupling rods were all brightly polished.

Collection of G.H.Platt

TOOLS CARRIED BY G.C.ATLANTICS

The tender documents of 1903, from Beyer, Peacock & Co. for the building of the first two Atlantics contains this very interesting list of tools carried by the engine. It is reproduced here complete with weights of all items.

LIST OF TOOLS

Description	Weight in LBS
1 heavy hammer	7
1 small hammer	2
1 copper hammer	5½
1 large pin punch	1¼
1 small pin punch	1
3 chisels(1 flat,1 cross cut,1 round nose	3
2 drifts	3½
1 steel pointed crowbar	5½
1 small steel pinchbar	5
1 gland packing bar	2
2 20-ton traversing screwjacks & levers	270
1.6 quart, 1.4 quart, 1.1 quart oil cans	7
1 long oil feeder	2¼
1 short oil feeder	1¾
1 fog signal case and flag holder	3¼
2 shovels, 1 long, 1 short	8
1 coal hammer	7½
1 hand brush	1
1 bucket with spout	8¼

1	sand sieve	3
1	monkey wrench	9
6	tube plugs	18
3	padlocks and keys	3
1	rake	15½
1	pricker	18
1	clinker bar	21
15	single ended keys	67
2	single ended keys 2¼ & 2½	18
5	double ended keys	13½
4	box keys	12
7	circular keys	6½
3	head lamps,1 water gauge lamp,1 hand lamp	38
2	torch lamps,1 watering pipe	1¼
1	key for drawbar nut	33

All of which added up to the impressive total of 5 cwts.,2 qrs. and 14½ lbs.of tools and should have meant that any locomotive crew was well-equipped for all contingencies. notice the word 'keys' for what we would nowadays term 'spanners' and the weight of the three fireirons. The all important water gauge lamp would have been the only cab interior illumination apart from the glow from the firebox. Small comfort indeed when the murky depths of Woodhead or Catesby tunnels were encounted.

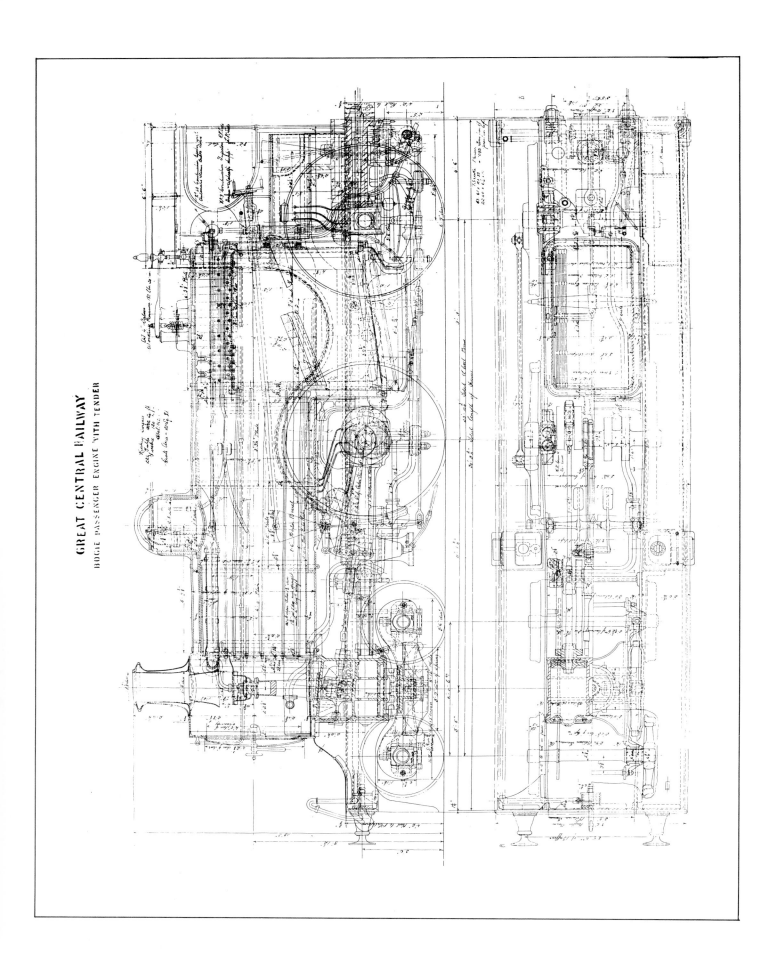

GREAT CENTRAL RAILWAY

BOGIE PASSENGER ENGINE WITH TENDER

GREAT CENTRAL RAILWAY

G.W.C. BOGIE GOODS ENGINES Nos 1105 – 1114

MAKERS PROGRESSIVE Nos 4806 – 4815

Acknowledgements

11A 4-4-0 no.875 in full forward gear, coaled-up and ready for the Liverpool road. Trafford Park shed, Manchester.

Collection of G.H.Platt

It is now well over sixty years since the Great Central Railway disappeared into the amalgam that became the London & North Eastern Railway, and just over forty years since that concern passed away to give birth to what is now known as British Rail. This means that even for such middle-aged juniors as myself, memories, even of apple-green engines are decidedly sketchy. Hence, the author of a work such as this relies, perforce, on what others have passed down to him.

We in Britain are fortunate in having at our disposal a well organised and efficient archive and library system with free and open access to all. I refer in particular to the Public Record Office at Kew, in London, the National Railway Museum at York and, in my own case, the Central Reference Library here in Manchester. To all these offices I pass my thanks, for without the help and support of such organisations, this work would be much the poorer.

The student of Great Central locomotives is already well served by the superb and incomparable RCTS reference books on LNER motive power and I would like to pay tribute to the gentlemen who, over many years of patient and diligent work, have compiled such volumes for the benefit of fellow enthusiasts. Reference has been made to the RCTS texts where appropriate and those wishing to extend their working knowledge of locomotives of any of the LNER constituents need look no further. In like manner, the late George Dow's monumental trilogy on Great Central history offers inspiration to us lesser mortals.

Manchester was the home base of the Great Central's 'Locomotive Department' and while readers may detect a hint of bias here, the southern half of the company has had comprehensive coverage over the last few years. Indeed, though the leafy bowers of the shires of Leicester, Northampton and Buckingham offer a stark contrast to a backcloth of seemingly dark, satanic mills and factory chimneys in Manchester, it was from this fount nevertheless that the Great Central sprang. Here was muck, sweat and toil-the daily work diet of the men of Gorton, Openshaw, Fairfield, Guide Bridge, Ashton-under-Lyne and Stalybridge. In the words of the historian G.M.Trevelyan:.....*all gone now like ghosts at cock-crow*; let us not forget them.

On a personal basis I must first pay thanks to my publishers: the 'team' of Chris Hawkins, John Hooper and George Reeve for having faith in this project of mine and for being so generous with space, and time! Likewise, Bill Rear, well known for his writings on the railways of North and central Wales and his encyclopaedic knowledge of train workings, has ploughed with fellow enthusiast John Kimberley through the archives of the late G.H.Platt for me with endless patience. We owe a debt to Geoff Platt for collecting so much 24 carat G.C. material; I was fortunate enough to have met this gentleman and anyone who had this privilege knows that he was always ready to pass on and share his very wide knowledge of railways to others.

The name of G.M.Shoults occurs in connection with photographs in the Leicester area. This gentleman lived in Whetstone and was an avid photographer at the lineside in that area before the First World War. His photographs have made a very worthwhile addition to this work and I would like to thank his son, Mr Charles Shoults of Buxton for the very generous help afforded me in giving access to his father's unique collection of material. This Derbyshire town has also been the source of other material, from Martyn Ashworth of Peak Rail who has generously loaned material by the late A.A.Torrance.

I pass thanks also to Ronnie Gee who began his railway career when many Great Central locomotives were still in operation. his expert knowledge of the former G.C.lines in the Manchester area, coupled with a wide-ranging expertise covering stations, signalling and junction layouts has been of immense benefit to me. Doug Darby and Raymond Keeley both knew and saw Great Central engines in both pre and post-war days and their memories of those eras have inspired and helped me in preparing this book. Bill Johnson, a colleague from South Trafford College, has helpfully come up with stories passed on by his late father, an ex-Great Northern driver from Trafford Park shed.

Valuable help has also come from my old friend Ray Hepner who freely loaned me books and archive material from his collection and Brian Hilton and Bob Fysh who provided me unfettered access to their material. Greg Fox, well-known as a writer and publisher, has also given help and has made useful suggestions regarding the text and compilation of the book. John Doyle parted with his very valuable Great Central engine diagram book so that unique and individual information could be inserted.

In like manner, Alan Brown, a renowned authority on Great Central locomotives, has given unstintingly of of his help, time and material. David Jackson, Richard Moreton and John Quick of the Great Central Society have all made generous and significant contributions. I offer my warmest thanks to them.

At home, here in Manchester, I must pay a loving tribute to my wife, Mary, who has given me much help and support while this work has been in progress. There have been many hours when I have been away from the family circle and she has willingly played host to our many visitors, to say nothing of keeping my never-diminishing piles of papers and photographs in check! Likewise, Sarah and Ian, my two children, have played their part in household duties when Dad has been 'otherwise engaged'.

To you all, my sincere thanks and good wishes.

E.M.Johnson, Burnage, Manchester. July 1989.